In the Way of the Story

In the Way of the Story

Reading Biblical Narrative

HUW THOMAS

WIPF & STOCK · Eugene, Oregon

IN THE WAY OF THE STORY
Reading Biblical Narrative

Wipf & Stock
An Imprint of Wipf and Stock Publishers
199 W. 8th Ave., Suite 3
Eugene, OR 97401

www.wipfandstock.com

PAPERBACK ISBN: 978-1-6667-1327-5
HARDCOVER ISBN: 978-1-6667-1328-2
EBOOK ISBN: 978-1-6667-1329-9

12/06/21

This book is dedicated to my mum, Sylvia,
my first and best storyteller.

Contents

Acknowledgments

Thanks to my teacher of Biblical studies, David J. A. Clines, for introducing me to "the Bible as literature" and inspiring a reading and understanding that has stayed with me for many years.

Thanks also to Ella Nutu-Hall at the University of Sheffield and Liz Bentley, librarian at the Wilson Carlisle Centre.

Much of the work in this book began life as work on story structures in education leaving me indebted to Poplar, Ellesmere/Byron Wood, Springfield, and Emmaus, my four schools. Thanks also to the Diocese of Sheffield, and Sheffield Hallam University, where I developed and taught some of the content, and to Matt Wimer, Emily Callihan, Caleb Shupe, Kara Barlow, Mike Surber, Savanah N. Landerholm, Ian Creeger, and Wipf & Stock Publishers.

Christ Church Pitsmoor remains a home for my own exploration of the Bible which I gratefully acknowledge.

Finally a big vote of thanks as ever is to my children, Jacob, Barnabas, and Carys, for many years of reading and stories. And, as ever, the biggest thank-you goes to Kate.

Introduction: In the Way

You'll be doing all the work.

This book will get you looking at the Bible with fresh eyes, reading stories and getting to work on the nature of narrative, but you'll then be doing the work. You may have experienced writers, preachers, or speakers dishing out their insights into a story. This book is about getting you to a place where you have the insights. Unlike some books that offer readings of Bible stories, this one enables the reader to come up with their own reading. This will include stories you may feel you know: in reality, none of us fully knows a Bible story and we can always revisit them to find they have something new to offer. We often assume we know what happened, until a rereading trips us up and we realize, we don't actually know what happened when five loaves became thousands.

The one commitment to agree on at the outset is that the stories of the Bible matter. Christians often talk about story being crucial to faith but in biblical reflection characters get reduced to examples or the story is chopped up and served as some spiritual or moral lesson. Hearing their profound stories minced into homilies of injunctions you can imagine a biblical author thinking "Why did I bother?" This book clears a way to and through Bible stories.

THE BIBLE

When Christians disagree, they are often disagreeing about the Bible. Some of the spikiest debates of contemporary church bust-ups find their ultimate home in the question "What do you make of the Bible?" This book is written to meet a broad sweep of readers who would answer that question in different ways, primarily because this is about how to analyze and unpick stories, as you find them on the page. The approach is literary, adopting what is sometimes described as a "Bible as literature" or "Literary Reading" approach. This is not to say that the Bible isn't also Scripture or to question it's importance: quite the contrary. What is offered here is a way of actually reading biblical stories rather than relying on what some other reader preaches about it. Within the Christian Church, the starting point for this sort of reading is best expressed by one of the lead exponents of literary readings, David Clines, who suggested that: "The church can properly hear its Bible as scripture only when it reads it as literature"[1]

LITERARY THEORY

This book draws upon contemporary literary theory. In particular it will delve into poetics. Poetics unpicks how texts work and how readers respond. As with approaches to the Bible, there are different schools of literary theory, and this book picks and distills some pointers about story structure and reader response, drawing on the work of theorists described as structuralists and reader response theorists, and drawing upon some of the debates in which they engaged. Along the way names will be dropped in, along with a few choice quotes from some of the big names in literary theory. One great thing about poetics is that this thinking applies to the full range of stories so, alongside the Bible, we'll end up dipping into well known stories like "Jack and the Beanstalk" and *Where the Wild Things Are* or films like *Toy Story* and *Thelma and Louise*.

Ways of Reading

Throughout this book sections labeled "Ways of Reading" take the reader back to stories with activities that take the literary theory covered and suggest ways in which they can work with the text. Many of these involve cutting up texts, doodling images, or creating diagrams and flip charts that lead the reader to reflect on the story through exploring how stories work.

HISTORY: DID IT HAPPEN?

In this book, we don't worry too much about historical fact and what did or didn't happen. Important though that question may be to some, this is about reading the text, as found on the page. If, as a reader, you struggle with the idea someone walked on water you'll still discover how that story has a life

1. Clines, "Story and Poem," 115.

of its own regardless of whether anyone ever really did. If you believe the Bible is all accurate history, you'll gain new insights into the event that is reported. In our reading of the stories, we will be accepting the worldview of the Bible.[2] If you struggle with a water walk, for the purpose of our reading, you are asked to suspend disbelief and see just how Jesus walks—because that's one story where readers often miss out what he's actually doing on that walk. There are some great books out there that approach the Bible, exploring its history.[3] Aside from insights that enrich a reading of a story, this one doesn't.

OUR FOCUS

While this book offers literary approaches that can be applied across all biblical narrative, including Old Testament stories, for the purpose of trying out the material encountered it helps to have a focus. For this reason, this text will mainly focus on the Gospel of Mark, dwelling on specific stories. This is to enable the reader to get to know certain stories as places in which to try out the ideas in this book. However, whatever is tried out in Mark can then be taken off and tried across the Bible, on any story.

PREPARING THE WAY

"In the way" is an ambiguous term, which can describe the manner in which something is done, as when we describe what someone offers in the way of support or challenge. There is also the sense of obstruction and the task of clearing the way. In this book both meanings are adopted. Biblical narrative offers a resource for reflection and growth, but sometimes other people or beliefs get in the way of the story Inspired by the story of Mark's Gospel that often refers to "the way" Jesus walks, this book places the reader in the way, in the sense of being "in step" with story, always remembering that the Bible never says "God so loved the world." It actually says "God so loved the world that . . ." and the rest is story.[4]

Let's get you to work.

2. Vorster, "Reader in the Text," 32.

3. E.g. Burridge, *Four Gospels*; Enns, *How the Bible*; Blevins, *How to Read*.

4. see Goldingay, "Biblical Narrative," 130.

Chapter 1

Events

At the start of time, Angel Gabriel bumps into God and asks, "Hi there, done any more of the creating thing?"

God says to Gabriel, "Oh yes. I've invented a unit of time, by which humanity can organize themselves, which I'll mark by the movement of the sun rising and setting."

"That's great," Gabriel replies. "So what are you gonna do now?"

God pauses and thinks, then says, "I think I'll call it a day."

FROM THE BEGINNING, BIBLICAL narrative is event-driven. Compared with the agonizing and internal struggles of characters in modern fiction, Bible stories contain a lot less character description and thematic discussion. They are driven by events. This chapter explores the nature of those events, with the chapter that follows exploring the way they connect into a plot.

⸱. ADDITION.

In a story something changes. The narrative of a cartoon sequence needs that frame where things change to become a story.

Just as time moves on and one day leads to another, so a narrative involves a sequence of event added to event, an addition the narrative theorists Cohan and Shires described in this way: "The events constituting a story do not occur in isolation but belong to a sequence. Every sequence contains at least two events, one to establish a narrative situation or proposition, and one to alter (or at least merely differ from) that initial situation."[1]

A starting point for analyzing stories has to be grasping the events that form the narrative sequence. Readers familiar with the Bible can sometimes miss them out or make assumptions based on what we remember of the story or comparison with similar ones. The reader may want to recall the story in Mark's Gospel of Jesus walking on water (Mark 6:45–52). It's a well known story in which the disciples are all at sea and Jesus walks out on the water and encounters them and the storm stops, but to really read it, the reader needs to check the actual events. For example, in Mark's story the disciples are not in danger. They do not face a storm, but a struggle. Jesus sees the disciples are straining against an adverse wind, but in Mark's Gospel there is no mention of waves, as in Matthew and John. However, they have been struggling for a number of hours.[2]

Another feature in the story—Jesus does not walk to them, he's walking past them: When he saw that they were straining at the oars against an adverse wind, he came towards them early in the morning, walking on the sea. He intended to pass them by" (Mark 6:48). Unlike Matthew and John's version of this story, Mark has this one odd detail: not that he was pretending to pass by, but that he fully intending to. Some commentators wonder whether he changed his plans mid-water walk, others that the description sees events through the eyes of his disciples.[3] An alternative reading is one in which Jesus, as Son of God, is passing people by, in a manner akin to God

---

1. Cohan and Shires, *Telling Stories*, 54.
2. France, *Mark*, 271.
3. Lane, *Mark*, 236–37; France, *Mark*, 272.

passing by to Moses or Elijah.[4] This is in keeping with a Gospel that opened "The beginning of the good news of Jesus Christ, the Son of God." We may even perceive in his "It is I" a reflection of God's "I am" revelation to Moses in Exodus 3:14.[5] For the disciples this is an experience of awe and fear, not because of waves, but simply because they think he is a ghost. It is he who speaks to them to reveal himself.

Such details could be missed and are worth catching. To really get into a story the reader needs to ensure a clarity as to what does and doesn't happen within it. This may throw up puzzling or challenging moments, but these can be worth seeking out.

Ways of Reading: Events

Getting in the Way

Throughout this book the theory is interspersed with "Ways of Reading" sections. These involve activities or questions that get the reader looking at stories. In some cases specific examples will be used, but the reader should keep in mind a few stories as ones where they can try for their own use of this material.

What Actually Happens?

Readers can take time with the events of the story. Printing out a story out from the Bible,[6] the reader could read it once. Then, by putting a mark after every moment that could be classified as an event, the reader is allowing each moment its own space.

---

4. Exod 33; 1 Kgs 9.

5. Lane, *Mark*, 237.

6. Online resources can be used to create such texts, including Bible Gateway.

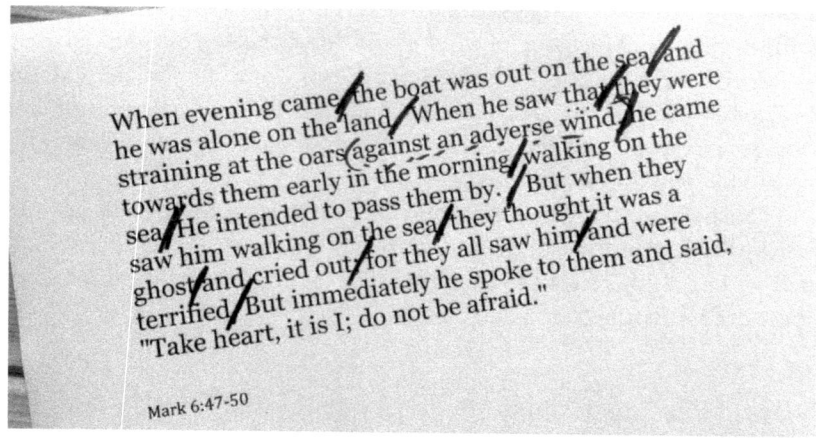

When evening came, the boat was out on the sea, and he was alone on the land. When he saw that they were straining at the oars against an adverse wind, he came towards them early in the morning, walking on the sea. He intended to pass them by. But when they saw him walking on the sea, they thought it was a ghost, and cried out, for they all saw him, and were terrified. But immediately he spoke to them and said, "Take heart, it is I; do not be afraid."

Mark 6:47-50

It is not uncommon for readers to read and race, skipping some details in a text—particularly seasoned Bible readers who have read a story before. We think we know a story but dividing verses like this can bring home the disciples' experience of believing they were being approached by something horrific, along with the noise they made in response.

2. TYPES OF EVENTS

The story goes that Prime Minister Harold Macmillan was once asked what was most likely to blow a government off course, to which he replied: "Events, dear boy. Events." There are different types of event, and when it comes to picking them out in a story there are some distinctions that can help readers explore them. A story event can be:

- an action or a happening
- a durative or punctual
- a hinge-point or a filler

a. Action or Happening

The first distinction asks: "Whodunit" or "Whodunto"? Literary theorist Seymour Chatman raises a question about characters doing events. Faced with events in a story, Chatman asks whether they are done by a character or ones done to or around them, that then affect them.[7] So in the story of

7. Chatman, *Story and Discourse*, 44–45.

Jesus walking on water, the disciples sail on ahead. Jesus makes them, but they do the action. Meanwhile, Jesus prays—also an action. However the adverse wind that arises is a happening. It is done to the disciples, and they don't like it . . . but stuff happens!

When Jesus gets into the boat, it is actually left open as to whether the cessation of the wind is an action or a happening. Did Jesus cause it as in the story of the calming of the storm (Mark 4:35–41), or did it just happen?

b. Durative or Punctual

Is the event an ongoing one that almost stands as a backdrop to other events, or does it occur once? Durative events are ones that are going on for a while, sometimes during other events. They are there for the duration. Mark's explanation that the disciples "did not understand about the loaves" (Mark 6:52) is an ongoing, durative event which the disciples start doing—or not doing—from the moment that feeding story ends. They continue to do it during Jesus walk on water (Mark 6:45–52) and afterwards. It crops up again in Mark 8:21 with the exasperated Jesus saying "And you still don't understand?" (Mark 8:21, GNB). His walk towards them is a single, punctual event, as is their cry and the wind ceasing. Such events have a clear start and stop within a story, whereas the disciples lack of understanding describes something ongoing. Another example would be the wind: it is a durative happening that spans much of the story of the water walk. During this durative happening they strain, Jesus walks, he almost passes, they see—and these more punctual events take place.

The distinction can matter to reading because durative events can create the backdrop to punctual ones. Indeed one cited above could be part of the backdrop to an entire gospel—the event of the disciples not understanding.

c. Nuclei and Catalyzers

One of the joys of appreciating stories is catching the things that matter and things that don't. There are also the ones that seem like they don't but they really do. If an action hero puts a rubber band down on the table, and the camera shows that action, watch for it later. Said hero will inevitably use it to bungee jump off a building or some such action. Think of how Bruce Willis uses his lighter at the start of *Die Hard 2*, E. T. takes a shine to a potted plant, and, in *Jaws*, of shark expert Hooper's early warning that his scuba tanks are dangerous and could explode. Seemingly trivial events can become critical.

In his brilliant "Introduction to the Structural Analysis of Narratives" the theorist Roland Barthes makes the distinction between *nuclei* that "constitute real hinge-points of a narrative" and *catalyzers* that "merely 'fill in' narrative space separating the hinge functions." Nuclei are events "of direct consequence for the subsequent development of the story"—take them out and the story won't work.[8]

Not all events fall clearly into one or other category, and in some cases we discover the importance of events only as they connect with the fuller narrative. Part of the fun is realizing, later in a story, why something mattered. When, in *Toy Story*, Sid is diverted from lighting a match that will rocket Buzz to doom, he tucks it into Woody's holster. Is that a catalyzer, or will that be essential? To answer that you'd need to watch the finale. Likewise Bruce Willis is shot at the start of *The Sixth Sense* and, while for the rest of the film he doesn't seem burdened by pain or trauma, we need to watch the end to see how important this was and whether he is, indeed, haunted by that event.

The reader is the one who decides whether a moment is a hinge or a catalyzer. It's an act of reading that figures out whether an event is more essential or more filling in. In the story of the water walk, it will be up to a reader to decide if Jesus going off to pray (Mark 6:46) is one type of event or the other.

A good example of the import following the event is the moment in Mark 1 when the leper disobeys Jesus and proclaims his healing story freely (Mark 1:45). That will affect the rest of the gospel, in which Jesus will avoid the cities of Galilee. Cities such as Tiberias and Sepphoris don't even get a mention, leave alone a visit. A mission plan was outlined by Jesus in Mark 1:38 in response to the disciples wondering what he's up to: "He answered, "Let us go on to the neighboring towns, so that I may proclaim the message there also; for that is what I came out to do." And he went throughout Galilee, proclaiming the message in their synagogues and casting out demons." That mission now has to be abandoned and Mark 1:45 makes it clear his plans are scuppered: "Jesus could no longer go into a town openly, but stayed out in the country; and people came to him from every quarter."

There are moments within this narrative that may appear catalytic but are not so: the event of Jesus reaching and touching the leper may appear to be just added detail, yet this touch has significant consequences.

8. Barthes, "Introduction," 94.

Ways of Reading: Types of Events

Pick Apart the Types

Using the distinctions between different types of event can provide interesting ways of reading a story. To raise one example, is the problem of a hungry multitude in Mark 6:30–34 and action or a happening? Is it caused by someone or is it just a collision of events? Pick apart the actual events of Mark 6:31–34 and there is an element of the resultant problem that is just a cock-up:

> [Jesus] said to [the disciples], "Come away to a deserted place all by yourselves and rest a while." For many were coming and going, and they had no leisure even to eat. And they went away in the boat to a deserted place by themselves. Now many saw them going and recognized them, and they hurried there on foot from all the towns and arrived ahead of them. As he went ashore, he saw a great crowd; and he had compassion for them, because they were like sheep without a shepherd; and he began to teach them many things."

Reading with a question like this in mind, the reader considers to what extent Jesus is the engineer or victim of occurrences, such that towards the end of each gospel we are asking to what extent Jesus does the crucifixion or whether it just happens.

To use another distinction, Jesus's compassion for the crowds forms the durative backdrop, against which punctual events of the feeding story take place. There is also a durative lack of understanding on the part of the disciples that is mentioned after Jesus walks on water (Mark 6:52) and remains in the background until a similar story follows later (Mark 8:1–10). These two stories provide the opening to a whole sequence of narrative about who Jesus is, that commences with him enigmatically revisiting these feeding stories and the disciples lack of understanding (Mark 8:14–21).

What Doesn't Happen

As Bible readers, particularly experienced ones, we sometimes need to take a good look at what actually takes place in a story. We also need to watch for what doesn't occur, but that we still assume takes place. The story of the Widow's Mite (Mark 12:41–44) is often read as one in which Jesus sees the rich giving of their abundance and commends a poor woman giving two coins. Readers may assume he commends her action. He doesn't actually do that, he just comments on the difference between the acts of giving. It raises the possibility he is not commending this action, and that something else is going on—more of which later.

Events in Mark 1:40–45

Looking at events, the reader can distinguish different types:

- an action or a happening
- a durative or punctual
- a hinge-point or filler

In Mark 1:40–45, a leper comes to Jesus for healing and kneels. Jesus performs the actions of stretching and touching. While these may be read as the actions, the leper is described on the receiving end of a happening: "the leprosy left him." However, at the end of the story the leper acts, going out and proclaiming his story, and the result happens to Jesus, in the form of a durative prohibition: from now on Jesus is unable to do what he planned in verse 38 and visit towns openly. The text leaves it open to the reader to imagine how that prohibition was realized. Did Jesus try visiting one, and get thrown out of a town? Did he discuss it with the disciples and realize any such visit was now impossible?

The whys and wherefores of this prohibition may be explained by one of the actions in the story: as was noted in picking apart the actual events, Jesus touched a leper. To explore the question of whether an event is a hinge-point or a filler we need to ask whether it has an effect on what follows, such that had it been left out the storyline would not make sense or appear radically altered. The "kneeling" in verse 40 may qualify as a filler. The touch isn't. After he touches the leper Jesus undergoes another burst of emotion: the Greek term used for his strict charge to the leper term can also denote the snort of a horse,[9] and elsewhere describes Jesus response to death.[10] In seeing this part of the story as a nucleus the reader will read it as having effects further down the line.[11] Jesus's response may be because he envisages the consequences of that touch.[12] A reading that connects events and sees Mark 1:45 as a scuppering of the mission outlined in Mark 1:38 presents

9. Guellich, *Mark 1—8:26*, 72.

10. John 11:33, 38.

11. Marcus, *Mark 1–8*, 206.

12. France, *Mark*, 119 doesn't agree with my interpretation but does suggest this is moment of foresight.

this possibility that, in touching the leper, Jesus made himself unclean.[13] The emphatic picking out of the event of the touch and the snorted indignation and plea to not spread this news all tally with the notion that Jesus made himself unclean.[14] Jesus crossed a line, touched a leper, declared him clean and scuppered his own mission. He goes home to Capernaum (2:1), stays in the rural settings, and does not enter a city, barring gentile Tyre (7:24) until Jerusalem at the gospel's climax (Mark 11:1).

Main Events

The reader can reflect and ask what are the main events are in a story. Given three pieces of paper to label or illustrate the three main events in a film like *Toy Story* which would you choose? What about the whole Gospel of Mark? Or Mark 1:35–45? Only three—no cheating.

This activity, using any story, scatters the focus from one single event. It is a variation on the old "That's the story, now draw a picture of it" activity beloved in school. By going for three the reader has to think across the story and sometimes gathers interesting events from the breadth of the story being recounted.

3. MICROSEQUENCES AND MACROSEQUENCES

It is possible that Shakespeare wrote in five acts, neatly spaced, because they roughly matched the amount of time before the candles in the theater needed replacement.[15] A narrative contains distinct sections that connect to a sequence. Such sequences bear different relations to each other as parts of the whole. To use the terminology, smaller events form *microsequences* that then line up to create a *macrosequence*. This is particularly evident in a Gospel, where the full story of Jesus appearing, ministering, encountering conflict, dying, and his tomb being found empty, all form a macrosequence. Within that macrosequence there are microsequences, such as the one in which the disciples return from their mission (Mark 6:30), begin a retreat (Mark 6:31–34), and the other events of the miraculous feeding. Such

---

13. See France, *Mark*, 118.

14. Malina, *New Testament World*, 161; Malina and Rohrbaugh, *Social-Science*, 185 provide rare and guarded support for this reading.

15. Yorke, *Into the Woods*, 35.

microsequences then create the one macrosequence, ultimately giving each gospel its distinctive storyline.

The terms are relative and in the example just quoted there are two events that form a microsequence within the macrosequence of the story of the miraculous feeding: within that story there is a story of a crowd appearing as the disciples take their retreat. The terms are relative but what the reader can grasp is the way smaller microsequences work within larger macro ones.

There are a number of ways in which microsequences can connect to form a macro, the two main ones[16] being a process of time running, through one event, into the other. The other is the way one smaller micro may cause, or be caused by, another micro.

When reading, instead of treating the shorter sequences in isolation, the reader can connect them to the bigger narrative. This involves figuring out how one sequence relates to another. There is also the crucial task of analyzing how events relate the overarching story in which they sit.[17] In Mark 1:36–45 the story begins with a microsequence in which Jesus goes to pray and is found by the disciples, at which point he announces and enacts a mission plan (Mark 1:38–39). Then something happens that scuppers this mission, such that "Jesus could no longer go into a town openly, but stayed out in the country" (Mark 1:45), raising the question of how the events in between relate to this frame, and also causing the reader to reflect on the context the frame brings to story it frames—that of the healing of the leper (Mark 1:40–44)

Ways of Reading: Microsequences and Macrosequences

Before and After

One activity that can be played with a story of any length involves labeling the middle of a sheet of paper with one moment from the story. If done with a group this can be done on a flipchart. Individually, it can just be any notepad.

16. Rimmon-Kenan, *Narrative Fiction*, 16.
17. Ryken, *How to Read the Bible*, 49.

This event becomes the marker: the task for the reader or readers is to think of events that happened before or after that moment and just note them either side. It brings out the change caused and the nature of that event. It also encourages the reader to look at the events from either side.

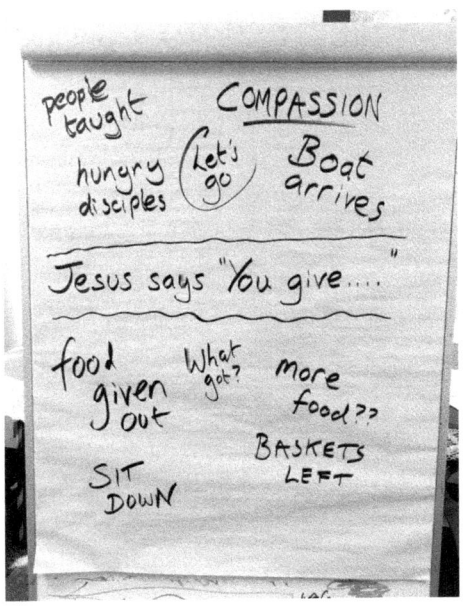

A refinement on this idea involves trying to distance the events an appropriate space away from the marker event.

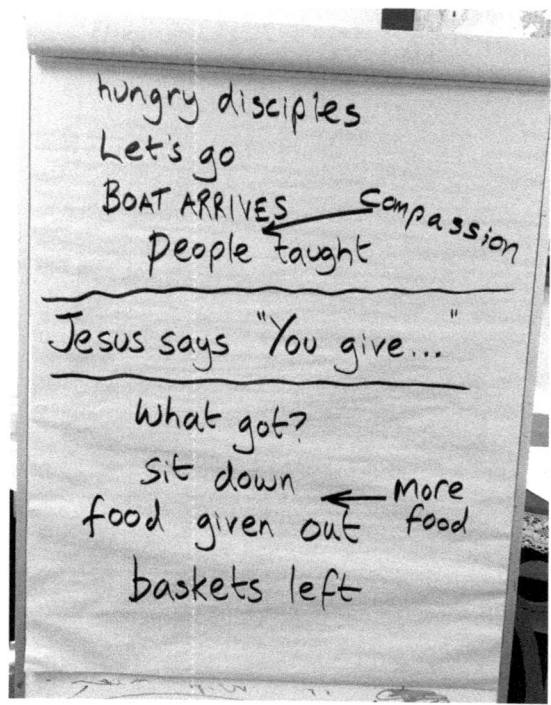

After a bit of notemaking it's worth rereading the list of events. Such a rereading raises the question of the degree to which the summary of events that is being compiled matches the overall memory of the whole story. Sometimes a crucial event has been omitted. It can also be interesting to vary the marker event. For example, if the marker is changed to "Jesus starts teaching" there is a different sense of before and after in that same story.

This example draws the line through the story higher up the biblical page, when "Jesus starts teaching." In many retellings and descriptions of the story, that's where it begins. Retellings can start at the point "One day Jesus was teaching" and in doing so miss many crucial, preceding events. Making this event the marker against which other events are placed involves noticing the disciples beforehand, in Mark 6:30–32; it involves noticing that before they set out to this deserted place there was a lot going on, and "They had no leisure to eat" (Mark 6:31). They are hungry. Jesus's words, "Let's go to a solitary place," are a response to that specific point made in the story. Is it like "Let's go and get something to eat"? The phrase in verse 31 is quite emphatic. He's saying "Just us." This is downtime for just the disciples and Jesus. When they arrive at the place, there is a crowd, so Jesus has compassion and starts teaching. Imagine the disciples at this point! So when they raise the food issue they raise an experience of being with the people. And when he feeds the crowd, an exercise like this may cause the reader to consider the multitude, including twelve famished and peeved disciples. They are perfectly matched to twelve baskets of leftovers, which may have been the feast left for the disciples after they had taken part in the miraculous

ₙg, each filling their own basket.[18] It can be read as a story of minister-
ᵤ to the needy, taking vulnerabilities into such activity, and being healed
with the healing of those joined with, in their need.

Is this why Jesus didn't just conjure up twelve lunches? Either way, the
stuff above the line is hugely important part of the opening of this feeding
miracle.

Micro the Macro

When stories narrate events that are significant but short they open the door
for the reader to both carefully note each event, and then also to imagine
events more fully. We end up splitting events so that a macro moment is
seen in micro. This can be done in a manner similar to the way the opening
to the story of the healing of the leper was unpicked above. The Bible is also
awash with glossed events where the reader can imagine what took place,
microstep by microstep.

The first chapter of Mark contains at least eight verses that condense a
much fuller story and, when seen in that way, can cause the reader to reflect
on just how much is covered in so few words. For example, a huge step is involved in the a verse like Mark 1:4: "John the baptizer appeared in the wilderness, proclaiming a baptism of repentance for the forgiveness of sins." Such
a one-line event invites us to reflect on what we know of the opposition this
would generate, and the life John would lead—including how it would end.

A one-line event like this can also lead us to consider the many different stages that must be packed into the one line, and this is fertile ground for
a readers imagination. It invites us to imagine what could have caused this
move on John's part, and to consider what it would have meant for him and
those around him: the sacrifices, the questioning.

Once we're done with verse 4, verse 5 opens up a similar vista, with a
whole load of other people: "And people from the whole Judean countryside
and all the people of Jerusalem were going out to him, and were baptized by
him in the river Jordan, confessing their sins."

Readers may want to play with the text before reading ahead and look
through chapter 1 and try finding other instances[19] where a single line captures a bigger sequence, hidden within the brevity of the text. One example
is verse 13 which is fleshed out in Matthew and Luke, but here still leaves
open forty days of imagination.[20]

---

18. Lane, *Mark*, 231.

19. Mark 1:14a, 18, 28, 39, 45.

20. See the example of "Simon Smith: 40" in *The Lent Project* blog.

Event Splitting

Working with the micro in the macro involves finding the smaller events that combine to create larger ones. One way to tease out the microsequence is to use rectangles of paper and, starting with two, split a story between them. The leper story (Mark 1:40–45) could be divided into:

A leper asks
for healing

Jesus heals
the leper

or, alternatively:

Jesus touches
the leper

The leper is
healed

There is no right or wrong division. So what about this one?

This could have been done in any number of ways: every reader has a reading.

Once that's done other splits can be made, breaking up the stages along the storyline. For example, that first event can be chopped again.

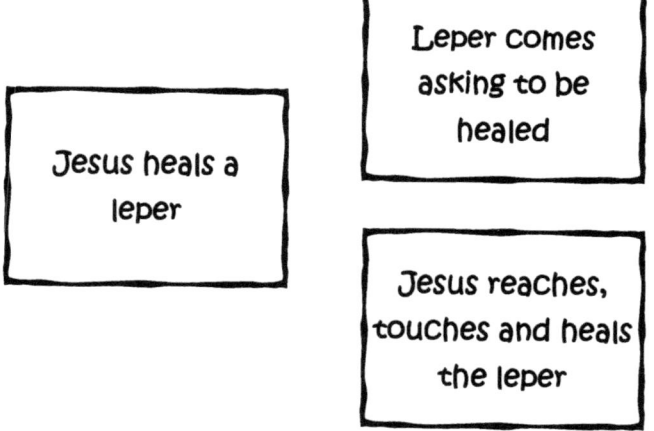

There are at least two bits to the healing box so we can tease out another . . .

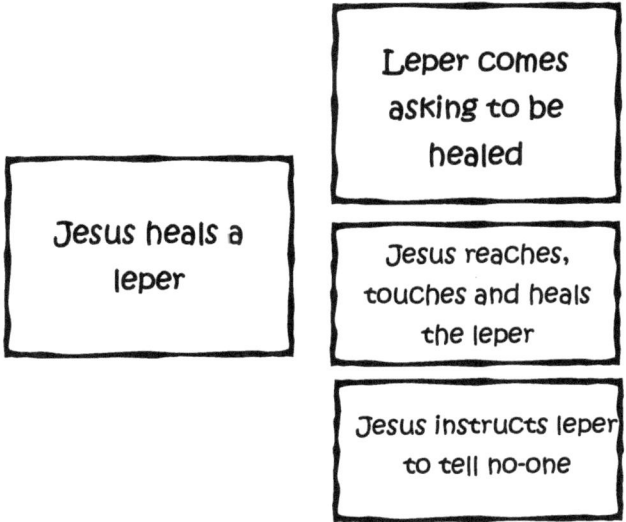

. . . leading up to a final two. Looking at the detail of verse 45 there are also two clear stages to the story's conclusion:

"Leper" goes and tells all about healing

Jesus no longer able to go into town

Events can be split again. For example, there are also two parts to that last event: "Jesus is no longer able to go into town openly so stays in the countryside." This involves branching out into a rejection or resistance to visiting towns, and the resultant resorting to the countryside. The reader could possibly split this even further . . . and further . . .

4. SEQUENCE AND TIME.

Normally "Once upon a time" leads to "and then" . . . or does it? The clock doesn't tick regularly forward in a story, and the variations on this norm are the stuff of anachrony.

Anachrony

In many modern television dramas the trend is for flashbacks and even flash-forwards that deviate from the timeline of the story, create a web of connections across time and also cause viewers to work at figuring out these deviations while watching the story. The narrative theorist Gerard Genette calls such flips in the timeline "anachrony."[21] Films like Quentin Tarantino's *Pulp Fiction* dance forward and backwards. *Orange Is the New Black* and *Lost* are just two examples of television series that maintain a storyline with dips back into the history of each character, shifting from regular passage of time to anachrony. Genette distinguishes between two types of anachrony: analepsis and prolepsis.

Analepsis is where the story flashes back to an earlier event. *Prolepsis* is where it flashes forward. Both are rare in biblical narratives so are worth noting when they arise. They tend to be more glancing references to events. The glance can be quick in the text but huge in what is described, such as the woman healed of a hemorrhage. There is an analepsis that describes the sad years of the woman who tried to be healed discretely, with flashes back through the previous twelve years, during which: "She had endured much under many physicians, and had spent all that she had; and she was no better, but rather grew worse" (Mark 5:26).

The story of Jesus meeting with the tormented Gerasene demoniac, earlier in the chapter (Mark 5:1–20) contains three verses of analepsis that flash back through a montage of his troubled life (vv. 3–5). Once healed, there is also a prolepsis, flashing forward to what he did in the days ahead in verse 20.

The Gerasene demoniac also contains an interesting flashback. On arrival, he saw Jesus from a distance and ran and shouted strange words: "What have you to do with me, Jesus, Son of the Most High God? I adjure you by God, do not torment me" (Mark 5:7) and verse 8 then explains: "For he had said to him, 'Come out of the man, you unclean spirit!'"

It's the quickest of flashbacks but here's an example of why a departure from the timeline is worth watching. This flashback leads the reader to ask:

---

21. Genette, *Narrative Discourse*, 48.

When? When did Jesus say that? Verse 2 makes it clear their encounter happened immediately when Jesus steps out of the boat, so the reader may now play around with the notion that, if Jesus is met by this, could it be that he had been saying "Come out" before he leaves the boat? Could he have known, as they sailed across the Sea of Galilee, about the demoniac and been saying this as they sailed? Is it even possible that this one encounter with the demoniac was the reason for the trip? Again, we need to not partition stories off and can allow our reading to be illuminated by also reading what happened during that boat trip (Mark 4:35–41). It's also worth noting that, once the man is healed Jesus goes back across the sea leaving the reader with no other reason for the jaunt to this other side (Mark 5:21). Imagine it. The reputation this young man may have had amongst the fishermen, the warnings not to land in that part of the sea where this tomb-dwelling possessed man dwells and the trip across and all that happened.[22]

There is a more extensive flashback of analepsis in Mark 6:14–29. By Bible standards this one's positively cinematic. Jesus's fame begins to spread and folks are speculating as to who this teacher may be. No speculation for Herod, who declares: "John, whom I beheaded, has been raised" (Mark 6:16), at which point the story flashes back to a retelling of how John had troubled Herod, a telling that builds our sense of the tyrant who is now hearing about the success of Jesus.

The time signal, "For Herod himself had sent men who arrested John," flashes the story back, anachronically, to an event the reader has encountered, briefly, in Mark 1:14. However, the reader now learns that Herod hadn't heard about Jesus until this point in the story. The beheading of John is then retold, after which, in Mark's Gospel, Jesus shies away from the territories of Herod Antipas.[23]

Shortly after this flashback, there are two feeding miracles (Mark 6:30–44; 8:1–10), followed by an enigmatic exchange about these events (Mark 8:14–21). The obscure exchange is precipitated by the disciples worries about lack of bread and Jesus warning to "Watch out—beware of the yeast of the Pharisees and the yeast of Herod" (Mark 8:15).

The whole thrust of a reading of this macrosequence propels towards the peak of the Gospel, when Peter declares Jesus to be the Messiah (8:29). For now it's worth noting the analepsis. The gospel that opens with Jesus mission following John's arrest approaches a peak moment following a flashback to John's death.

---

22. The request of the people, in Luke, is still consistent with this being the sole purpose of the visit.

23. France, *Mark*, 254.

Ways of Reading: Sequence

Order

In the story of the casting out of Legion, if we remove all time signals such as the flashback of "Jesus had been saying"(Mark 6:14) and just look at the events as they appear in the story, the list looks like this:

- Jesus arriving in the country of the Gerasenes.
- The demoniac living among the tombs.
- The demoniac breaking his chains.
- The demoniac howling and bruising himself with stones.
- The demoniac meeting Jesus.
- The demoniac seeing Jesus at a distance.
- The demoniac running and bowing down.
- The demoniac pleading with Jesus.
- Jesus saying, "Come out of the man."
- Jesus asking, "What is your name?"

As readers we encounter this story in a totally different, anachronic order. The crucial discovery that Jesus has been calling out the demon all along is reserved until we are well into their encounter (Mark 6:14).

For the individual reader, scraps of paper can be deployed again to show the events, and can be shuffled into the order of the text's discourse:

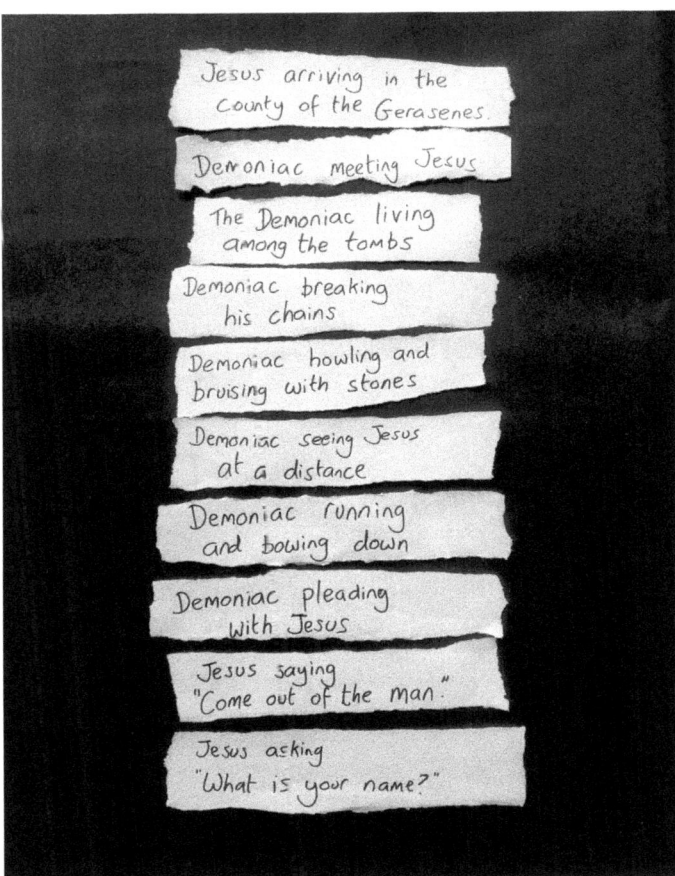

and the order of chronology.

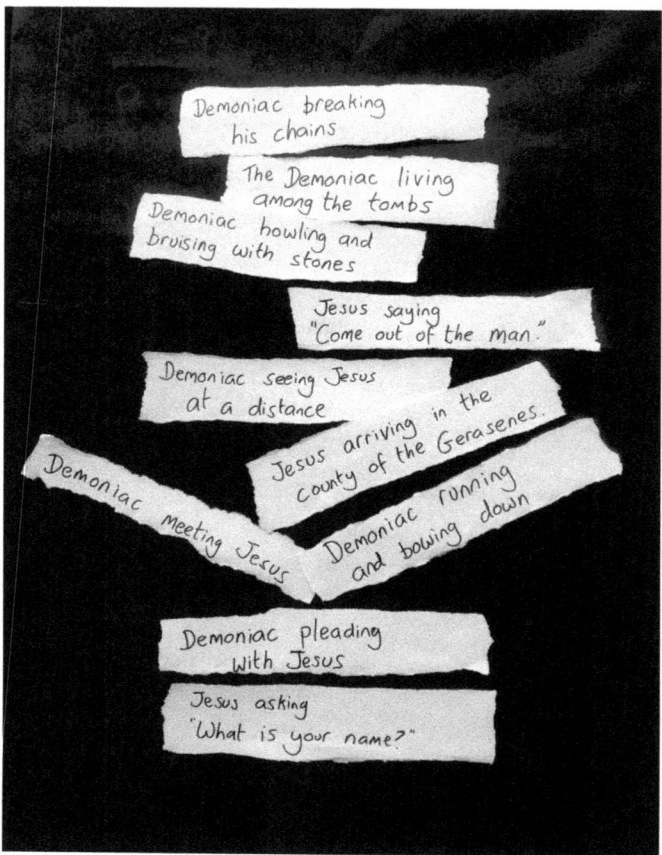

When working with readers in shared study of a text the clarification of what happened when, and the order in which events both happened and are told, can prove interesting. Sequencing a text can also present opportunities for active working together. Printing a story out, or summaries of the events, as in the demoniac example above, can provide a resource that readers are then encouraged to place in the order found in the text, or the natural chronological order.

Line Up

One game I play in services, classes, or workshops is to take a reading and split it into chunks of between one to three verses, which are randomly handed to as many people as there are chunks.[24] These five or six people then stand in a line and read their chunk, one by one. The listeners have to hear the complete jumbled version before they are allowed to move the readers, telling them things like "You need to go at the start" and "You stand between those two." It's literary theory with assertiveness!

As the listeners do this they'll be thinking back to cues like a story opening or one event following another, even in well-known examples. They will often figure out who has the story's beginning and ending. They shuffle folks in the line and then we read again. Sometimes the jumble is resolved, but it sometimes requires a further shuffle before, finally, we have a line that sounds like the story. With every runthrough the listeners actively listen for the connections that make up the sequence in a narrative.

Primacy and Recency[25]

In stories, as the events unfold each new one reshapes the one before it. In some ways, an event is changed by what follows. This phenomenon has been called the *primacy and recency effect*, describing the relationship between events that come earlier and have primacy in a narrative and those that we then read, that then acquire a recency, because their reading was more recent.

Primacy can connect to recency in different ways. As one event connects to another there can be continuity between the two, so when Jesus declares the leper to be clean (Mark 1:41), the leper is clean (Mark 1:42). It is also possible for a recency event to completely alter a primacy one in a way that can undermine or demolish it. The earlier reading of Mark 1 saw the mission of verse 38 significantly changed by verse 45, such that the story becomes one of a thwarting rather than expansion.

The Gospel of Mark opens with an example of a story in which time is somewhat fractal (Mark 1:1–9).[26]

- The declaration that this is the gospel.

- Isaiah prophesies.

- John appears and proclaims.

- The way is prepared and the paths straightened.

---

24. Chunks I use for the story of the Demoniac are as follows: Mark 6, verses 1–2, 3–5, 6–8, 9–10, 11–13, 14–16, 17–20.

25. Resseguie, *Narrative Criticism*, 209–13.

26. Shepherd, "Narrative Role," 160–61.

- John proclaims baptism.
- People go to see John.
- People are baptized.
- John wears camels hair and eats locusts and wild honey.
- One who is more powerful is coming after John.
- The coming one baptizes with the Holy Spirit.
- Jesus comes and is baptized.

The big announcement up top is that this is "The beginning of the good news of Jesus Christ, the Son of God" (Mark 1:1) but the next person we meet is not Jesus but John, the messenger. For a moment, it is as if the focus has shifted completely.[27] What happened to Jesus? Drawing on a bit of literary history, this is the stage at which an early biography would have talked about the subject of the story, with some background that outlined ancestry and possibly told of their birth and youth.[28] Greek and Roman prologues grounded their character in context, as do other gospels in the New Testament—think of the nativity stories. In the opening of Mark, the central character Jesus isn't missing out on that grounding. It's being done in a different way. He is being grounded in the work of God, "As it is written in the prophet Isaiah" (Mark 1:2a). Here the stage is being set with Isaiah's prophecy of John, preparing for Jesus.[29] What we have here is a reading journey of primacy and recency, guiding the response of the reader:

- It starts with the announcement, "The good news of Jesus Christ";
- then the reader is flipped back over five hundred years to "As it is written in the prophet Isaiah";
- and then a switch to "John the baptizer appeared";
- and a proleptic promise about "The one who is more powerful than I";
- before all this is modified by the arrival: "Jesus came from Nazareth."

Read playfully, it's a rollercoaster.

27. Shepherd, "Narrative Role," 154: "The evangelist begins with incomplete focalization of Jesus and leaves with incomplete focalization of John the Baptist."

28. Burridge, Four Gospels, 6–8.

29. Johnson, Form and Function.

4. STORY TIME

Readers read at a particular pace but the time it takes for us to read rarely matches the time it takes for the activity in the text. The activity of Genesis 1 takes six days of creation, but the text can be read in a minute. There is a difference between text time and story time, such that gospels tend to move at a fair pace. A journey across a sea or even a forty-day wilderness sojourn can take one verse. The mapping of the pace with which the narrative covers a time can vary.

At one end of the scale there are ellipses. An *ellipsis* takes place when the text omits or implies events that would have taken time in the story. In Matthew and Luke a good example of this would be the life of Jesus through from childhood to appearance at the Jordan. In these Gospels, Jesus grows up in an ellipsis: in Luke 2:52 he goes from 12 to 30 in one verse.

Closely linked to an ellipsis is a *summary*, as when a longer event is skirted over with a line like Mark 5:14, after the demons leave Legion and enter the pigs:

> The swineherds ran off and told it in the city and in the country.
> Then people came to see what it was that had happened.

At the other extreme there is a *pause*, when the clock stops ticking in the story, giving the narrator time to describe or provide information. This happens in Mark 5:11 when, in the middle of demoniac confrontation, the text narrates: "Now there on the hillside a great herd of swine was feeding."

One further interesting example is the way the start of that story pauses at the moment when Legion meets Jesus and uses a flashback to describe him. In reality this is still a ticking clock sweeping summarily over Legion's life, but also a description of the character who now meets us, pausing the story of the meeting.

Closely related to the pause is the *slowdown*, when the narrative slows down for something that would have been quicker than its narration. Proust's famous description of eating a petite madeleine takes longer to read than to eat, with a detailing of the soaked morsel of cake and changes in palate the cake evokes:

> No sooner had the warm liquid, mixed with the crumbs, touched
> my palate than a shudder ran through me and I stopped, intent
> upon the extraordinary thing that was happening to me.

This leads to questions about how to capture this bite of cake:

> Whence could it have come to me, this all-powerful joy? I sensed that it was connected with the taste of the tea and cake, but that it infinitely transcended those savours.[30]

That's some cake!

Mark 1 contains a good example of a point where the narrative notably slows as healing takes place: "Moved with pity, Jesus stretched out his hand and touched him, and said to him, "I do choose. Be made clean!" (Mark 1:41). This may roughly match the time the action took, and it noticeably slows down the narrative to a pace more detailed than the story around it.

In a *scene*, the duration of the narrative and time of the story are more similar,[31] an example being dialogue that takes as long to read aloud as it takes to say it, such as the lines from Mark 5:7–9:

> And he shouted at the top of his voice, "What have you to do with me, Jesus, Son of the Most High God? I adjure you by God, do not torment me." For he had said to him, "Come out of the man, you unclean spirit!"
> Then Jesus asked him, "What is your name?"
> He replied, "My name is Legion; for we are many."

This dialogue presents what was said in a timespan that matches the saying, whereas what follows, "He begged him earnestly not to send them out of the country" (Mark 5:10), returns the narrative to a summary.

It's helpful to see these types of duration as a continuum rather than trying to make hard and fast distinctions between them, and one way to play with the idea to listen to someone relating events that have taken place in real life, listening out for a story at length or a summarization.

Ellipsis	Summary	Scene	Slow down	Pause
A lot of time passes in the story but little or nothing in the text	A lot of time passes in the story that is summarized in the text	It takes almost as long to read me as it takes to happen	Something that happened at a regular speed is given more words and narrative in the text	Story time stops but the narrative carries on, as when there is description or reflection on events

In his literary study of another Gospel, R. Alan Culpepper points out a fact that can be applied to the Gospel of Mark: it is mostly a switch between

---

30. Proust, *Remembrance*, 48.

31. Bal, *Introduction*, 74.

scenes and summaries,[32] and the reader can watch for where the story speeds up and slows down. The opening of the Gospel in Mark 1:9–12 includes a good example of a summary that packs many events into one verse. Following the baptism, which receives a bit more story time, there is a summary in which the Spirit whisks Jesus away in the space of a verse:

> In those days Jesus came from Nazareth of Galilee and was baptized by John in the Jordan. And just as he was coming up out of the water, he saw the heavens torn apart and the Spirit descending like a dove on him. And a voice came from heaven, "You are my Son, the Beloved; with you I am well pleased." And the Spirit immediately drove him out into the wilderness.

Two points of interest are those times when the text moves quickly over slower events and also when the text slows down, in a way not wholly characteristic of Gospel writing, and so stands out. The quick coverage opens certain texts to the imagination. Mark 1:13 takes a biblical forty days, and during that time "he was with the wild beasts; and the angels waited on him." That's a lot packed into a small space, leaving readers to speculate on what may be summarized in those words. There are stories of Satan's temptation, as told in Matthew and Luke, but a verse like this Markan one opens the imagination to wild beasts. The reader may also note the text doesn't actually say whether being with the wild beasts was a good or bad experience. "The Testament of Naphtali," an apocryphal book found among the Dead Sea Scrolls, dates to just before the birth of Jesus and contains a different image to play with: "the devil will flee from you, wild animals will be afraid of you, and angels will stand by you."[33] What was told in short opens up a vista to long imaginings.

There are also instances of narrative slowdown, when moments of real time are itemized with greater detail. A classic example of this is in the book of Jeremiah, when Jeremiah buys a field of his relative, even though the land, and field, are about to be invaded. This symbolic act is told with loving detail:

> And I bought the field at Anathoth from my cousin Hanamel, and weighed out the money to him, seventeen shekels of silver. I signed the deed, sealed it, got witnesses, and weighed the money on scales. Then I took the sealed deed of purchase, containing the terms and conditions, and the open copy; and I gave the deed of purchase to Baruch son of Neriah son of Mahseiah, in the

---

32. Culpepper, *Anatomy*, 71.
33. T. Naph. 8.4, cited in Black, *Mark*, 62.

> presence of my cousin Hanamel, in the presence of the witnesses
> who signed the deed of purchase, and in the presence of all the
> Judeans who were sitting in the court of the guard. (Jer 32:9–12)

In the weighing and signing and sealing there is something of the moment of this action that is broken down, such that the reader can almost see each small step. There is something of this sort of loving and momentous slowdown in the story of the healing of the leper too (Mark 1:40–45).

Ways of Reading: Story Time

Speed and Slow

Readers can root out speedups and slowdowns. Slowdowns rarely get as slow as life itself. It is usually quicker to read something than do it. He may have been fast, but I can read the story "Roger Bannister Ran a Mile in 3 Minutes and 59 Seconds" quicker than he ran it. Slowdowns in biblical narrative are worth watching out for—one might ask, why this added detail?

In Mark 7:33–34 Jesus heals a man with details: "He took him aside in private, away from the crowd, and put his fingers into his ears, and he spat and touched his tongue. Then looking up to heaven, he sighed and said to him, 'Ephphatha,' that is, 'Be opened.'" Much slower than, for example, Matthew's healing of two blind men in Jericho, where he just touches the eyes and, it's done![34] Why the spit?[35] The reader can take time and look at the detail—the taking aside, the physicality of it. To be clear it isn't that these each mean something, and woe betide the sermonizer who tries to squash meaning into each wrinkle, but the reader needs to slow down with the slowed-down details. To pick up on this example, in Jesus's time saliva was believed to have curative properties, so this then raises the question, "What sort of a healer is this?" Is Jesus doing divine intervention or the general practice of the day?[36]

Speedups take the opposite end of this spectrum. Contrast the loving description of Jeremiah's act of faith in purchasing a field with the awful one-verse speed in Bathsheba's story: "So David sent messengers to get her, and she came to him, and he lay with her. (Now she was purifying herself after her period). Then she returned to her house" (2 Sam 11:4). One aspect of such speedups can be the space opened for the reader to consider what took place. In Bathsheba's case there is some debate as to whether this was

34. Matt 20:34.

35. Mark 8:23; Matt 9:1–7.

36. Craffert, *Galilean Shaman*, 293.

consensual. A happier speedup is in Mark 7:30, the climax of the story of the Syrophoenecian woman who pleaded for her child, where

> She went home, found the child lying on the bed, and the demon gone.

So much happens in that short summary.

Chapter 2

Plot

Lions, witches, and wardrobes would have come to nothing without the English weather.[1] In C. S. Lewis's classic, *The Lion, the Witch and the Wardrobe*, much happens, following Lucy's initial visit to Narnia through the wardrobe. That visit might never have happened had the English weather not resulted in the evacuees in the story playing hide-and-seek, causing Lucy to hide in a wardrobe, with the effect that she enters Narnia, and the plot thickens. Of course, Lucy needs to enter the wardrobe because, while there are any number of ways she could have got there, the plot needs to get to Narnia.

Plot is a thread through a story that connects the events, like beads on a string. While the string may not be visible it is evident in the way the beads appear strung together.

1. PLOT, COMBINATION AND CAUSALITY

The last chapter looked at addition of one event to another. This chapter looks at combination, and how those events are plotted together. In a story one event is followed by another. The reader takes these nuclei, the key points along the storyline, and experiences a holistic structure that holds events together.[2] The plot is the way the reader connects and combines these

1. Lewis, *Lion, the Witch and the Wardrobe*.
2. Chatman, *Story and Discourse*, 53.

bare bones into a structured unit.[3] One of the main ways this connection is made is through causality, with one event causing another. The novelist E. M. Forster came up with the classic distinction between "plot" and "story" when he suggested that:

> "The King died and then the Queen died" is a story.
> "The King died and then the Queen died of grief" is a plot."[4]

It is possible for stories to move along without such causal connections. *Alice in Wonderland* may be such a story. Dylan Thomas's classic radio play *Under Milk Wood* is also a good example of a story in which one event adds to another but the holistic combination arises more from the listener's consistent experience of a sleepy town. There are also stories that are mainly unified by the repeated presence of a particular character, resulting in an episodic narrative.[5]

The Gospels may sometimes appear to typify a storyline in which different small and unconnected stories follow one another, held together by the central character.[6] The connections between stories can sometimes be clear. Sometimes the connection is less clear, as may be the case between the two stories looked at in the previous chapter, of Jesus planning a mission (Mark 1:35–39), followed by the healing of the leper (Mark 1:40–45). Here, there may be a connection of plans being hatched in the former story that are then scuppered as a consequence of events in the latter one.

A sense of plot can be experienced across larger biblical narratives, such as the way Gospels build up of events of hostility and confrontation, leading to the confrontation of the final week.[6] This book sees plot as part of the work of the reader. It's what readers do. There is something almost habitually and playfully human about making plotted connections: faced with only the first of Forster's two mini-stories above, many readers will smell a rat and ask whether there's a royal conspiracy afoot. This is the role of the reader, an active role in the process of "event turned into plot."[7]

Concepts of cause, effect, and causal connection are a useful starting point in understanding the workings of plot, but alongside these there is also a sense of the thrust of the story and the narrowing of possible outcomes. Films like *Speed* and *Armageddon* both present a somewhat similar sense of massive problem hurtling along such that many viewers may not remember

---

3. Dannenberg, "Plot," 436.

4. Forster, *Aspects*, 87.

5. Ryken, *How to Read the Bible*, 44.

6. See also Resseguie, *Narrative Criticism*, 201–2.

7. Chatman, *Story and Discourse*, 43.

the events along the way, or even the eventual outcome, but retain a recollection of the crisis that was somehow averted.

Beginnings and Endings

Whether it's the English rain and liberation of Narnia or a hungry crowd and miraculous abundance of food, the defining bookends of a story provide the ends of the string that is the plot. Stories commence with an inciting incident, but defining a Bible story's beginning isn't always straightforward. Looking at a story like the widow's offering, the seemingly obvious boundary for this string of pearls in Mark chapter 12 is to start at verse 41, when Jesus is watching people make their offerings in the temple. There appears to be a natural ending at verse 44, when he commends the fact that "she out of her poverty has put in everything she had, all she had to live on" (Mark 12:44). The historic chapter divisions insert a break at that point and the reader may find here a simple tale of extra special sacrificial giving. However, there were no chapters in the original text, and no paragraphs and verses either, so in considering any narrative it is always worth reading to the sides and seeing just how extended in either direction the string of beads may be. In this story, immediately before the traditional start, Jesus has lashed out at the very system that exploits such women. He warns about the scribes and lists various hypocrisies of the system including, in verse 40, immediately before the story in question, railing against the way "They devour widows' houses." As traditionally read, Jesus is sitting at the temple offering watching rich people tossing in money they can spare, then he sees this woman putting in a lot less. Jesus's response has been read as him saying: "Isn't that great? Look, she's given more. She's given all she had." This could be read as Jesus trotting out a platitude and stating the obvious: just a bit of maths. Exercising the disciplines of chapter 1, the reader can note what actually happens (and may want to take a moment for this exercise). Jesus doesn't actually commend or rejoice in what he sees here. It could be alarming if he did, for to be a widow back then was a perilous situation and effectively meant you were destitute. Jesus passionately cared for the poor so it would be an odd reading that sees him giving a big thumbs up to someone becoming destitute, right before his eyes.

Switching to the other end of the string, immediately following the event of the widow's offering, Jesus issues his denunciation of the temple system and foretells it's destruction, prompted by one of the disciples, as they exit the temple, saying: "Look, Teacher, what large stones and what large buildings!" to which Jesus responds: "Do you see these great buildings? Not one stone will be left here upon another; all will be thrown down" (Mark 13:1–2).

The condemnations above are the beads at either end of the string of the story of the widow, and the reader could look again at Mark 12:41–44 in this light. Reading along this thread, the story can become one of a widow being exploited by a temple system that Jesus predicts is going to be destroyed along with the building,—something that actually happened, a few decades later. Could it be that the story of the widow's offering is not one in which Jesus commends what he is seeing, but rather one in which he laments it? This may not be a commendation, so much as a warning to recognize an abusive and exploitative system or power that can consume a person, and to see it as fleeting, passing, and slated for destruction.

The story exemplifies the general prompt to look at the events on either side of any Bible story.

Teleological

Aristotle used the term teleological, combining "telos" (end) and "logos" (word or reason) to describe the notion of the reason or purpose of something being perceived by looking to its ending or completion. Like a goal, the ending of the storyline defines what takes place before it. This applies to longer stories and whole gospels. The ending can shape the reading of the individual stories, along the way. If the widow's offering is an event in a story about a commendation from Jesus then the two coins the widow drops in the offertory almost have a different currency if they are the oppressive action of the temple system. The part an event plays in the whole story can define that event. Narrative theorist Jonathan Culler frames a lovers' fallout in just this way: "After a severe quarrel hero and heroine may either be reconciled or go their separate ways, and the suspense which the reader might feel at such moments is, structurally, a desire to know whether the quarrel is to be classified as a testing of love or as an end to love."[8]

Whether it is a larger biblical narrative, or one story within, the plot provides the "because" and "so" of events. It could be that Jesus's comment on the Widow was because of his previous speech, and maybe the response about the stones of the temple is a "So . . ." that follows on from her story. As readers, we don't get access to the thinking of Jesus or any other character, but as we string the beads together, it's worth being mindful that these are not just stories separately following each other on a page. The time signals here create a succession within a single passage of time, with the story of the

8. Culler, *Structuralist Poetics*, 211.

widow placed after "He sat down" (Mark 12:41) and the exchange about the stones of the temple similarly taking place "As he came out of the temple" (Mark 13:1a). These events connect in the story.

Ways of Reading: Plot

Framing

Readers should check the frame around any Bible story. While the separate stories of the gospels may be threaded like beads, there is a renewed sense in modern criticism of the narrative string that combines them. Allowing the events on either side to speak to the reading of a story can enrich the content that is so framed. The story of the leper's healing is framed by Jesus's plan for mission, and then followed by Jesus at home—possibly his own—when the roof comes in (Mark 2:1–5). Another example is that of the rich man who enthuses about eternal life but does not follow Jesus (Mark 10:17–22). The texts on either side can offer illumination on this moment. Immediately before he has said: "Truly I tell you, whoever does not receive the kingdom of God as a little child will never enter it" (Mark 10:15). There is also a discussion with the disciples immediately after, about riches, camels and the eye of the needle, directly related to the story. The reader may also push the frame further, as far as the incident that follows and the amazement and fear as Jesus heads for Jerusalem (Mark 10:32).

Reading benefits from the framing of the story, a quality enhanced in settings where Bibles are opened so that readers can scan whole pages rather than hearing stories read as isolated chunks.

Asking "Why"?

The question "why?" can be posed at any point in a narrative. In terms of biblical text this simply involves reading a verse and ending with the question "Why?"

> A poor widow came and put in two small copper coins, which are worth a penny. (Mark 12:42)

Why?

The question opens onto a few levels, starting with the immediate cause and effect in the story, such that the answer may be because she was coming to the temple, or because it was her turn in the line. The reader may note that the rich folks were in the plural while this woman comes as a sole example.

This question also opens up the "why?" of the entire story and the tension Jesus is in with the authorities, throughout Mark 12, with an incendiary parable (12:1–12) and denunciations (12:35–40). These all add up towards answering the question, "why?"

There are bigger "why?" questions that are opened. In the case of the widow's offering there is the reading that sees here the answer "Because she was so devoted and sacrificial" but there is also the bigger "why" of spiritual abuse, which may resonate with the "why?" the reader may throw at contemporary religious situations. The bigger answer incorporates the system that dominated this woman and others at the time—a further answer to the question "Why?"

The basic idea is to stop at any moment in a story, whether selected or at random, and ask "Why?"

Opening Lines

It is up to the reader to delineate the starting point of a story, but having done so it is worth taking time with the opening lines. In the same way the scanning of a range of stories can enhance a reading of a book or long section of biblical narrative, so the collecting of opening lines or scenarios can offer a montage of the a series of events. The choice of starting point may be arbitrary, but opening lines still offer a border.

In those days when there was again a great crowd without anything to eat. (Mark 8:1a)

Six days later, Jesus took with him Peter and James and John, and led them up a high mountain apart, by themselves. And he was transfigured before them. (Mark 9:2)

As he was setting out on a journey, a man ran up and knelt before him, and asked him, "Good Teacher, what must I do to inherit eternal life?" (Mark 10:17)

He sat down opposite the treasury, and watched the crowd putting money into the treasury. Many rich people put in large sums." (Mark 12:41)

What questions are raised by such openings? To answer, the readers will need to try approaching the opening of this moment as if they did not know the actual course of events that follow. Only then can the list be added to with questions about what Jesus may do and how characters may respond.

Working Backwards

The theorist Leland Ryken once observed: "For me, the most convenient test of whether a story has such causal coherence (as in Forster) is to begin at the end of a story and march backwards through the main events"[9]

In the end of the feeding of the multitude in Mark 6 the disciples do finally get their food, and they actually get enough for one basket each. In a manner that is somewhat beloved of an Agatha Christie whodunit, the end contains the strands that led there and the reader can home in on the end outcome of a story and work back through all the elements that drive towards that point. In an individual biblical story these can provide a vital connection to the wider vista, as when the walking on the water story ends on the note that the disciples "did not understand about the loaves, but their hearts were hardened" (Mark 6:52).

Links

One way of homing in on the causality, connecting cause and effect within a story, is to simply scribble a few linked circles on a piece of paper

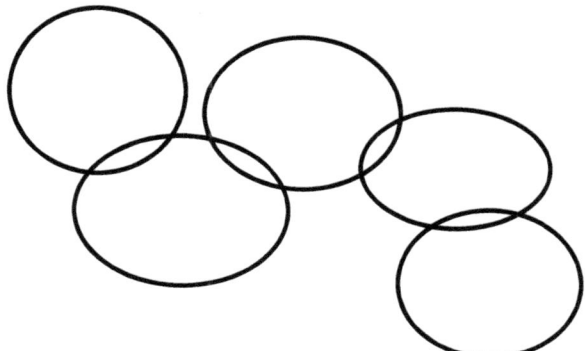

and place one event in one circle.
This could be the middle

9. Ryken, *How to Read the Bible*, 47.

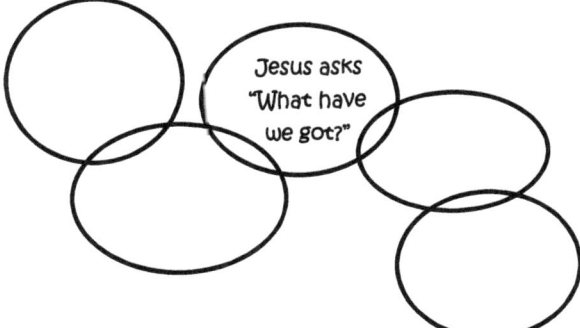

or ending

The event itself could be one that commences a story or something that takes place in the middle. Whatever is chosen, the task is then to look to empty links either side and make the connections to this moment.

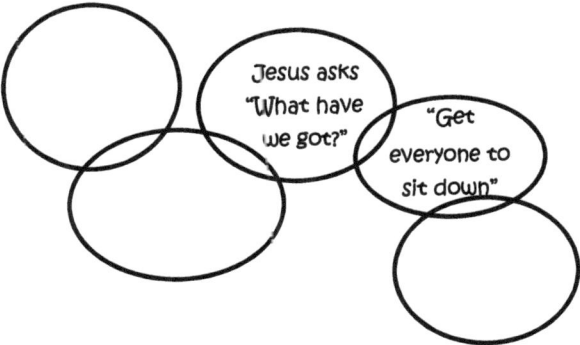

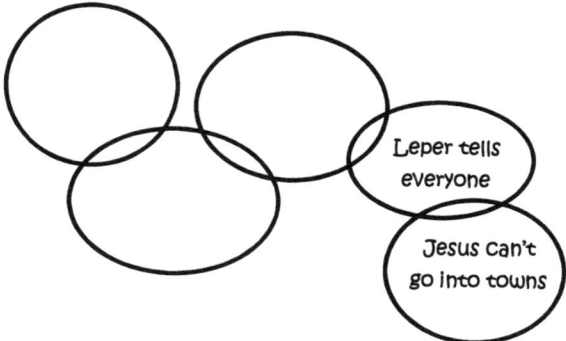

It can cause reflection on what causes and what follows an event and prompt thoughts about, for example, why the counting of what was available mattered when there were so many people to feed or why the leper's telling people about his healing may stop Jesus going on his mission. It can also raise a connection that isn't directly causal: the widow's offering is not, in one sense, caused by the offerings of the wealthy people. In another sense, it very much is. The exercise guides the reader's sense of connection and plot within stories, that will look to how actions like that of the wealthy givers both cause and exploit the widow's offering.

Plot Boxes

Similar to the links, a further way to tease out the connection and plot of a story is to take a few scraps of paper or sticky notes and plot the story out. This can take the form of note words or doodles—whatever works.

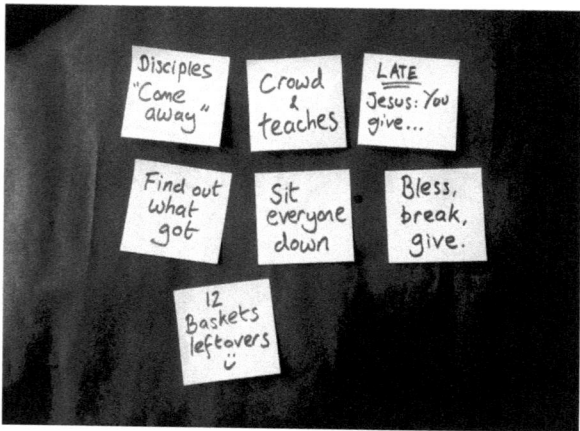

Straightway seeing the story represented this way can highlight what a cursory scribbling has left out, particularly when held against a rereading of the text.

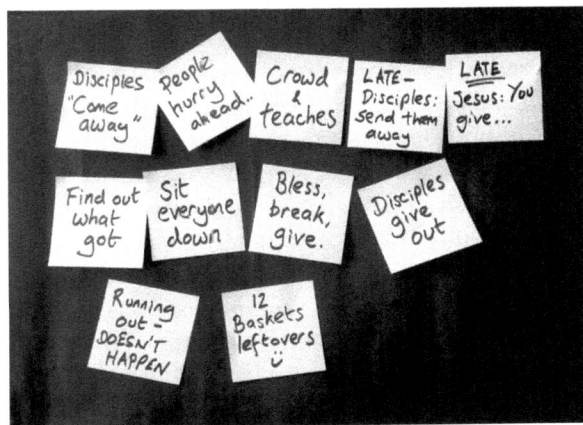

This can cause the reader to see a vital connection with one event leading to another. In this example, Jesus is not out to feed the crowd until the disciples say: "This is a deserted place, and the hour is now very late; send them away so that they may go into the surrounding country and villages and buy something for themselves to eat" (Mark 6:35b–36). Would he have fed them otherwise?

This bit of text play also casts a light on gaps such as the one clearly puzzling the plot boxer in the example shown: does Jesus actually feed anyone, or do the disciples give out the food? How this happens is not depicted but the two added boxes build up a disciple shaped role of concern and panic met by something unspecified—a plot line that may have something to say to discipleship today.

2. SHAPE OF STORY

There's a shape to the way stories work. For writer and director, David Mamet,

> Dramatic structure is not an arbitrary—or even a conscious— invention. It is an organic codification of the human mechanism for ordering information. Event, elaboration, denouement;

thesis, antithesis, synthesis; boy meets girl, boy loses girl, boy gets girl; act one, act two, act three.[10]

One of the classic outlines of such a shapes is that of

situation-complication-resolution.

Alternatively, in his *Grammar of Stories* Gerard Prince described "a minimal story as consisting of three events, the third of which is the inverse of the first."[11] Within such a shape there will be the events, but there is also a sense of the shaping of the events, and that's a crucial added factor. While the image of beads on a string partially represents the nature of story plot, there is more to it, otherwise a story could end up being strung along ad infinitum. Plot is also the shape of the whole story. A teller can tell the story, event by event, but there is also a sense in which one can tell the plot by telling the overarching action or disclosure to which the events drive, in a teleological manner. To say "twelve people are all suspects in a murder, and it transpires they all did it" or "a detective investigates a murder but, at the end, one of the suspects unmasks the detective as the murderer" is to tell the plot that strings together everything else that occurs.[12] The triumph of *The Lion King* or tackling of *Jaws* are examples of the way the constituent events of the story build towards the ending and are defined by the shape that carries the reader towards it.[13]

For the writer and producer John Yorke, there may be a variety of shapes and structures to stories but he boils them down to one simple, underlying structure:

JOURNEY THERE: JOURNEY BACK.

Sometimes this is literally so, as in "Jack and the Beanstalk," but at other times the journey is an inner movement of a character but, Yorke observes, stories involve a leaving to go and get the solution to a problem, and bring it back. In some the protagonist doesn't get what they seek until the end of the tale. Yorke cites *E.T.* and *Saving Private Ryan* among examples of such stories. However, Yorke demonstrates that, while the apparent journey may end at the final spaceship or the finding of Ryan, in such stories "The archetypal 'journey there; journey back' structure is buried within the more obvious outward journey."[14] In such cases there is a surface destination, such

10. Mamet, quoted in Yorke, *Into the Woods*, 28.

11. Ryken, *How to Read the Bible*, 52.

12. I'm not footnoting either of these as it will give the games away.

13. Merenlahti, *Poetics*, 100.

14. Yorke, *Into the Woods*, 70.

as a spaceship home or Private Ryan, but Yorke directs our attention to the point at which Elliot enables E.T. to phone home, or when the troop charged with saving Private Ryan resolve to continue their mission, having initially found the wrong Ryan and discovered it will be almost suicidal to continue towards the right one. He sees these as the character's actual, personal journey and observes that in stories like these, "We know the midpoint of each film is the moment when each protagonist embraces for the first time the quality they will need to become complete and finish their story."[15] They have journeyed there.

The reader may be able to think of their own examples such as the venture after *Jaws* or Simba's turnaround in *The Lion King*. It's also an insight that lights up old films like *The Third Man*. On another level, in traditional British pantomimes it is not uncommon for the all-important turn in character plans and fortunes to happen just before the interval, allowing the second section of the performance to play out the change to the character.

It is also worth noting that, with this internal goal in mind, Yorke also reminds that: "A well-designed midpoint has a risk/reward ratio: a character gains something vital, but in doing so ramps up the jeopardy around them."[16]

A turning of the story at a midpoint can operate on the level of a larger biblical narrative and also within individual stories. In the former, it can be seen in Jonah (2:1–10), when God remembering Jonah changes the story and sows the seeds for God remembering Ninevah (3:10) and Jonah's final argument about the sheltering plant (4:6–11). It is also there in the fate of King Saul when, having been made king (1 Sam 9), there is a turning point when he disobeys a commandment (1 Sam 13:8–14), and the stage is set for the outcome of God's rejection. It can also be found in the structure of the whole Gospel of John, when the raising of Lazarus (John 11) leads to a chapter that marks a midpoint, as Jesus restores a friend he loved to life, immediately before entering Jerusalem (John 12). In the Gospel of Mark, as a whole there is a definite sense of movement to a midpoint which, for reasons of geography, is covered in a later chapter on story settings. It involves a journey to the midpoint and top of the map at Caesarea Philippi (Mark 8:27–29). There is more on this in the section "A Background and One Reading" in chapter 7.

Within the individual story there can also be a critical moment of mid-pointing, It may not be as dramatic as the Lion King's encounter with his own identity or the moment of revelation in *The Third Man*, but it is

15. Yorke, *Into the Woods*, 70.
16. Yorke, *Into the Woods*, 59.

still worth looking within an individual Bible story and seeking the midpoint that carries the seeds of the outcome. This is the moment in which the
story embraces what will be needed for the outcome. In the Old Testament,
Leland-Ryken describes some of the heroic tests that confront the courage,
resourcefulness, and mental and moral resources of protagonist in stories.
Examples include the story of David and Goliath, when the resolve to face
the Philistine champion (1 Sam 17:26) comes well before the concluding
sling of the stone or the way Ruth's choice to stay with Naomi, though early
in the story, is a choice that shapes what follows (Ruth 1:16–17). Leland-
Ryken observes the centrality of choice in such stories, observing that "Stories concentrate on the person at the crossroads."[17]

In the gospels the extent of the narrative can be more concise but
similar points within a story can still be located. When confronted by the
Gerasene demoniac, before the demons are cast out, the wild man of the
tombs is met by, and responds to, a question.

> Then Jesus asked him, "What is your name?" He replied, "My
> name is Legion; for we are many." (Mark 5:9)

The belief that knowing someone or something's name involves gaining
some power over them was prevalent at the time, and is present in the way
humanity names the animals (Gen 2:19–20) and also in the demand for a
name when Jacob wrestles with the Angel of the Lord (Gen 32:39). It's also
present in the way the name of God is revered (Lev 24:16). In other cultures,
this power also there in the traditional tale of *Rumpelstiltskin*. In the story of
the demoniac the giving up of the name reveals his pitiful level of possession
and the turning point from which Jesus will find an alternative multitude of
pigs to which to send the Legion. The reader may just reread and reflect on
the way that question and answer turns the whole story.

Another example of a turning point within a particular Bible story can
be found in the first feeding of a multitude. Before even one fish is shared
there is a key turning point in the confrontation between Jesus and the disciples, when he meets their request to send the people way with his absurd
command:

> You! You give them something to eat. (Mark 6:37b, author translation)

The original Greek has an added emphasis that is clearly turning the
matter back to the disciples, with the sense of "You! You give them" with
the resultant, amusing check on what they have, then the requirement to

---

17. Ryken, *How to Read the Bible*, 51.

get everyone seated. The shift from sending the people away to sitting them down is as much a miracle as anything that happens to a fish.

In Bible stories these mid-points can be the moment when something of depth kicks in, even though the outcome hasn't yet emerged, whether it's the cry of disciples who think they see a ghost (Mark 6:49) or the determination to press on with a healing in the face of despair (Mark 5:36).

Ways of Reading: Shape of Story

Basic Structures

The children's novelist Janni Howker once categorized stories into three diagrammatically represented structures.[18] Howker labeled them the relationship, the invited/uninvited guest, and the quest, and suggested that "the entire canon of the world's stories may be based on three or four such structures."[19]

The relationship	The invited/uninvited guest	The Quest
Y	(circle with arrow)	(bar chart)

The relationship involves the basic structure of a meeting and the storyline created by that encounter, with both *Romeo and Juliet* and *Lady Chatterley's Lover* as two such stories.

The invited/uninvited guest sees a preexisting circle affected by an arrival, be it invited, such as a new member of family, or uninvited, like a monster or large shark. Howker observed the way Stephen Spielberg used this structure in *E.T.*, *Jaws*, and *Gremlins*, adding: "It is the basis of most genre writing—horror, ghost stories, crime, westerns and much science fiction. As a culture we are obsessed with this pattern."[20]

18. Howker, "Plot."
19. Howker, "Plot."
20. Howker, "Plot."

Finally, "a quest is a journey with a purpose" and, alongside such human journeys as seeking the love of a father or school qualifications, Howker places the quests of Sir Galahad and Indiana Jones.

For a gospel as a whole the quest arrow entering the circle can provide an overall image, and is certainly one that applies to notions of incarnation. There are also elements of the quest that feature in the overall structure of Mark's Gospel and that will be explored in chapter 7. However, these shapes also have much to offer the reading of an individual story within a longer biblical book. Mark 1 begins with the arrow entering the circle, whether it be the appearing of John or the emerging of Jesus, whereas the encounter with the first disciples and their calling has more of the relationship "Y" shape to it. The mission of Mark 1:35–39 then becomes something of a quest.

The shape of the leper story (Mark 1:40–45) is open to some debate. This could read like a "Y" shaped relationship but there is an element of arrow into circle about it. However, is this the apparently obvious arrow of Jesus the healer coming into the lives of people like this leper? The story also reads as an established mission into which the leper steps and disrupts. Is he the arrow? The same question as to who is the arrow and who is the circle is present in Mark 2:1–12, when the paralytic quite literally breaks into the story. Other healings may have a similar direction to them, as when a woman in need of healing invades another healing (Mark 5:21–34) or another woman crashes in on Jesus (Mark 7:24–30). In considering stories this way, the reader begins to discover the application these shapes have across the Bible as a whole: there is no set answer, but they offer ways of reading.

Doodle the Story

Folks who study the Bible as literature seem to love a good graphic, and while Howker's images are overarching, the doodling need not stop there. One of the most effective ways of playing with a story is to doodle out the tale. The idea here is not to draw an illustration, but a graphic that scribbles out the text, with messy shapes or arrows. In the example below, doodling out the Gerasene demoniac, the arrows of who comings and goings raises the question around when, precisely, Jesus had done verse 8, in which: "He had said to him, "Come out of the man, you unclean spirit!""

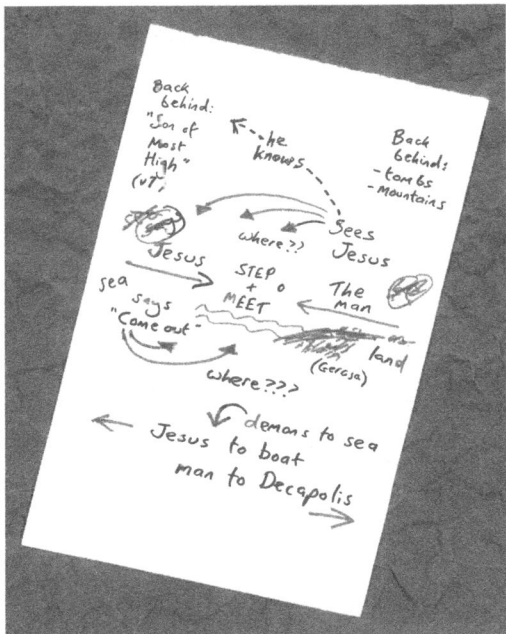

One guide for this is to use stick people or graphics, simple symbols, and lots of arrows. The other is to start somewhere other than the top left of the page, where English writing would often commence.

This example, with the feeding of the multitude, and the bracket over the moment when food is set before the disciples draws attention to the suggestion it is the disciples who, in the end, feed the crowd, asking whether they do the miraculous.

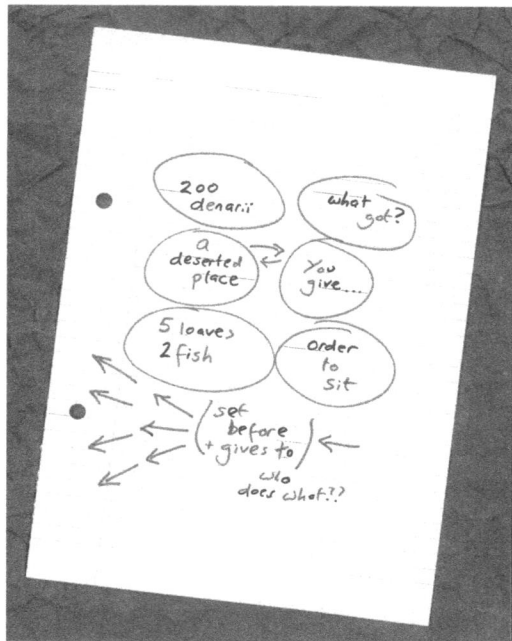

The aim here, as with all such narrative tinkering, is not that some stunning and hitherto unseen lesson or meaning will emerge. The task is just to explore the story. If anything does emerge from such a graphic, great, but the main task is to doodle through the story.

Longer Strings

Returning to the image of a plot as a string of pearls, in exploring biblical narrative there are strings of story that span a number of Bible chapters, if not a whole book. Certain critical theories, outside the scope of this book, explore how different smaller stories came to be strung into larger biblical narratives,[21] but for the reader focused on poetics, one way of reading involves considering the longer chunk, such as a whole Gospel, and exploring something of the particular way in which that longer story is shaped.[22] To give one example, Matthew's Gospel can be read as "five great blocks" of teaching that echo the five books of the Law of Moses, structuring the narrative.[23] John's Gospel has much longer specific stories that build around

21. See Barton, *Reading*, particularly the Vanishing Redactor of 56–58.
22. Brown, *Gospels*, and Burridge, *Four Gospels*.
23. Burridge and Gould, *Jesus*, 60.

themes and sayings. Both are examples of bigger pictures of a chunk of biblical narrative illustrating the value of exploring the string that holds the beads.

Point Within

When Jesus calls the disciples, the significance of the way that "immediately they left their nets" (Mark 1:18) captures something of the whole call. Reflecting the nature of the midpoint, above, a reading of a story can involve looking for a turning point within it. This may not necessarily be near the halfway mark in terms of Bible verses, but rather the point at which the story turns. Identifying such a point will be subjective, but the idea is to find that point in a story when that which is needed for its completion is reached.

In the reading of the leper story in Mark 1:40–45 the moment when Jesus stretches out his hand and touches him (Mark 1:41), though comparatively early in the story, is one of those midpoints when a character "embraces for the first time the quality they will need to become complete and finish their story."[24] Locating this point involves isolating a moment within a story that captures the whole of its plot. This requires looking at each event in the sequence and asking how it relates to the story as a whole, and looking for that one moment that carries the story as a whole.

3. POSSIBILITIES AND DISPLACEMENT

In a story the events are forged out of the array of possibilities between one event and another. The events that come between the opening and ending of a story form a pathway through a series of possibilities; this is where much of the fun lies. In Mark Lawson's novel *Idlewild*, the priest preparing to administer John F. Kennedy's last rites following the assassination attempt in Dallas in 1963 experiences "a sudden sense of this moment as one of history's hinges. Events can swing to either side from here."[25] And in Lawson's story, Kennedy lives and the priest is sent away.

Part of the exploration of story structure involves analyzing how a situation in which anything can happen narrows down to something happening, and how that something is then shaped. When it comes to the

---

24. Yorke, *Into the Woods*, 70.
25. Lawson, *Idlewild*, 10.

process of a story: "In the beginning anything is possible; in the middle things become probable; in the ending everything is necessary."[26]

Throughout a story, alternatives present themselves and the story forges a way through pathways of complete possibility to narrowed probability. Jack sells his cow for five beans or and so won't be auctioning it at the market. The beans could grow or waste away outside Jack's window. Jack could climb the beanstalk or stay safely down at the bottom. One set of possibilities follows another and a story is plotted through them, narrowing down to what is necessary, now that the story has plotted a path through the alternatives.

In his article on "The Logic of Narrative Possibilities" Claude Bremond analyzes the elementary sequences at work in stories. From the first three actions or events in a story, an "elementary sequence"[27] opens, forming this pattern:[28]

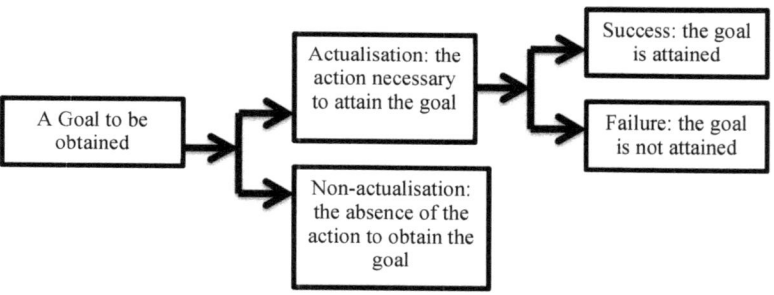

Based on Bremond, 1980

A goal is to be obtained and that attainment may be actualized or not. Assuming someone sets out to attain it, that actualization itself may succeed or fail. Within this structure Bremond sees the ups and downs of a narrative—what he calls "amelioration" and "degradation." Amelioration involves a plan or goal being attained and in degradation it is thwarted or missed.

In the healing of the paralytic story in Mark 2:1–12, the unnamed paralyzed man is brought by friends, with a goal to be obtained: to get their friend to Jesus. They are frustrated at first by the crowds and the absence of actualization, but when they dig through the roof (Mark 1:4) they attain their goal of reaching Jesus.

---

26. Goodman quoted in Chatman, *Story and Discourse*, 46.

27. Bremond, "Logic," 63.

28. Bremond, "Logic," 63.

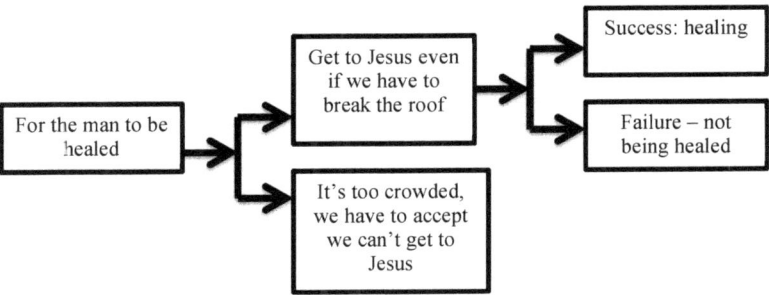

Based on Bremond, 1980

The logic of this cycle can branch further,[29] in that they reach Jesus, but he then forgives the man's sins which, though important and opposed by the scribes, was not their goal. The story goes off in a different direction to the goal of these characters. However, in the process of debating authority with the scribes Jesus then also heals the man (Mark 1:12). Bremond also observes that it is possible for a narrative sequence to be the amelioration for one character while also being a degradation for another.[30] The story of the healing of the leper in Mark 1:40–45 clearly accomplishes the goal of the leper but also sees a frustration to the goal of Jesus.

Unpicking the logic of possibilities, Bremond uses the phrase "the network of possibilities" to describe the way in which a story is made up of basic units in which there are varying possibilities and a path that is actualized. The path followed through them is plotted towards the teleological goal, mentioned earlier, running through the story. When the magic beans sprout, Jack is presented with a possibility: should he go up the beanstalk, or not? Of course, the absence of actualization would leave us with a dull story called "Jack Stays at Home," so he climbs it. At this point it is worth referring back to chapter 1 and the distinction Barthes makes between nuclei and catalyzers, because nuclei "constitute real hinge-points" in a story.[31] Nuclei open up the network of possibilities in a story. They can form a focus for asking "What could Jack do about the Beanstalk?" In the Bible, questions arise like "What will Eve do?" and also asking "What could Jesus do?" (possibly more fun than asking "WWJD?")

In the healing of the paralyzed man, the course followed seems not to be actualizing the goal of the man and his friends. Up till this point Jesus has

29. Rimmon-Kenan, *Narrative Fiction*, 27.

30. Bremond, "Logic," 65.

31. Barthes, "Introduction," 93.

been healing quite a bit (Mark 1:26, :31, 34, and 39). This is the first instance in which, instead of healing, he pronounces the forgiveness of sins. It is also the beginning of his conflict with the scribes, because he is assuming the authority to bring God's forgiveness, with the eventual healing then offered as a demonstration of this authority (Mark 2:10).

Asking what characters could do focuses the reader on their choices and the actualization of those choices. As with the healing of the paralyzed man, Jesus's healing of the leper, in (Mark 1:40–45), is set in the context of the belief, referenced elsewhere in the New Testament,[32] that afflictions could result from sin, and a remedy involved both forgiveness and healing, along with sacrifice to restore disrupted relations.[33] When the leper approaches Jesus in Mark 1:40, Jesus tackles, not just the leprosy, but also the social repercussions of leprosy.[34] Here was an illness perceived as threatening to the community and its holiness, such that the sufferer must be cut off and ostracized.[35] Faced with the leper's request, Jesus does not just heal; he tackles the very system that pushed such people away, by choosing to reach out and touch the man. He also declares the man as clean (and in doing this he is trespassing onto the territory of the priests of the day).[36] It is a big choice with significant actualization. As observed earlier, in touching the leper, Jesus made himself unclean.[37]

> Moved with pity, Jesus stretched out his hand and touched him, and said to him, "I do choose. Be made clean!" Immediately the leprosy left him, and he was made clean. After sternly warning him he sent him away at once. (Mark 1:41–43)

The choice is a tense one and a textual footnote presents the alternative in verse 41, that Jesus was moved with anger or pity. Either way, feeling is high. Likewise, the stern warning to the leper of verse 43 emphasizes feeling on the part of Jesus, as does the narration of the reaching and touching, with slow, physical detail. The word used for that stern warning is the Greek *embrasinemos*, a term denoting the snort of a horse,[38] and elsewhere describing Jesus's response to death.[39] Anger, snorting, emphatic narrating of

---

32. John 9:2.

33. Craffert, *Galilean Shaman*, 289.

34. Kazmierski, "Evangelist and Leper," 41.

35. Pilch in Myers, *Binding*, 145; see also Craffert, *Galilean Shaman*, 289.

36. Craffert, *Galilean Shaman*, 291.

37. France, *Mark*, 118.

38. Guellich, *Mark 1—8:26*, 72.

39. John 11:33, 38.

the touch, and the plea to not spread this news all tally with the notion that Jesus made himself unclean,[40] and is aware of the scuppering of his mission that is to follow.[41] Could it be Jesus is aware of the long-term implications of his action: he has crossed a line, touched a leper, declared him clean and scuppered his mission?

The Needs of the Plot

Possibilities in a story are like branching pathways, with the track that is followed reaching a particular destination. Looking at such possibility, Rimmon-Kenan asks why Pip helps the runaway convict Magwitch, in Charles Dickens's, "Great Expectations" and presents two answers to this question and, in doing so, delineates two ways in which plot is at work. One reason is that the child, Pip, was frightened: "Hold your noise!" called a terrible voice, as a man started up from among the graves at the side of the church porch. "Keep still, you little devil, or I'll cut your throat!"[42] However, Rimmon-Kenan adds to this another reason. Pip has to help Magwitch: "according to the structural needs of the plot: this act is necessary for Magwitch to be grateful to Pip so as to wish to repay him; without it the plot would not be the kind of plot it is."[43] It's also why Luke responds to Leia's message, Thelma and Louise stop at a bar and Lucy enters the wardrobe. In Lucy's case, this is also why it rains. Rimmon-Kenan refers to this second reason behind Pip's help as "teleological (i.e. concerned with purpose)" and describes it as a 'forward causality.'[44] The "Why?" of this occurrence is to be found in the string that links the beads of the plot into the rest of the story.

At some times the actual goal is less consequential than at others. The film maker Alfred Hitchcock spoke of the McGuffin,[45] which was the thing everyone was after in his films. He described it as the thing that the spies are after but the audience doesn't care about and spoke amusingly of the way it just provided a reason for Cary Grant to climb Mount Rushmore or Robert Donat to climb out of moving trains, observing: "The MacGuffin is nothing."[46] However, in such stories there is still that teleological thrust. The

40. Malina, *New Testament World*, 161; Malina and Rohrbaugh, *Social-Science*, 185.
41. France, *Mark*, 119.
42. Dickens, *Great Expectations*, 3.
43. Rimmon-Kenan, *Narrative Fiction*, 18.
44. Rimmon-Kenan, *Narrative Fiction*, 18.
45. Springer, "McGuffin."
46 Springer, "McGuffin," para. 4.

audience are rooting for a character to find the McGuffin, and to survive the quest.

In biblical narrative the end or goal often matters hugely, but this thread can become hidden within the beads of the biblical narrative. Though presenting a historical life, the Gospels are nonetheless strung together with an overarching plot. In the same way the aid Pip gives to Magwitch happens according to the structural needs of the plot, the healing of Mark 2:1–12 contains a moment that is forward looking in its causality. Why does Jesus forgive the man's sins? Here again, two answers can be given. Jesus is offering this liberation to the character lowered down in front of him, but this act is also done in keeping with the structural needs of the plot: here begins a conflict that will heighten, and lead to the Passion narrative. Elsewhere in the Bible such structural needs can be traced in the way, through Genesis, a succession of ancestresses survive danger[47] or the way Saul's fate runs through 1 Samuel.[48] In the Gospels this inner thread is made explicit when Jesus reveals the inner dynamic of the events with a forward causality. There is an example immediately after Peter's "confession": "You are the Messiah" (Mark 8:29). Jesus orders them to tell no one and "then he began to teach them that the Son of Man must undergo great suffering, and be rejected by the elders, the chief priests, and the scribes, and be killed, and after three days rise again" (Mark 8:31).

From the initial nod to the reader that we are reading "good news of Jesus Christ, the Son of God" (Mark 1:1), the opening out of who Jesus is will unfold alongside this plotted conflict, culminating at the cross (Mark 15:39). Within the events of the story a revelation is taking place and even though Jesus says "tell no one" the plot drives towards discovery (Mark 8:30, c.f. 1:34).[49]

Displacement

> It is characteristic of stories that they do not end where they began. Change, growth and development are the very essence of stories.[50]

47. Clines, "Ancestor in Danger."

48. Gunn, *Fate of King Saul.*

49. Merenlahti, *Poetics*, 105.

50. Ryken, *How to Read the Bible*, 52.

Leland-Ryken is here describing the way stories have openings and endings, but also the displacement that takes place between. Cohan and Shires explain this, in their engaging and accessible guide to narrative poetics:

> When a story sequence combines more than two events (and most do), the addition of other events advances or amplifies the sequence to widen the space between opening (i.e. the possibility of an outcome) and ending (i.e. the realization of an outcome).[51]

Such displacement is the filling out of the story, which in biblical narrative can involve forty years in a wilderness. It is also displacement that gives the gospels life, in which Jesus isn't simply revealed as Son of God in a "Tah dah" moment, but instead goes the way of stories that unpick something of what this means and how this revelation grows. It is the dynamic within all stories:

> What initiates a story is the placement of an event in a sequence to mark the beginning; what ends a story is the *replacement* of the initial event by another one to mark the ending . . . what keeps the story going as a sequence of eventualities are displacements of both the initial and the closing events.[52]

For the paralyzed man this displacement means his lowering through the roof and request for healing is sent in a different direction by Jesus pronouncing forgiveness, followed by thoughts of the scribes and challenge of Jesus, all of which displace the eventual healing (Mark 2:1–10).

Without such displacement and change, nothing really happens. If the stories were simply a paralyzed man wanting to be healed and Jesus healed him, or a load of people needing food so Jesus fed them, then the Bible would be very different and a lot duller. There is more to a story. In the healing of the paralyzed man, there is a crowd in the way, so his friends take to the roof. Such roofs were workspaces and were "not flimsy in construction." The language used to describe the way the friends literally "unroofed the roof . . . digging it out" is a significant act and "suggests a major demolition job."[53] There is then further displacement when Jesus pronounces "Your sins are forgiven" (Mark 2:5). This is the only time in this Gospel that Jesus will actually forgive the sin of an individual. It's not crystal clear whether he does the forgiving or declares this forgiveness is already available. Is he saying: "I am doing the forgiving" or "I've got news for you, your sins are forgiven"? Whichever it is, given the response of the scribes, he's clearly and personally

---

51. Cohan and Shires, *Telling Stories*, 65.
52. Cohan and Shires, *Telling Stories*, 65–66.
53. France, *Mark*, 123.

doing something outrageous, though the Gospel has already opened with John "proclaiming a baptism of repentance for the forgiveness of sins" (Mark 1:4).

Displacements of this sort discover the changes that navigate a path through possibilities of the story.

Markan Sandwiches

Focusing on Mark's Gospel, one distinctive feature of displacement is the presence of Markan Sandwiches.[54] These are moments when a story is interrupted by a bit that falls within it. The clearest example of this is the story of Jairus's daughter (Mark 5:21–43) which is seemingly interrupted by the intrusion of the hemorrhaging woman (Mark 5:25–34). However, this is not a random interruption, and there are similarities between the two women depicted in both the bread and filling of the sandwich. Similarly, between Jesus prediction of his betrayal (Mark 14:17–21) and disciples abandoning and denying him (Mark 14:27–31), there is a filler as Jesus shares and hands them the last supper (Mark 14:22–26). There are also the women at the end of the Gospel who are there at the crucifixion, with Mary Magdalene specified (Mark 15:40–41), who then faithfully return, again name-checking Mary (Mark 15:47—16:1). In between the burial occurs through the secret action of Joseph, the disciples having fled. In Markan Sandwiches there are connections between the slices and filling, such as the twelve-years timescale shared in different ways between Jairus's daughter, dying at twelve years old, and the woman who has suffered a living death for twelve years. Edwards goes so far as to suggest that the middle bit in these sandwiches is the section that sheds light on the slices on either side.[55]

Markan Sandwiches

3:20–35 the conflict with the scribes as filling and the issues with his family as bread

4:1–20 a discussion about parables and the parable and interpretation of the sower

5:21–43 Jairus's daughter and hemorrhaging woman

6:7–30 Herod beheading John sandwiched by the mission of the disciples

---

54. Edwards, "Markan Sandwiches."

55. Edwards, "Markan Sandwiches," 196.

11:12–21 the cursed fig tree and the cleansing of the temple

14:1–11 the anointing at Bethany between the plot to arrest Jesus

14:17–31 predicting betrayal and denial either side of the last supper

14:53–72 Peter at the trial sandwiches the trial of Jesus

15:40—16:8 the women with Jesus at his death sandwich Joseph's obtaining and burying the body

Prediction and Comprehension

One day, Jesus was teaching in the temple when the wife of Pilate ran to him and said, "Teacher, my husband has fallen ill and is close to death, but only say the word and he shall be made whole." And what do you think Jesus did?

Within the network of possibilities in a text, the act of reading involves constant prediction and comprehension. Describing the very act of learning to read and comprehend, reading guru Frank Smith summed up this cycle: "Prediction is asking questions—and comprehension is getting these questions answered."[56]

The reader starts from that point where anything can happen, starts asking what will happen, and works through the plotted possibilities and path taken to what does happen. As Chatman outlines the way through the possibilities, "The working out of plot (or at least some plots) is a process of declining or narrowing possibility. The choices become more and more limited, and the final choice seems not a choice at all, but an inevitability."[57]

As readers of the Bible we are often faced with a text we know well, but part of the process of comprehension is to still see where the plot with which we are familiar takes the turns it takes. Read in this way, even the well-known story generates the unexpected:

- a paralyzed man seeks healing, such that his friends lower him through a roof, but Jesus forgives his sins (Mark 2:1–10);
- a healed demoniac seeks to do what numerous others have done this far in the Gospel and follow Jesus, but is sent back home (Mark 5:19);
- Jesus intends to walk right past a struggling band of disciples as they try and row across the sea (Mark 6:48);

56. Smith, *Reading*, 83.
57. Chatman, *Story and Discourse*, 46.

- the response Jesus gives to the Syrophoenician woman, and her response back to him (Mark 7:24–30);

- having experienced one miraculous feeding, the disciples panic when Jesus asks what he should do about a second such crowd (Mark 8:4).

The points at which expectation and prediction gets defied may bring out the depth to a healing story or the miraculous feeding. They also chart the surprising way the story goes.

Suspense and Surprise

Without plot-spoiling, a few citations may prompt memories of the moments of surprise in *Psycho*, *Jaws*, and *The Empire Strikes Back*. Suspense, on the other hand, is the stuff of *Witness* and *Rebecca*, where we are held waiting for prolonged viewing time for something we are anticipating, sometimes sat on the edge of our seats.

Surprise throws an audience momentarily, whereas suspense holds them for a painfully long time. In biblical narrative, familiarity with a story can restrict the chances of this. However, familiarity should not preclude an awareness of moments when suspense has kicked in: the paralyzed man is literally left hanging there in a theological debate and Jairus and Jesus get interrupted on their way to his daughter. Similarly the moments of surprise come when someone feeds a multitude or walks on water. Part of playful reading is to rediscover some of the emotion present in the text. Imagine being Jairus, or imagine seeing someone walking on water. And we may know what is going to happen, but Mark 16 is still quite breathtaking.

Ways of Reading: Possibilities and Displacement

Track Changes

Ryken's comment that "Change, growth and development are the very essence of stories"[58] leads to the simple task of looking at a story for the changes that occur, asking who or what is changed by who or what? One way of doing this is to print the text of a particular story and annotate the changes as they occur with a simple tick in the margin or a one-word label for the change, such as "healed." An activity like this can highlight changes that develop and grow the story, such as the leper coming, begging, and kneeling (Mark 1:40), contrasted with those that change the story, such as

58. Ryken, *How to Read the Bible*, 52.

when the healed leper who is told to "say nothing to anyone" (Mark 1:44) instead goes out and proclaims his news freely.

This activity raises the question for the reader of whether a particular event within a story is a change and if so, to what degree it is a departure from before. The reader could even grade the changes with an informal one-, two-, or three-tick system to denote minor and major changes. In the context of the leper story the touch is, at first, not as dramatic a departure. It is after the leper tells everyone that Jesus finds his mission scuppered, possibly as a result of that touch. If that is the case, it was even more of a change than may first be recognized.

A leper came to him begging him, and kneeling he said to him, "If you choose, you can make me clean." Moved with pity, Jesus stretched out his hand and touched him, and said to him, "I do choose. Be made clean!" Immediately the leprosy left him, and he was made clean. After sternly warning him he sent him away at once, saying to him, "See that you say nothing to anyone; but go, show yourself to the priest, and offer for your cleansing what Moses commanded, as a testimony to them." But he went out and began to proclaim it freely, and to spread the word, so that Jesus could no longer go into a town openly, but stayed out in the country; and people came to him from every quarter.

[Handwritten annotations: appears; moved; touch ?; sent; healed; tells; scuppered!; stayed]

These key points of change are the nuclei of the story, so this also raises the chance to ask, "What if?" What if the disciples hadn't noticed the hungry or Jesus hadn't touched the leper? Entertaining the alternative possibilities is one way in which light may be shed upon the path the story actually follows.

Possibilities and Predictions

The more outlandish the better! Look at the start of a biblical story and ask what possibilities there are. It could be that, on having the paralyzed man lowered to him, Jesus would refuse to heal him. This may seem counterintuitive . . . though interestingly he actually doesn't heal the paralysis at first. Likewise, in the story of the Syrophenician woman, his response is not what may have been predicted (Mark 7:37). What if he had stuck to his original response?

To enter into this sort of text play, the reader needs to take on the mantle of the virgin reader, approaching the story for the first time, and explore what could have been predicted and is more or less likely within a story. Even when a story is well-known, it is still possible to take on such tensions as part of a reading, such as the buildup of Legion's description, leading to the moment of confrontation (Mark 5:1–26). After all that buildup in verses 1–5, Legion's first encounter is a surprise.

Probability

In basic math the nature of a probability is indicated using a scale.

Impossible   ----   Less   ----   Even   ----   More   ----   Certain
                     likely   chance   likely

Looking at a Bible story, one way of plotting the possibilities in a story is to come up with some possibilities and place them along a scale like this. This involves pausing a story and considering, what could happen?

In Mark 2:2 the paralyzed man is lowered to Jesus and "When Jesus saw their faith, he . . ." What?

- Got angry?
- Climbed up the ropes and out the hole?
- Said "Why would I help a dog like you?"
- Asked the people stood around, "What should I do?"
- Said to his disciples, "You heal him"?
- Was distracted by somebody else?
- Recognized they had faith?
- Reckoned these folks lacked faith?
- Had compassion?

Creating, and then rating, the likelihood of a range of actions provides a way of exploring the possibilities and paths followed by a plot. It's worth taking two steps back and trying this exercise with the friends of the man, in 2:4a: "And when they could not bring him to Jesus because of the crowd, they . . ." (Mark 2:4a), or, having read the buildup in the Legion story: "When he saw Jesus from a distance, he . . ." (Mark 5:6a).

Looking at the list above, it's worth noting that elsewhere in the Gospel Jesus does refer to a woman seeking healing as a dog (Mark 7:27—see the next chapter on "character"). He also gets distracted on the way to a dying child (5:30), throws a miraculous need back at the disciples, twice (6:37; 8:2,3), and possibly, as we will discover in one textual variant of the leper story, gets angry. Then, in the actual story of the paralyzed man, Jesus doesn't heal him at first, but recognizes faith and has a debate, which leads to the healing. Whether he would have done this anyway is not made explicit, so is he guided by the crowd as to what he should do?

T Fold

John Yorke highlights the change as the basis of narrative, observing that "Change is the bedrock of life and consequently the bedrock of narrative."[59] Between the placement of the first event in a story, and replacement at the other end, by the final one, various events occur that displace one end from the other. One way of graphically focusing on this is to take a strip of paper and fold it in half, then halve these halves by folding down two wings to make a T shape, in which two frames are hidden and two flap outwards.

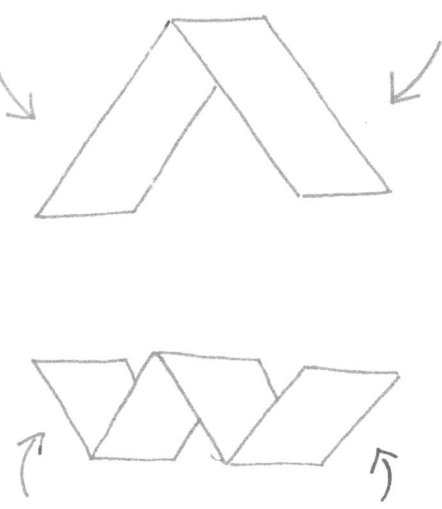

The reader can use these two flapping frames as space to note the opening and closing of a story, and jot or doodle the main points from either end.

59. Yorke, *Into the Woods*, 46.

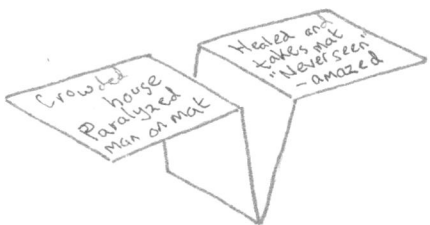

Once these are opened out the displacement is graphic, and begs the question: what happens to move from the first and last frame? The reader can jot out the events between.

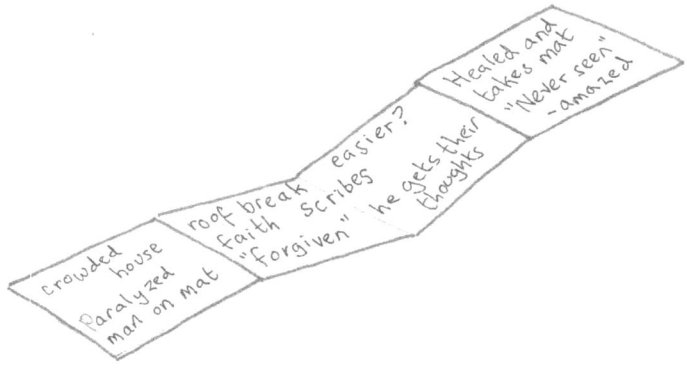

In the instance shown, this brings out the parallel stories of the paralyzed man and the crowd—because this is also the story of a crowd. It's the crowd who have the last word. Their amazement at the "never seen" (Mark 2:10) is notable, given the claims in chapter 1 of John the Baptist, and then of Jesus, about forgiveness of sins. The crowd bears witness to the fact that, which has not been seen before, and which can be disputed, is now here and now visible.

And I like that he takes the mat on which he was lowered.

Chapter 3

Character

Think of a Bible character. For the moment, put God and Jesus aside (it's a big ask) and think of a character from those remaining in the Bible. Can you imagine that person appearing in front of your eyes? Can you picture them? Imagine them speaking?

The Bible is full of stories populated by amazing characters, and a grasp of their personality and the way this shapes stories is an essential component of literary reading because, as John Yorke, the television drama producer, reminds us: "Flesh and blood makes things more refreshingly complicated."[1]

If there's one activity that evidences the vital place of character in biblical reading and illustrates how much life this can bring to faith, it's this: a few moments ago you saw someone who lived a few thousand years ago, and heard them speak. The coming four chapters will focus on five terms about character and explore ways in which a grasp of each idea can enliven reading.

FIVE TERMS ABOUT CHARACTER.

Character: A word is used freely but are folks clear what they mean by it? In one sense characters are nothing more than text on a page or names attached to actions that make a story, so how is it a reader can get a sense of a them being somebody?

1. Yorke, *Into the Woods*, 139.

Traits: Chapter 4 explores what a particular character is like. Character traits are the features of a character's identity that readers build up as they read. These traits, and consequently these characters, stand outside the timeline of the story and build up the image we form of a character as a person.

Paradigm: Readers build up a sense of a character, but what happens when a character changes? Readers develop a sense of what a character is like that can be altered and revised as readers progress in the reading of a text. Chapter 4 also explores how the paradigm of traits readers build up for a particular character alters as they read a story.

Characterization: Chapter 5 asks the question, how do readers know whatever they know about a character? Characterization is the makeup of characters readers respond to as they read the story.

Role: What do different characters do? Chapter 6 explores the different roles characters play within stories. Through looking at models that unpick how such roles are structured, this chapter will offer insight into the way in which characters fit together to collectively work within the story.

CHARACTER

The starting point to engaging with the concept of character involves three small excursions that have cropped up in narrative theory, each of which shows something of the complexity of this literary construct and also calls into question our own sense of what we encounter when we meet characters in Bible reading.

Mini Excursion 1: Being or Doing?

The crux of this excursion is the question of whether, in narrative, a character has an identity aside from what they do? Structuralist theorists explore the sorts of story structures we have been working with thus far, such as the nature of events in a storyline and how events combine in a sequence. They can be dismissive of the idea of characters having an identity or personality and relegate such talk to a secondary place. What really matters, they say, is the actions the character performs. For structuralists like Barthes, therefore, their only importance lies in the actions they perform to move along the thing that really matters: the events of a story. Such thinking dismisses what is seen as the bourgeois romanticizing of characters' roles and has, as

Barthes observed, "shown the utmost reluctance to treat the character as an essence."[2] Instead the emphasis has been squarely placed on what they do.

However, as readers we do come away from a story with a sense of the personality of Lyra Belacqua or Mr. Micawber, and John Yorke is clear in his view that all great drama is character-based.[3] For Christian readers of the gospels, this is all quite tricky when the character is someone you love. Is Jesus functional to the plot? Christian readers tend to relate to the characters as lived experiences, seeing in Mary, Paul and Peter[4] people to whom they relate as examples and whose existence they affirm as real people. As with many such debates in this book, the tension between being and doing is not to be decisively finalized but appreciated for the way it prompts reflection on reading. In this case, there are three ways of finding some resolution in this tension.

Firstly, this debate highlights the interdependence between who characters are and what they do—a genuine interdependence in which each feeds the other. In offering a resolution to the above debate, the theorist Rimmon-Kenan quoted the great novelist Henry James and his questions: "What is character but the determination of incident? What is incident but the illustration of character?"[5]

There is no way a reader of *Mary Poppins* is going to lose that sense of the great woman, but this excursion alerts the reader to maintain an awareness of the two types of reading and be aware that there are times when character will be subordinated to action, and vice versa.

Secondly, this debate serves as a healthy reminder that the Jesus we get to know—or the Esther or Mary we get to know– will be known through the network of glances and glimpses afforded by the narrative, and in biblical narrative primarily through what they do. This matters because on the one hand it can check a reader's sense that they know a character and have effectively "got 'em." This debate reminds us to let their traits construct, change and challenge the character we think we have got to know. This is particularly important for reading in a spirit of faith. The reader may have sung songs about a beautiful Jesus but the way he dismisses the Syrophoenician woman as a dog (Mark 7:27) may challenge the characterization offered by creeds, worship songs or other sources. It's not that readers should lose their love of characters in the Bible—if anything, deeper reading should rekindle

---

2. Barthes, "Introduction," 105.

3. Yorke, *Into the Woods*, 124.

4. In reverse that's a folk band.

5. Rimmon-Kenan, *Narrative Fiction*, 35.

that sense of knowing them: if Peter, says something ignorant, he becomes a guide to everyone who stumbles.

Thirdly, as ever there is a middle ground, in the debate between being and doing. Narrative theories are a bit like takeaway menus: just because you have pizza one night doesn't mean you'll never eat Thai again. While we need to avoid the simplification of a character's identity, readers are still going to form that sense of somebody arising from stories. Wallace Martin offers the wise view about characters that "Though fused with the action . . . they are not dissolved in it."[6] They are fused by their significance in the workings of the plot. A good example in the Gospel of Mark is the way the disciples feature as a functional means of the dynamic of the plot. They are often characterized in a lumpen way, as if they all speak with one voice at the same time. However, a reading of their function in the story presents a group who can offer insights into belief and unbelief and who present a dynamic in their development.

Ways of Reading: Permission to Be

Nobody can stop you enjoying a character's being, and when reading the Bible the reader is free to let a character be, and be with that character. Two things to note when getting to know one. Spiritually minded readers will often go with the big name exemplary characters, like Peter and Jesus, but the leper who scuppers the mission of Jesus and demoniac who meets him on the shore are vivid enough for us to allow their doings to give an insight into their being. Secondly, there are those who appear a few times across a few chapters of Bible and the reader can get to know them. This can involve starting at a first or appearance of a character and reading onwards into the story, just finding them within it, considering what image of the character you is formed across the story, and what it is they do that forms that image.

Mini Excursion 2: Open or Closed Constructs?

In Mark 6 there is a moment of analepsis that tells the story of the beheading of John the Baptist. Within this flashback (Mark 6:17–29) there is this revelation about Herod's imprisonment of John the Baptist: "When he heard him, he was greatly perplexed; and yet he liked to listen to him" (Mark 6:20). It is a doorway to a story not told: that of Herod's meetings with John. For a moment, the reader can picture such an exchange, and maybe read the story

6 Martin, *Recent Theories*, 122.

again in the light of picturing it. Doing so requires imagination to supply the looks on their faces and tones in their voices. In doing so, the reader is going well beyond the text. But why not? Is a character open to us imagining a life beyond and outside the scope of the discourse we read or are they closed up and restricted to what such reading affords? That's the debate between characters as closed or open constructs.

There are literary theorists who would query such speculation,[7] in a manner similar to the previous mini-debate's assertion characters are only what they contribute to the furtherance of the narrative. Others would leave the option open to speculate and imagine outside the frame of the story. The former approach regards characters as closed constructs and the latter as open. They are either closed off to such speculation or open to it.

Like the last mini-excursion, this debate is answered by the reality of reading. When a woman with a flow of blood approaches Jesus in the crowd, the reader, noting she had spent money on physicians and things had just got worse (Mark 5:26), may instinctively imagine her rejection by her failed healers. And why not? Seymour Chatman puts the challenge: "In short, should we restrain what seems a God-given right to infer and even speculate about characters if we like? Any such restraint strikes me as an impoverishment of aesthetic experience."[8] He goes on to suggest this is more than emotional reaction to characters. Imaginative speculation like this is a way the way in which readers construct their characterization:

> A viable theory of character should preserve mere openness and treat characters as autonomous beings, not mere plot functions. It should argue that character is reconstructed by the audience from evidence announced or implicit in an original construction.[9]

Such reconstruction is important for reading stories, as biblical narratives can lack much of a rubber ducky moment. Film director Sidney Lumet and writer Paddy Chayefsky coined the term "rubber ducky moment" to describe the incident earlier in life that explains who a character is now and why they are the way they are.[10] Examples in film include Ilsa leaving Rick in *Casablanca*, Bruce Wayne's parent's murder in *Batman*, the problems of the older generation in *Star Wars: a New Hope*, and Clarice Starling's trauma with *Lambs*. However, it is also the case that there are Bible characters who

---

7 Chatman, *Story and Discourse*, 117.

8 Chatman, *Story and Discourse*, 117.

9 Chatman, *Story and Discourse*, 119.

10. Yorke, *Into the Woods*, 145.

appear with enough to cause the reader to speculate on experience before the story. When a paralytic is carried in by friends, a demoniac breaks his chains, or a woman who has suffered hemorrhaging for twelve years appears the reader gets a sense of a doorway to a story that remains untold. The hemorrhaging woman has two verses of back story (Mark 5:25–26) but it's a massive story, and the character of Legion was shackled and broke chains, such that "no one had the strength to subdue him" (Mark 5:4).

When it comes to background outside the story, this is also one of those areas where commentaries and background information can help fill out a character. In Mark 1:40–45 Jesus meets, reacts to, and heals a leper. We are told little about this character, get no name and no back story. However we do know that the leprosy of the day, although not the modern Hansen's disease, carried many miseries to it. Lepers were classed as living corpses[11] and effecting a cure was held to be as difficult as resurrection from the dead.[12] In addition to the malaise, this leper could have been considered ritually impure[13] and people like him were ostracized.[14] They were not allowed to live in Jerusalem or any other city walled from antiquity.[15] Instead, they begged outside such walls[16] One further, critical bit of background: a chance encounter between the leper and the non-leper could render the latter unclean.[17] None of this is in the text of that story but, in encountering a character, readers are invited to open up their speculation.

Ways of Reading: Open Up

For readers of the gospels, the open view is not essential, but playing in that field can enrich reading, though it's worth noting the crossing point when moving outside the frame of the story. To take an example, I don't know what Herod's relationship with John the Baptist was like other than the bits afforded in Mark 6:14–28, when John is finally beheaded. Personally, I still have an image of a troubled Herod listening to John from beyond a grill, such that John is preaching out and possibly can't even see for sure that Herod is there. However, for all I know the two engaged in hours of meaningful conversation. In the hands of a good scriptwriter the conversations

11. Schweizer, *Matthew*, 57; Marcus, *Mark 1–8*, 208.

12. Schweizer, *Matthew*, 57.

13. Lane, *Mark*, 85.

14. Lev 13:45–46.

15. Lane, *Mark*, 85.

16. Malina and Rohrbaugh, *Social-Science*, 184—see 2 Kings 7:3–9.

17. Lane, *Mark*, 85.

they held could be a good two-hour script before Herod is cornered by his wife and his cowardice. In the frame the text creates there is the mention that: "When (Herod) heard (John), he was greatly perplexed; and yet he liked to listen to him." In various translations the term "greatly perplexed" rendered as "puzzled" (NIV), "confused" (CEV), "greatly disturbed" (Good News), and the King James is closest to the Greek with "he did many things."

There was no simple experience here and the idea that Herod's hearing was perplexing is one that the reader can take back to their reading of the story. What is imagined is based on what is read, and could enlighten the reading. Features like this, along with the small insights into the relationships between Herod, John, and Herodias and the quick violence of the girl's question are all like doors to backstories open to the reader's imagination. Such imaginings involve constantly bouncing back and forth, in and out of the frame of the story: if I start to perceive these two sat together, even laughing at a difference of opinion, or a conversation that challenges Herod, I should always bounce back and read the story asking, what is allowing space for this (and there is such a space)? I should also ask what that open moment says to the rest of my reading. For example, how would any nascent respect and care have felt when the girl asks Herod: "I want you to give me at once the head of John the Baptist on a platter."

Mini Excursion 3: Flat or Round

The novelist E. M. Forster gave us the distinction between flat and rounded characters, and on hearing the terms folks often know precisely what he meant. Some characters appear and do little, even though they are significant people. Zebedee just stays in a boat while his sons go off and follow Jesus (Mark 1:20). The man with the withered hand (Mark 3:1) gets healed but the conversation that follows is between Jesus and the bystanders. Neither character leaps out from the page. In contrast, the Syrophoenician woman outwits Jesus in a verbal exchange and has some life to her (Mark 7:24–30).

Forster described rounded characters with the observation that "The test of a round character is whether it is capable of surprising in a convincing way. If it never surprises, it is flat. If it does not convince, it is a flat," and he also observed that a rounded character "has the incalculability of life about it—life within the pages of a book."[18]

Just by using the term "rounded," Forster delineates a character the reader can look around—someone where there are aspects to their character and more than one angle can be taken in looking upon them. Possibly a

18. Forster, *Aspects*, 81.

minimal example of such roundedness would be Peter's mother-in-law who is the first healing in Mark's Gospel (Mark 1:29–31). She then, straightaway, gets up and serves. Not much, but there's a lot there. The relationship to other characters, the simplicity of the hand taken, and serving early in a Gospel that will celebrate service (Mark 9:35, 10:43) and in which angels were the last to undertake such an action for Jesus (Mark 1:13), coupled with the fact this is all happening on a Sabbath (1:21), making it a debatable action—put together all this rounds her out.

Adele Berlin expands on this flat/rounded distinction by adding a third option. She accepts the round full-fledged character and describes the flat character as a *type*: into this schema she adds a third category of character who acts as a functionary, who she labels the *agent*.[19] For Berlin, flat characters simply represent a type of character, whereas an agent acts as a function of the plot. A great Old Testament example would be the fellow who tells Joseph where his brothers are (Gen 37:15–17). That's all he does—but if he hadn't there would have been no Joseph story.[20] What Berlin is drawing out is the fact that round and flat is not a binary distinction. There is a continuum between the two, with varying ways in which the flat character can round out a bit. In the Gospel of Mark, Rhoads, Dewey, and Michie draw out the way typical characters map onto the types of seeds in "the riddle of the sower"[21] (Mark 4:14–20). Seeds "on the path" typify the authorities, with the typical pattern that they "hear the word, but immediately Satan comes and takes away the word." But Rhoads, Dewey, and Michie also point out that, in Mark's Gospel, there are exceptions to this categorization. One group that exemplifies this is "The seeds on the rocky ground" who are "like the disciples who hear the word with joy but stumble when trouble comes." They also cite the rich man (Mark 10:17–22) as akin to the thorn seeds who "because of the desires of the world [are] fruitless" and then see the good soil as typifying disciples and characters "who proclaim and reap results."[22]

Within Mark's Gospel there are exceptions to the typecasts: lepers disobey the rules (Mark 1:40–45), the authority figure Jairus needs Jesus (Mark 5:21–43), disciples succeed in their mission (Mark 6:13), centurions can say the profoundest things (Mark 15:49) and the council that crucifies Jesus includes the member who rescues his crucified body (Mark 16:43).[23]

---

19. Berlin, *Poetics*, 23.

20. Abrams uses the term "stock characters"; Powell, *What Is Narrative Criticism?*, 55.

21. Rhoads et al., *Mark as Story*, 100.

22. Rhoads et al., *Mark as Story*, 100.

23. Amit, *Reading Biblical Narratives*, 78.

Ways of Reading: Depictions of Jesus

A reader's characterization of Jesus will influence every approach to the Gospel stories they read. With this in mind, anyone exploring character in the Gospels would do well to think through depictions of Jesus in cinema and television, and their significant impact on us, as readers. Different tastes and generations alight on different representations of Jesus, from the "teeny Jesus" of Tab Hunter in *King of Kings* or Max von Sydow's serious Jesus in *The Greatest Story Ever Told* to the glam rock *Jesus Christ Superstar* or troubled character in *The Last Temptation of Christ*.

There are varying degrees of flatness and roundedness in such portrayals are. In a study of depictions of Jesus in cinema William Telford opens his consideration of the problems of portraying Jesus with the observations that: "It is difficult . . . to imagine either Arnold Schwarzenegger or Danny De Vito in the role of Christianity's founder"[24] and over time there have been sensitivities concerning the actor playing Jesus.[25] The interesting issue, for readers looking at Jesus as a character in the Gospels, is the difficulty screen writers have expressed turning the Jesus of the Gospels into a screen character. For such writers, the use of the biblical text is actually a problem. The words of Jesus may make for inspirational teaching but they don't make for great script. Consequently, screenwriters often play off another character to provide tension and conflict: Barabbas in the film *King of Kings* is a foil to Jesus, with the narration describing the two of them as "the left and right hands of the same body."[25] In *Jesus Christ Superstar*, it is Judas who expresses the tension between the "Jesus" and the "Superstar"—and who arguably gets the funkiest songs. When filmmakers do tackle this dilemma of making Jesus a character of tension head on, the results can be engaging, though controversial, with examples including Denys Arcand's "Jesus of Montreal"—and possibly the most controversial example, Martin Scorcese's *The Last Temptation*, wherein the very temptation is between Jesus's life and a possible, tempting alternative.

When exploring different portrayals and the insight they give into Jesus as a character in the Gospel story, Telford's analysis of different types of filmed Jesus can be instructive for the reader exploring the image of Christ brought to the reading of a text and some of the issues they create when reading Jesus.

24. Telford, "Jesus Christ, Movie Star," 127.

25. Telford, "Jesus Christ, Movie Star," 129, quotes Cecil B. DeMille recounting that, during the filming of the 1927 film *The King of Kings* only the director was allowed to speak to Jesus.

26. Telford, "Jesus Christ, Movie Star," 129.

There is . . .

- the Patriarchal father figure, sometimes played by an actor well over thirty-three years of age;

- the adolescent figure at the other end of this scale, like the "I was a teenage Jesus" version in *King of Kings*;

- pacific Jesus, a passive figure, like Robert Powell's *Jesus of Nazareth* and many Jesus films made for Christian evangelistic purposes;

- subversive Jesus undermines the world in which he's presented, the classic example being Daniel, the Christ-figure in *Jesus of Montreal*, throwing television monitors around and recruiting porn voiceover artists;

- mystical Jesus—very wondrous and sometimes lit from behind;

- musical Jesus, of *Superstar* and *Godspell*—though I'd suggest these also fit other categories in the list;

- and, finally, controversial Jesus of *The Last Temptation*, and a category in which I'd place Brian in *Life of Brian*, even though he's not the Messiah.[27]

The controversy surrounding Scorcese's *Last Temptation* offers an interesting challenge to the debate about characters being or doing. Scorcese's Jesus, drawn from the novel by Niklos Kazanistasis, is very much being as well as doing and an open construct who became rounded enough to spark protests. Complainants objected to the fact this Jesus was a sexual individual and one with a human fallibility and doubt. He also is seen to be formulating his gospel as the film progresses, struggling his way into parables with the line: "I've got something to tell you . . . uh . . . I'm . . . I'm sorry but . . . the easiest way to make myself clear . . . is to tell you a story."

Incarnation and Character

The reader needs to decide to what extent they are going to be influenced by other aspects of belief and thinking about Jesus. Faced with the leper there is one reading of the text that sees Jesus becoming angry. Why this may be will be explored in chapter 9, but a Jesus who doubts or gets angry is, to some readers, not possible. There are those who are resolute on such things, even in the face of the text. Faced with the character of Jesus a dynamic reading of the Gospel stories may be subjected to other texts, such as Hebrews 4:14–15:

27. I know, I know.

Since, then, we have a great high priest who has passed through the heavens, Jesus, the Son of God, let us hold fast to our confession. For we do not have a high priest who is unable to sympathize with our weaknesses, but we have one who in every respect has been tested as we are, yet without sin.

One approach is to recognize a growth in Christian belief about Jesus, acknowledging that the views expressed in such verses may be in conversation with the stories of the gospel. It is then down to the reader whether they pit Hebrews in tension against gospels or seek to harmonise the two. If a reader thinks anger is a sin then the curse of a fig tree (Mark 11:12–14) and cleansing of the Temple (Mark 11:15–18) may give something with which to wrestle. There is also the option of allowing the character of Jesus to be himself and to challenge notions of what is and isn't sinful—to allow the reader to weigh him up as you would any other character but also let this character cast a challenge at the scales whereby they are weighed.

Ways of Reading: Character

Catch Characters

Note each character: one first step for the reader is simply to be aware of their vital role in a biblical text. Though not as agonized as the characters of modern literature, and while there is also some tension between reading this way about people when you believe they were historical actors in a story that shapes life, it is nonetheless rewarding to clock their presence in story. When approaching any story take time to consider, who's here? The reader can list them, being sure not to miss one out. Getting used to reading Bible stories as literature involves tuning in to the presence of characters, and noticing their presence—including the slightly hidden ones that get few lines of text. The story of the healing of Simon Peter's mother in law lists a few characters entering the house (Mark 1:29), and Herod's execution of John sends another character to actually get the deed done (Mark 6:27). When encountering a story it can be interesting to list all the characters present, even in the shadows, making sure we include those who had attempted to restrain the demoniac (Mark 5:3), swineherds (Mark 5:14), unclean spirits (Mark 5:12) other leaders of the local synagogue (Mark 5:22), people who are pressing in a crowd (Mark 5:31), and those wailing and weeping (Mark 5:38). And not to forget Jairus's unnamed daughter (Mark 5:23, 35, 41–43) whose actual experience is narrated while she herself is often overlooked by readers.

Drama Techniques

Some of the drama games that have been deployed in exploring literature offer scope for playing with characters in a biblical story. Four of particular use (with variations for the solitary reader) would be:

FREEZE FRAME

This involves a group work to recreate one moment from the story with different participants stepping into different character roles. So readers can take a moment like Mark 5:31: "And his disciples said to him, 'You see the crowd pressing in on you; how can you say, "Who touched me?"'" Freezing it requires different folks to construct the scene by adopting places in it, before freezing still. It involves noticing who is present and imagining their expressions and actions, frozen in the moment. Don't worry too much about numbers. If you haven't got a crowd, one individual can represent a "pressing" crowd.

For the solitary reader, if uninhibited they can try forming the pose or expression of any one character. An alternative is to doodle a diagram of the scene, scribbling in who is standing where and what is going on for them in that moment. One example in Mark 5:31 would be the question as to where the woman is, at that moment. Do we imagine her stood right next to Jesus hearing this exchange? Behind him? Or is she making a break for it?

THOUGHT TRACKING

Thought tracking takes place when an actor breaks off from acting and talks to an audience about the thoughts and feelings of the character they are playing, at that moment. This is sometimes referred to as breaking the fourth wall—a reference to the fourth wall being the barrier between stage and audience in theater. Characters in Shakespeare do it, as does *Fleabag*. From a freeze frame or a solitary reader doodle, readers can then thaw the scene and allow some insights. Any one of those characters can stop and say, for them, what is going on and how it looks and feels at this moment. Done with two scenes within a story, this activity can capture moments within stories that move, homing in on the thoughts of characters in the moment.

HOT SEATING

In a group setting, someone playing the part of a character in a story takes to the hot seat whilst everyone else gets to quiz them with questions about the activity and emotions of their character in the story. They remain in role. If it is the woman of Mark 5:25–34, the person being the character simply has to imagine what answers could be given. Following this questioners and character can discuss the responses and what insights they offer to this very real character, with life opened beyond the frame of the story.

For a solitary reader, the same is possible but the suggestion would be to list five or six top questions for that character, take a short break, then return to them and respond to them one at a time, in character.

This activity involves imagining more than the text offers so the hot seat occupants can vary from a character like Jairus, who get's quite a bit of time center stage in the story, to a character like one of the weepers and wailers, who get bundled off in one verse (Mark 5:40).

CORRIDOR

Participants line up in two parallel lines, facing inwards, to create a corridor down which someone acting the role of a character walks. Whoever is being the character takes their time and as they walk by those standing to the side offer thoughts, opinions, and advice about the story or at a particular point in the story. The words offered relate to the story and that character's place within it.

The individual reader can jot down an array of such thoughts and advice—keeping as random and disjointed as a corridor of people would be.

Representation

The representation of the Bible in the creative arts is a whole avenue in itself worth exploring but two areas merit consideration by the reader. One is the different ways a character can be represented. The use of internet search engines presents a wealth of imagery. Watch out for the interesting variations. The hemorrhaging woman sings through Sam Cooke's spiritual "Touch the Hem of His Garment,"[28] John Martin's painting expands the storm on the sea,[29] and the dance at Herod's birthday is captured in varied artistic presentations of the story.

28. Cooke, "Touch the Hem of His Garment."
29. See John Martin's painting *Christ Stilleth the Tempest*.

Choosing Images

This idea is based on an activity spoken of by John Bell of the Iona Community. The idea is to have available an array of photographs or images
of people. One resource I use is secondhand books of portraiture, sliced
and guillotined into cards of people (old BP Portrait Award booklets are
particularly rich in faces).[30] Postcards of this nature or images from maga-
zines can be collected and collated for this purpose. These can be used for
different exercises, such as spreading many diverse images out and asking
folks to take their reading of a particular story and find, amongst all these
people, one who grabs the viewer as an image of a particular character in the
story. Another option is to limit the images—say four images of women—
and following a reading of the story ask readers to look at their image and
ask whether the person in a photo matches what the character in the story
might have looked like. One participant recalls a group, following a reading
of the Cana story (John 2:1–11), looking at images with the possibility they
may depict something of Mary, the mother of Jesus: "There was a silence,
followed by laughter. One person near me had a picture of a crabby-looking
Middle Eastern woman in her fifties, with few teeth, but a determined look
on her face" prompting him to reflect, "Why do we see Mary as the perpet-
ual 16 year-old, waif-like and dressed in lovely blue, when at the wedding in
Cana she was clearly in her late forties or early fifties and had been widowed
for a couple of decades or so?"[31]

Just to free up the play a little: the reader can mix the genders. So a
woman with the look of Jairus for them can be Jairus, and, yes, it is fine to
play this game with Jesus as a character, and, yes, this may mean he ends up
being seen as Danny de Vito-like. And why not?

Excursion Destination: A Bottleneck

In the excursions into debates, mapped out above, much of the above distinctions involve a narrowing or widening of the sense of a character. This
will often be down to the playfulness of the reader. Introducing the analysis
of characters, Rhoads, Dewey, and Michie observe the natural tendency to
"recall Hamlet and Juliet as if they were real people" leading to their observation: "We can analyze not only what characters 'do,' but also who they
'are,' treating them as autonomous figures in the plot and assessing them

---

30. National Portrait Gallery, *BP Portrait Award*.

31. Baines, "Seeing Through," paras. 9, 11.

as we assess real people."[32] The reader can do just that, and when doing so, engagement with the text of the Bible can act like a much needed bottle-neck. Not many verses are devoted to the Syrophoenician woman (Mark 7:24–30). Nonetheless, the reader can widen out and encounter her as a person. There is little of the exchange between Herod and John (Mark 6:20) but it intrigues and widens the reading, and Simon Peter's unnamed mum-in-law does enough to round away from flatness (Mark 1:30–31). Just like the bottle, there is a wider capacity in the reader's imaginings and infer-ence but there is also the discipline of the neck of the bottle. The interplay between the sense of the identity of a character, an ability to imagine be-yond what the text offers and the experience of rounding a character out can all be creatively held in tension with the reader's reading of the text. Speculations that Jesus was teasing the Syrophoenician woman or that the dance of Herod's stepdaughter was sexual or that Simon Peter's mother in law was delighted at all these guests and wouldn't have rather had the rest of the night in bed are all just that—speculative. The discipline of sharing a text, even playfully, is the bottleneck it provides to flights of fancy. To offer one good example, consider old song "Gentle Jesus, Meek and Mild." Is that character in the Bible?

32. Rhoads et al., *Mark as Story*, 98.

Chapter 4

Character Traits and Development

What was Judas like? Or Peter's mother in law? Or Esther? Or Jonah? Having explored the way characters stand out and how the reader relates to them, this chapter asks: exactly what is it that stands out and how these folks change. To understand this we explore the concept of character traits and the way a character develops.

TRAITS

A trait is the answer given to the question: what was Judas like? In illustrating character traits, Chatman asks his readers to follow a simple story:[1] (1) Peter fell ill. (2) He died. (3) He had no friends or relatives. (4) Only one person came to his funeral.

It's sad . . . but at point 3, Chatman isolates the trait that underpins the whole of this mini-story. Point 3 is not an event. It stands outside the events, whereas statements 1, 2, and 4 relate events that happened. Statement 3 tells a trait of Peter's. Diagrammatically the story could look like a line, with the 3 to the side.

---

1. Chatman, *Story and Discourse*, 43.

3

Statement 3 is a trait, not an event; there is a sense in which it shouldn't be on the diagram at all. It is something about a character that we might have pieced together from event 4, but it is not one of events in the story. To quote Chatman again: "Events travel as vectors, 'horizontally' from earlier to later. Traits, on the other hard, extend over the time spans staked out by the events."[2]

Chatman's diagram provides one helpful way of appreciating the place of the character traits in relation to the reading of stories. Over the course of a text, that third point is built up and, as is noted below, challenged and altered. In the Gospel of Mark Judas has just one trait: he betrays Jesus (Mark 3:19). Whereas the woman with the hemorrhaging brings a back story, thinks, plans, performs actions and changes, all within nine verses.

Ways of Reading: Traits

Trait Thinking

Recalling the first mini-excursion, in chapter 3, about whether characters are "being" or "doing," the reader can allow a trait to be a point of reflection or discussion. To do this, readers need to allow what the story offers to be translated into what we can say about a character. There are things we are told directly about a character, as when we are given a general overview of the woman in Mark 5:5: "There was a woman who had been suffering from hemorrhages for twelve years." The question is, what traits do we, as readers, form in response to that news. When the hemorrhaging woman thinks, "If I but touch his clothes, I will be made well" (Mark 5:28), the reader can consider what character quality is emerging. Is she beset with fear, showing humility or is this down to the notion that she is ritually unclean and will, in doing this, potentially make Jesus unclean? Or does she just want to get this over and done with quickly and without having to talk to anyone? Might

2. Chatman, *Story and Discourse*, 129.

this be a shame borne of years of being considered unclean, or a cynicism born of being ripped off by other healers? When told her faith made her well (5:34) might she be as surprised as anyone else at this fact?

Traits Backwards

The interesting reverse to this is to explore a trait and see how it plays out in the characters of the Bible. This involves considering a trait like humility, fear, shame, or cynicism and considering what we see of such traits in other characters. Where do we see a quality like humility? It can also be interesting to follow up a trait we assume a particular character may have. Sometimes, having been schooled in a story, readers can pick up common assumptions about characters that don't bear well under scrutiny. Which qualities does the Syrophoenician woman in Mark 7:24–30 actually show? Is she humble or cynical? Between her and Jairus, there is a difference in the demands they make on Jesus: one goes home, the other makes him go with them. And in his response to her, what traits does the character of Jesus display?

Follow the Trait

As a story progresses the trait changes, presenting, potentially, some interesting tracking to be undertaken, following characters through their storylines. The disciples are an example of characters who feature and change over a whole Gospel, as do characters who appear intermittently, like the specific disciples, James and John, or John the Baptist. Such tracking can also take place through a single story. We've noted the changes in the hemorrhaging woman, from her backstory of ritual uncleanness and enduring physicians without healing to her thinking about touching. But she changes. Having acted surreptitiously she is healed and "the woman, knowing what had happened to her, came in fear and trembling, fell down before him, and told him the whole truth" (Mark 5:33). She steps forward and Jesus says her faith has made her well, giving an indication of a trait that was there when she secretly touched him. For her, it is on "knowing what had happened to her" that she reveals herself. So does he see a trait that was there before she touched Jesus—one that she only sees after he identifies it?

Thesaurusing

One approach to exploring characters traits is to begin with an extensive list of them. Chatman's example of friendless Peter is quite specific, but there is the possibility of devising a fairly extensive list of traits that a character in a biblical story could have. A quick skim over such a list, after reading a story such as that of the hemorrhaging woman, may throw up a few unexpected trait words: is she arrogant? Bold? Creative? If pushed to select ten traits she exemplifies, which would a reader select and why?

Adventurous	Alert	Ambitious	Angry
Arrogant	Attentive	Authoritative	Bold
Boring	Brave	Calm	Charismatic
Compassionate	Confident	Confused	Cooperative
Courageous	Creative	Creepy	Cruel
Cunning	Cynical	Daring	Deceptive
Deferential	Determined	Devoted	Diligent
Discerning	Dishonest	Disloyal	Disrespectful
Dopey	Duplicitous	Enduring	Enlightened
Enthusiastic	Evil	Fair	Faithful
Fearful	Fearless	Forgiving	Friendly
Funny	Generous	Gentle	Graceful
Grateful	Greedy	Grumpy	Honest
Hopeful	Hospitable	Humble	Hurt
Idolatrous	Immoral	Impatient	Joyful
Kind	Loving	Loyal	Lustful
Meek	Merciful	Misguided	Murderous
Obedient	Patient	Peaceful	Persistent
Persuasive	Prickly	Quarrelsome	Reckless
Reliable	Resourceful	Ridiculous	Rude
Self-controlled	Shamed	Silly	Sincere
Single-minded	Spiritual	Strong	Stubborn
Tolerant	Tough	Truthful	Unforgiving
Unhappy	Unkind	Unmerciful	Vengeful
Weak	Wild	Wise	Witty

Likewise a look at a list like this may cause us to ask whether a word finds a home in the traits of a character encountered in the Bible. Imagine rooting out all the wild ones? And who is stubborn? Is anyone 'silly' in scripture?

PARADIGM

Chatman uses the phrase *paradigm* as a label for the collection of traits that readers collect together in our reading about a character. This is an interesting term to use, because a paradigm is the collection of ideas people form on the basis of experience, which become the standpoint for understanding other experiences. However, a paradigm can also be shattered and changed by further experiences. There was a time when experience dictated the accepted paradigm that the Earth stood still and the Sun went round it, and sure enough at sunrise onwards, it looked like that was happening. When astronomers started showing the problems with this paradigm, it broke down and shifted to a new paradigm backed up by new experience.

In character terms, there are points at which the reader has gained an impression of a character and that impression become the basis on which other encounters take place. As people, we characterize people. It is the same with story characters. We form opinions that can alter. The theorist Raman Selden put it:

> At any given stage in reading there are a number of possible ways of building a provisional interpretation of the characters and their situation. . . . Our construction of meaning is likely to be open and provisional at the outset, but to become gradually less open and more definite.[3]

The degree to which characters change will vary. Merenlahti describes how: "Before the reader's eyes, the characters take shape gradually, often in unexpected ways, so that there is usually a notable difference between the first impression and the last."[4] This is different when it comes to God, who in the Gospels remains relatively unchanged. As Merenlahti puts it: "While God is, humans are only in the process of becoming what they are."[5]

The Syrophoenician woman appears on the scene with the odds of her paradigm quickly and fairly comprehensively stacked against her.[6] The action takes place on gentile turf. She's female, so many teachers of the time

---

3. Selden, *Reader's Guide*, 124.

4. Merenlahti, *Poetics*, 81.

5. Merenlahti, *Poetics*, 81.

6. France, *Mark*, 297.

would not have engaged with her. France adds: "Her daughter's condition might be expected to inspire fear and/or disgust, while the 'uncleanness' of the demon suggests ritual impurity."[7] It is from such a position that she comes in and bows and, at this point, the reader could be forgiven for having formed a paradigm of humility and submission, particularly as the daughter's condition is there up front. There is therefore a tension for modern sensibilities, schooled in a Gospel where "uncleans" are included, gentiles are reached and women are the eventual heroes of the tale when Jesus says those outrageous words: "It is not fair to take the children's food and throw it to the dogs" (Mark 7:27).

He calls her a dog? At this point the reader is also forming their view of Jesus. Up to date he carries a track record of loving gentiles and receiving the touch and company of women, but this comment changes his paradigm.

The woman then uses wit, not dissimilar to that Jesus deployed on regular occasions—and he appreciates this. It could be that Jesus has been wittily playing to the assumption of her behavior in bowing down, but he is clearly influenced, and changed, by her and tells her: "For saying that, you may go—the demon has left your daughter" (Mark 7:29).

To fully appreciate the story the reader needs to follow the change in the way we read this woman. over the course of these few verses. With regards to Jesus, there are dogmatic reasons why some would balk at the suggestion Jesus held the views of his time and was challenged and molded by a character like this. Interesting to note that for reasons of belief located outside the story there are those who have to assume, faced with a story like this, that Jesus is playing devil's advocate, because he could not have learned a more open approach from a woman's response.[8] For others of us, it is just this that makes it such a treasured story.

Collective Characters: The Disciples

In Mark's Gospel, the disciples wiggle their paradigm more than most, and do so as a collective group. It is possible to look at the life of individuals like Peter and Matthew. Depending on the Gospel there are illuminating examples such as Thomas, who, in the Gospel of John, is at times genuinely funny. Groups like "the crowd" or "the disciples" are also good examples of how collective characters work in the Gospels. While individually called, sometimes in controversial circumstances that add to their character, the disciples are formed into a collective that act as something of a sidekick, or

7. France, *Mark*, 297.
8. Paul, "Did the Syrophoenician Woman. . .?"

foil, to Jesus. In Mark's Gospel they demonstrate the genuine struggle between the life to which Jesus calls them and the natural, human response to challenges of this calling. In this regard they hold a place of tension that can resonate with the reader. They follow Jesus (Mark 1:16-20) and even chase him (Mark 1:35–37). He appoints them (Mark 3:14), adopts them (Mark 3:34) and teaches them what others will not hear (Mark 4:10–12). He also puts the wind up them (Mark 4:35–41) and throws ridiculous challenges in their direction (Mark 6:37). From these opening scenes the journey of the disciples takes them from Galilee to the cross, via a desertion they assured Jesus would not happen (Mark 14:31). Yet at the resurrection when his female disciples attend the tomb the promise to them from the young man therein is: "Go, tell his disciples and Peter that he is going ahead of you to Galilee; there you will see him, just as he told you" (Mark 16:7). As a collective the disciples embody the paradox between what they desire to be and how, in reality, the behave.[9]

Within collective groupings there often are exceptions to the rule. There is also good reason to hold the rule cautiously. Collective ascription should always be handled with care, particularly as association of an uncritical grouping of "the Jews" with the death of Christ has contributed to anti-Semitism. Within the authorities of the day there are paradigm-busting examples such as Jairus, driven to speak from within the leadership of the Synagogues. Also, ultimately, when all others desert Jesus, it is a member of the same council that plotted Jesus's death (Mark 14:55; 15:1) who saves the body for burial, an act the Romans often didn't permit for a victim of crucifixion.[10]

Jesus

It is in the nature of a Gospel and of an incarnational faith that the character who is declared Son of God provides a thoughtful, emotional, frustrated, and changing character that can act as a window to the nature of God. Any portion of the Gospel can and should lend itself to allowing the personal and characterful nature of Jesus to be a full part of a reading. Within chapter 1 he appears, is baptized and strange occurrences follow: God calls him "my Son." Next thing the reader knows, he's off to the wilderness to be tempted. Readers familiar with the story may be used to these changes but it's worth reflecting just how much happens to this character in just four verses (Mark

9. Yorke, *Into the Woods*, 133.

10. Malbon, *Mark's Jesus*, 227.

1:9-12). While God may not change much in the narrative, the Son of God experiences and responds in a way full of change.

The change in Jesus sometimes needs more careful teasing out, and again, towards the end of Mark 1, the leper story provides an example of such subtle change. Jesus finds himself holding audience to a whole city (Mark 1:33) and so, after this, goes off to a deserted place to pray. There, his disciples find him and he declares a plan to visit neighboring towns. When the disciples ask what he's up to, this is his clear intention and he follows through on it. Verses 38 and 39 may be short but this character is doing a lot (Mark 1:38): "He answered, 'Let us go on to the neighbouring towns, so that I may proclaim the message there also; for that is what I came out to do.' And he went throughout Galilee, proclaiming the message in their synagogues and casting out demons." Then one leper approaches him and Jesus is deeply moved (Mark 1:41), touches, and heals him, and as a result can no longer openly go into these other towns. During that story, Jesus is changed.

Ways of Reading: Paradigm

Follow a Character

One of the simplest ways to enjoy this facet of biblical narrative is to follow a character, tracking Moses through the opening of Exodus or Ruth through her tale. A concordance or search engine can provide instances of their name but the more enjoyable way to undertake this task is to skim or read through an extended Bible story or Gospel, looking both for where they occur and sometimes imagining how they feature in those moments when they are unnamed. To imagine Joseph of Arimathea, though unnamed, as part of that council that arranges the death of Jesus adds to the moment when he retrieves the body. It's a tension that leads to some commentators suggesting that Joseph skipped the actual trial hearing.[11] But the reader can work with the narrative of Mark, and ask: what if he had been there?

Traits

Different instances of character appearances will result in different traits being highlighted. Considering a character at different stages along a storyline, the reader will experience contrasting traits. This can be explored over chapters of the Bible, with recurring characters such as the disciples.

11. France, *Mark*, 666, who directs readers to Luke 23:51—though this does not rule out Joseph's presence at the trial.

It can also be explored during a single story: how, for instance, does the hemorrhaging woman change over the course of her story (Mark 5:25–34)? Traits may change over the course of the story. Also the reader may respond imaginatively with thoughts as to how traits may change: how would Jairus feel when Jesus, the successful healer, went with him to his daughter who was at death's door? Or how would he feel as they hurry along, when Jesus turns (5:30)? That turn is a chilling prospect and the imagination can then play further with this fact: when dread news comes he still takes Jesus back home with him.

Character Lines

There is a dynamic at work between characters and, as they make their separate ways through stories, they can be enjoyed in parallel. Both *Frozen* and *Toy Story* are studies in characters developing together, such as the point at which Buzz Lightyear gives up in despair, which is also the point at which the cynical Woody becomes the great encourager. Woody then sinks into despair as Buzz becomes the optimist. The changes work in a neat parallel.

At the start of their time in a particular Bible story, two characters can be selected and lines drawn down a sheet of paper to track, not just each character, but each in relation to the other. In the walking-on-water story (Mark 6:45–56) an activity like this can bring home the fact that the disciples don't see Jesus, they think they are seeing a ghost (a detail sometimes overlooked). Paralleling Jesus and the disciples also raises the question of who precisely does what when the thousands are fed (Mark 6:33–44).

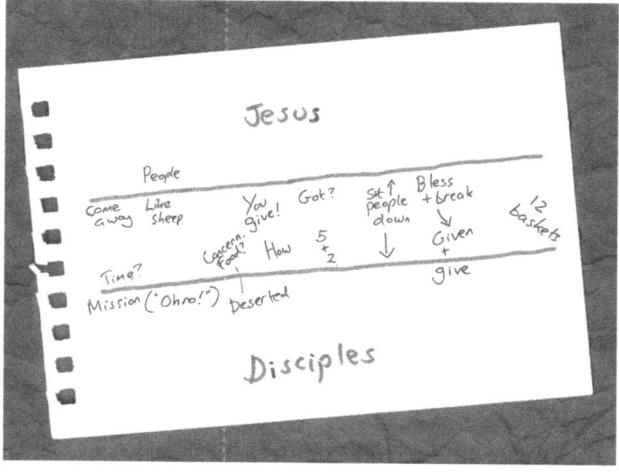

Pause

At a particular point in any story the reader can press the pause button. Stopping at any point, the reader can ask how a character has changed and, if familiar with the tale, what is still to come. In the moment before she touches Jesus's cloak the text presents what the hemorrhaging woman was thinking (Mark 5:28). The reader can pause here. This is a point where the reader can explore how this moment must be for one who has already endured much and spent all that she had on various physicians.

The reader who rereads a story also has the knowledge of what is still to come, such that the conversation with James and John about their drinking the cup Jesus will drink (Mark 10:39) can be read in the light of their actual desertion in the final stages of the story. Pausing a reading involves reflection on the way a character changes and how they have acted and will act throughout the wider story.

First and Last Impressions

Readers undertake the rollercoaster ride of character change. One activity that plays with this idea is to contrast the impressions of a character at the start and end of a story. We have seen the way the Syrophoenician woman starts and ends. What about the Gerasene demoniac when first encountered and how finally left? A piece of paper divided in two can provide a frame to explore first and last impressions.

Comparing

As mentioned in the introduction, this book is very much in favour of allowing each story to stand on it's own. However, when it comes to biblical characters there is also something enriching about readers referring across Gospels and other texts. Luke's version of the crucifixion gives a different take on Joseph of Arimathea, not mentioning the whole council meeting (Luke 22:66; cf. Mark 15:1) and, when he appears to request the body, observing: "There was a good and righteous man named Joseph, who, though a member of the council, had not agreed to their plan and action. He came from the Jewish town of Arimathea, and he was waiting expectantly for the kingdom of God" (Luke 23:50, 51).

Similarly there is an interesting task to be undertaken tracking the development of the character of Judas through various texts,[12] running in the order they may have been written and possibly representing the way the tradition about the character grew.[13]

A Reflective Reader

The characters of the Bible offer much scope for reflection. The hemorrhaging woman allows her belief in what may happen to overcome her supposed shame and Joseph of Arimathea asks for the body of the man condemned by his own council, yet the disciples flee—and this is without us looking further afield at characters like Ruth or King David.

For the spiritually minded reader, the gap John Yorke explores "between how a character wishes to be seen and who they really are"[14] provides a rich seam of reflective material within Bible reading. That contrast between the façade and the real is well caught in the moment in Oliver Stone's biopic, *Nixon*, in the moment when President Nixon stands in front of a White House portrait of JFK and laments: "When they look at you, they see what they want to be. When they look at me, they see what they are."[15]

When the disciples get it wrong or run away, they remind me of myself. In the Bible, this gap between want-to-be and reality can be the stuff of reflection, tied up with our understanding of our false and true self and our integration of sinful self with new creation. In his letter to the Romans, Paul put it differently when he described the two persons in tension within himself (best cited in the King James Version), leading to his declaration "O wretched man that I am"(Rom 7:24):

> For the good that I would I do not: but the evil which I would not, that I do.
> Now if I do that I would not, it is no more I that do it, but sin that dwelleth in me. . . .
> For I delight in the law of God after the inward man:

---

12. Merenlahti, *Poetics*, 86–88.

13. To follow Judas in the growth of the tradition: in 1 Cor 11:23 he is unnamed but his action is featured, then some of the texts that grow his story can be found in Mark 3:19 and 14:10 followed by Matt 26:14–16; 27:3; Luke 22:3; 22:47, 48; John 13:2; 13:26–29; 18:5.

14. Yorke, *Into the Woods*, 133.

15. Cited in Yorke, *Into the Woods*, 129.

But I see another law in my members, warring against the
law of my mind, and bringing me into captivity to the law of sin
which is in my members.
(Rom 7:19–20, 22–23, KJV)

Following traits and paradigms involves asking how a character changes a story but also, crucially, how a story changes a character. Asking after
both changes can make for an insightful reflection. Yorke describes all the
great archetypal stories as journeys towards completion and his summary
of how central characters develop can be borne in mind when reading the
stories of many biblical characters: "It is not enough for them to assume an
entirely new personality—they have to learn how to merge the good from
the new with the good from the old."[16]

The reader, whether Christian or otherwise, who finds within the Gospel some spiritual guidance may want to take note of what such character
development has to offer, finding in the way of characters encountered in
stories reflections for journeys of our own.

16. Yorke, *Into the Woods*, 137.

Chapter 5

Characterization

Flick back to the start of chapter 3.

    Who was your character?

    What did you make of them?

    Writing about the character of Sarrasine in Balzac's story of the same name, the literary theorist Roland Barthes wrote:

> We occasionally speak of Sarrasine as though he existed, as though he had a future, an unconscious, a soul; however what we are talking about is his *figure* (an impersonal network of symbols combined under the proper name "Sarrasine"), not his *person*.[1]

Characters are indeed constructs but, still, even in fiction those constructs can be spoken of as people with an existence and life of their own. For many Bible readers this relationship has the added dimension of the characters being looked to as people who lived and carry a faith story. However, the relationship is one that is constructed by the act of reading: readers pick up those traits and build up that relationship. This raises the question: how are characters constructed? Where character is concerned, one of the key distinctions in narrative theory is between indirect showing and direct telling, and the way in which the reader experiences a character through a building up of their traits.

---

1. Barthes, *S/Z*, 94.

DIRECT, INDIRECT, TYPE, AND COMPOSITE CHARACTERIZATION

"Their names were Aunt Sponge and Aunt Spiker, and I am sorry to say that they were both really horrible people. They were selfish, lazy, and cruel.[2] That's direct. In establishing the traits of characters, there is a basic distinction between direct and indirect characterization. For the purposes of biblical literature, to this distinction we can add the category of "type characters" and also include "composite characters."

In *direct characterization* the narrative just states the trait of a character. Such indications are rare in the Gospels but do appear in other biblical literature. Such labeling of characters tends to happen at their introduction, and can be blunt, as when Nabal and Abigail are introduced in 1 Samuel: "Now the name of the man was Nabal; and the name of his wife Abigail: and she was a woman of good understanding, and of a beautiful countenance: but the man was churlish and evil in his doings; and he was of the house of Caleb" (1 Sam 25:3, KJV).

Other examples include

"Noah was a just man" (Gen 6:9, KJV).

"Esau was a skillful hunter, a man of the field, while Jacob was a quiet man, living in tents" (Gen 25:27).

In the Gospels such directness is rare, though Joseph is clearly described in Matthew and Judas is labeled in John:

"Joseph, being a just man" (Matt 1:19, ESV).

"He was a thief" (John 12:6).

To grasp *indirect characterization* the reader just needs to think of a memorable character in literature or film and ask "How do I know what I know about them?" The answer will often include features such as the appearance of E.T., or his actions, such as the way he scratches his nose, indirectly building up the feeling he's a sweetie. Indirect characterization describes the way in which a reader builds up the traits of a character through indirect indications. Various schema unpick the way this happens. Rimmon-Kenan itemized her list of these indirect ways in which character is constructed:

- actions
- speech

2. Dahl, *James*, 1.

- appearance

- environment

- analogy.

I would add two more:

- other characters

- the undone and unsaid.

The meaning of some of these will be self-evident and the analysis below will pick out precisely how environment and analogy work, in this context.

This distinction of direct and indirect characterization can be applied to all examples of the construction of characters occurs in stories. However, there are two more ways in which biblical literature characterizes that are worth adding alongside: type and composite characters.

Type characters populate a type scene. The 'type scene' is a phrase taken from the study of classical literature and applied to biblical literature.[3] Alter relates the ways in Homeric literature includes stories of visits to locations that follow a regular pattern.[4] In biblical literature he finds a number of such typical and patterned scenes in Old Testament narrative, such as betrothals at wells and dangers in the desert. He also labels one type "annunciations," acknowledging the term has a New Testament connection.[5]

Typicality of this sort was picked up by Rhoads in a study of healing stories in the Gospel of Mark, all of which have a degree of similarity among them. There are shared behaviors exhibited by type-characters in these stories that could be given the umbrella term, "A Suppliant with Faith."[6] These can include the times when the character is said to have heard about Jesus (Mark 2:1; 7:25; 10:47); there are also a number of stories in which they kneel before Jesus (Mark 1:40; 5:22; 7:25). In a number of such stories a suppliant brings someone other than themselves, to Jesus (Mark 5:23; 8:22; 9:17). Rhoads also notes the way Jesus often gives instructions not to broadcast the news of the healing at the end of such stories (Mark 1:44; 8:26).[7]

One repeated feature is the presence, and overcoming, of obstacles by suppliants. These can include the problem of non-leper touching leper (Mark 1:40, 41), the crowd surrounding a house (Mark 2:2), news that the

3. Alter, *Art of Biblical Narrative*, 50.

4. Alter, *Art of Biblical Narrative*, 51

5. Alter, *Art of Biblical Narrative*, 51.

6. Rhoads, *Jesus and the Syrophoenician Woman*, 39–40.

7. Rhoads, *Jesus and the Syrophoenician Woman*, 39–40.

person needing healing has died (5:35–36), sight only being partially restored (Mark 8:24), or the failings of the disciples (10:18).

Type characters may act in ways that are in keeping with their type. Their characterization can also highlight variations from the typical. In casting the idea of type Alter cautioned: "As is true of all original art, what is really interesting is not the schema of convention but what is done in each individual application of the schema to give it a sudden tilt of innovation or event to refashion it radically for the imaginative purposes at hand."[8]

Examples of tilts and refashioning include the responses to obstacles suppliants encounter. These differ in ways that breathe a particular liveliness into these characters: de-roofing a roof (Mark 2:4), answering back with a witty reply (Mark 7:28), being declared dead (5:35; 9:26), or even just shouting louder (10:48). These variations develop the characters further. In an example such as the healing of the blind man at Bethsaida, we have a unique example of a healing that appears not to work first time (Mark 8:23–24), a tilt so stand-out and unusual that this story doesn't appear in the other gospels—possibly being left out because of the apparent failure.

In addition to type characters, there are *composite* characters. These are groups of two or more characters that are gathered together and can be characterized in terms similar to those that could be applied to an individual. One double-act that fits this bill would be the midwives, Shiphrah and Puah, who deceive the King of Egypt. Though individually named and honored at the start of their part in the Exodus story (Exod 1:15) their actions thereafter are presented in composite fashion: "The midwives feared God; they did not do as the king of Egypt commanded them" (Exod 1:17a). They act and speak as one (Exod 1:19).

Some collectives can be larger and almost serve as a shorthand for a stance by a group. The religious leaders of the Gospels are lumped together, even though there were differences and sub-groups within this collective.[9] The disciples can also appear as a collective, albeit one that is more rounded and changeable than some other such groupings. Their collective nature is evident in instances such as the first feeding miracle—a story in which the disciples act and speak as one (Mark 6:35, 41)—and also in their response to the miracle of walking on the water, when the storm calms:
"And they were utterly astounded, for they did not understand about the loaves, but their hearts were hardened" (Mark 6:51b–52).

Later there will be a second miraculous feeding, followed by a gradual restoration of one man's sight (Mark 8:14–21) That miracle kicks off a run

8. Alter, *Art of Biblical Narrative*, 52.
9. Powell, *What Is Narrative Criticism?*, 58.

of stories which include the eyes of the blind being opened (Mark 8:25) and Peter's declaration—a different, gradual seeing (Mark 8:29). Three disciples will also experience the transfiguration (Mark 9:1–8) as Jesus and the Gospel story turns towards Jerusalem (Mark 10:32). So the collective characterization of these disciples at the outset of this run of stories is significant. Immediately following that second feeding, setting out by boat, the disciples demonstrate that they have collectively failed to see in Jesus the successor to Moses, the other great provider of bread in the wild place. They collectively realize their failure to take any bread with them (Mark 8:14) and when Jesus warns them against the yeast of the rulers, they have collectively said: "It is because we have no bread" (Mark 8:16). From that point the narrative turn towards gradually seeing Jesus for who he is, and where he is headed. It continues right up to the empty tomb where a young man tells the women: "Go, tell his disciples and Peter that he is going ahead of you to Galilee; there you will see him, just as he told you" (Mark 16:7). It is in these stories that the disciples are not just characterized but developed, in concert, as a collective.

INDIRECT CHARACTERIZATION

As readers, we encounter characters and construct our understanding of them through various ways.

Action

Peter's mother-in-law is one of the unnamed women of this Gospel who is known to the reader through just one thing: her actions. She is healed and she serves Jesus (Mark 1:31b). The reader of a Bible story encounters various actions that characterize those within it. This includes those such as Peter's mother-in-law, who has one action ascribed, as well as characters with a series of actions that build up their characterization. Over the course of the Gospel of Mark, the disciples will follow Jesus and take off on their own preaching journeys, doing the sort of exorcisms and healings Jesus has done (Mark 6:12–13). They will feed multitudes, desert Jesus at his arrest, and be directed to meet him again by going to Galilee, and progressively their characterization builds up.

The one-off action can also be powerful. Little is related about the friends who brought the paralyzed man to Jesus, but un-roofing a roof gives us a way in. It has been noted above that those coming for healing often do something to overcome an obstacle, and these hole-makers provide a memorable example.

Alongside the actions characters perform are the actions they don't do or the actions we, as readers, may think they should have done. In some cases such omissions indicate a positive choice to the contrary, as when the failure of the religious leaders to see is presented as a positive act—they are choosing not to see.[10] This failure to act is also seen in the characterization of the disciples, who develop in part through their failure to do what they could have done. The degree to which we may judge such actions and the way Jesus responds to them creates an interesting dynamic in reading. When the disciples argue, rather than feeding a multitude (Mark 6:45), readers may understand their point of view. However, we may ask why this massed feeding option doesn't spring to mind when, shortly after, a similar crowd appears (Mark 8:4). Similarly, shortly after Jesus commends to the disciples the welcoming of a child (Mark 9:36–37) the disciples encounter people bringing children to Jesus and rebuke them (Mark 10:13). Stories like these, particularly so close to each other and tagged to discussions that follow, about the sufficiency of bread (Mark 8:9–21) or the nature of status (Mark 11:41–45), build up this characterization of the disciples. Later in the story their big omission and action to the contrary will be to run away at the arrest of Jesus (Mark 14:50). Care needs to be taken about making a realistic assessment of what we could expect of these folks in that situation, but as a reader the humility with which a reader acknowledges the possibility that we would also have got things wrong or made a run for it enhances our appreciation of the development of these characters.

Speech

Who said these?

"If I but touch his clothes, I will be made well."

"The head of John the Baptizer."

"Sir, even the dogs under the table eat the children's crumbs."

"Truly this man was God's Son!"

The answers can be found in Mark 5:28; 6:24; 7:28; and 15:39, but it's worth noting that this is all each of these particular characters say. Not too many words are required, but they characterize them.

In biblical stories, the reader should watch for limited but loaded speech. Things a character says can contribute to this build up of characterization, and once again this can be a one-off story, but there are also

10. Rhoads et al., *Mark as Story*, 120.

interesting examples of the way this contributes to characterization over the course of a longer narrative. The book of Jonah is a cracking example.

In longer stretches of story, the reader can take stock of what characters say at different stages, and here again the disciples provide a rich seam of characterization. Often they model misunderstandings, in a way with which readers may sympathize. Twice, they point out the problems regarding a need for food for the multitude in the wilderness (Mark 6:35; 8:4). You would have thought when this crops up in chapter 8 they'd remember the story in chapter 6. In fairness, the disciples also develop as characters, and there are times when individual voices emerge. When asked about Jesus's identity—"Who do people say I am?" (Mark 8:27b)—the group offer various answers (Mark 8:28), but from among them, Peter calls Jesus the Messiah (8:29). He then messes up by telling him what sort of a Messiah to be (Mark 8:32). Later the collective argue about who is the greatest (Mark 9:34). In these ways, the disciples stand in contrast to other characters, such as the Syrophoenician woman who believes there is enough bread for all (Mark 7:28) or the silent woman who, Jesus declares, anoints him for the death this Messiah will undergo in a tale that "will be told in remembrance of her" (Mark 14:8–9b).

Silence also speaks. The anointing woman contrasts with the disciples. She is also a prime example of the way in which, as with inaction, the absence of speech can also be significant. She performs this act that connects more fully than any other character with Jesus intention for his way as Messiah. By contrast, the disciples' moment of silence follows their argument about who is the greatest, when Jesus has to ask what they had been arguing about and "they were silent, for on the way they had argued with one another about who was the greatest" (Mark 9:34). Their silence following such arguing contrasts with the anointing woman who remains silent, yet performs the action that others will tell in memory of her (Mark 14:9b).

A character's speech is a window into their inner life of thoughts and feelings and, in biblical narrative, action and speech stand as the two main ways in which indirect characterization takes place.

Appearance

As modern readers we are used to full and fascinating character descriptions. Celie, the narrator in *The Color Purple*, describes the singer coming to town:

> Shug Avery standing upside a piano, elbow crook, hand on her hip. She wearing a hat like Indian Chiefs. Her mouth open

showing all her teef and don't nothing seem to be troubling her
mind. Come one, come all, it say. The Queen Honeybee is back
in town.[11]

In the Bible, character description seems almost avoided. Berlin points
out that objects such as temples and arks receive fulsome description, but
characters do not receive the same treatment.[12] There are descriptions of
characters in the Bible but they are rare. One example would be Jacob's summary of himself and his brother: "And Jacob said to Rebekah his mother,
Behold, Esau my brother is a hairy man, and I am a smooth man" (Gen
27:11, KJV) This reminds the reader of their birth. Even then, Esau was
declared hairy all over (Gen 25 25).

There is a difference between the stories of the Old Testament and
those in the New. In the Old, there are character descriptions. They tend
to establish features of a character early in their story. We noted above that
Esau is born hairy. Similarly, in the very verses in which they are introduced,
Goliath appears as a huge (1 Sam 17:4), Abigail is clever and beautiful (1
Sam 25:3), and Naaman suffers from leprosy (2 Kgs 5:1). Sternberg alerts
us to the way in which characteristics like this, once described, are "like
a ticking bomb, sure to explode into action in the narrator's (and God's)
own good time."[13] In the Old Testament, such early descriptions will feature
significantly, later in the story. Sometimes, as Sternberg points out in relation to Esau's hairiness: "The effect is so long delayed that the impatient
reader may begin to suspect that it will never materialize."[14] The reader has
a patient wait from Esau's hairy birth (Gen 25:15) to Jacob's hairsuit disguise
(Gen 27:16), though along the way there are other moments when Esau
behaves more like an animal than a smoothie.

Within the New Testament, description of appearance is rare. We have
no physical description of Jesus. Where a character's appearance does occur
it is often at the outset of a story, and again the details are significant. In the
Gospel of Mark, the clothing and diet of John the Baptist emphasize that he
is a wilderness character,[15] resembling Elijah (2 Kgs 1:8). Such introductory
characteristics are also prone to change once the story gets going,[16] and this
is a feature that arises in the Gospel, particularly in healing and miracle

11. Walker, *Color Purple*, 24.

12. Berlin, *Poetics*, 34.

13. Sternberg, *Poetics*, 339.

14. Sternberg, *Poetics*, 339.

15. Lane, *Mark*, 51.

16. Sternberg, *Poetics*, 339, highlights women depicted as barren as an example.

stories: a character with a withered hand (Mark 3:1) or born blind (Mark 8:22) are examples of characters presenting as ones who come for healing.

The reader will also garner something of a character's appearance from their actions. Something of their composure and manner arises from the way they appear on the scene. The character of the Gerasene demoniac (5:1–6) appears in a combination of actions and howls, with bruises and broken shackles. Likewise there is something to be inferred in the way a character appears and can instantly be designated a poor widow (13:43) or the image evoked by someone who silently anoints Jesus (Mark 14:3). For an imaginative reader there is almost something balletic about such moments and we can take such actions as prompts to the way we imagine a character's appearance.

Environment

> Old Scrooge sat in his counting house. It was cold, bleak, biting weather: foggy withal: and he could hear the people in the court outside go wheezing up and down. . . . The door of Scrooge's counting house was open that he might keep an eye upon his clerk, who in a dismal little cell beyond, a sort of tank, was copying letters. Scrooge had a very small fire, but the clerk's fire was so very much smaller that it looked like one coal.[17]

This classic encounter fixes the character in the reader's thinking. Likewise, though with less descriptive language, the encounter with Levi "sitting at the tax booth" (Mark 2:14) or the Gerasene demoniac emerging as "a man out of the tombs" (Mark 5:2) are examples of characters characterized by their setting.

One of the questions that arises from such settings is the degree to which the character creates the setting or is molded by it. With Levi the reader may be assume he has chosen his occupation but the Gerasene demoniac's situation is a combination of his own strength in breaking his chains, and his torment, that sets him howling on mountains (Mark 5:5). The Syrophoenician woman is encountered in a gentile setting—hence Jesus's response to her about dogs and food. Clearly she has not chosen to be born a gentile, and Jesus's engagement with her takes place on the trajectory headed towards a second miraculous feeding of another multitude, but with this feeding taking place in a Gentile location (Mark 8:1–8). Her

---

17. Dickens, *Christmas Carol*, 11–12.

insistence that there is enough food for all beautifully challenges division and exclusion.

The settings of stories will be explored in chapter 7, but one further feature in relation to characterization is to note that settings do not need to be places. A social setting can also contribute to the construction of character, as when Peter make his declaration about Jesus, within the setting of a bunch of disciples (Mark 8:27–30). The other feature to note is that settings can be as momentary as a character's appearance. The first disciples are encountered in their regular settings: Simon Peter and Andrew are fishing (Mark 1:16) and Levi is encountered at his tax booth (Mark 2:14). Both are settings that characterize. Furthermore, Levi and his relationship with Jesus is also characterized by the dinner they then share. The description of the setting is actually ambiguous: "And so it was as he reclined to eat in his house, many tax collectors and sinners also reclined with Jesus and his disciples" (Mark 2:15).[18] Although some translations pin the house of "his house" to Levi, it could have been Jesus's. This could be his house party. Equally he could be a guest of Levi. In either reading, the environment further characterizes Jesus and Levi.

Ways of Reading: Characterization

Understanding Characterizations

Characterization is one of those concepts in literary theory where just grasping the idea, and how it works, lends itself to further thinking. With these features of characterization in mind, the reader can review their experience of any character within any story. If a character appears in more than one story, the reader can also look at how characterization builds up over that series, but there is also much to be said for homing in on a serial character in the one moment of characterization. Those characters who say one thing or Peter's mother-in-law doing just what she does still build up a sense of character. With this focus in mind the reader can ask what it is that characterizes a character. What do they do? What do they say? How do they appear? Where are they? And as ever, where the text does not provide an answer, the reader can root their thinking in the text but branch out in their own imagination.

18. My translation. See France, *Mark*, 133.

Isolating Characterization

Characterization involves a buildup of various features, all coming together in one individual. One activity the reader can pursue is to focus on one particular strand featuring in a character. This works well if they appear over a few stories, so that the reader can focus on what a character says or the environments in which they appear.

One fruitful focus of significance in biblical narrative will be the decisions a character makes. In biblical narrative, the choices a character makes are a vital source of characterization. Looking through a portion of their story, the reader can keep a track of the choices with which they were presented and the decisions they made.

One small take on this involves working characterization backwards. The reader can reflect on their impression of a character and ask, what one action or one spoken sentence might have had the greatest bearing? What moment or moments have led the construction of that characterization?

What Don't We Know?

The characters the reader encounters in narrative will sometimes be characterized directly. They will also be directly commented on by other characters. This opens the possibility for readers to ask: how well do we know what we know about a character? The reader could produce a two-columned table headed "What I know" and "Don't know/not sure." The first will record characterization, the second will show the gaps that remain. We read of the Syrophoenician woman as confidently understanding the sufficiency of what was on offer and that there was enough bread for all, including the dogs. We don't know how she formed that view, or how she heard about Jesus, and it's a characterful gap. The simple two-columned chart could be expanded outwards to become a continuum that demonstrates those facets of a character the reader perceives as surer than others.

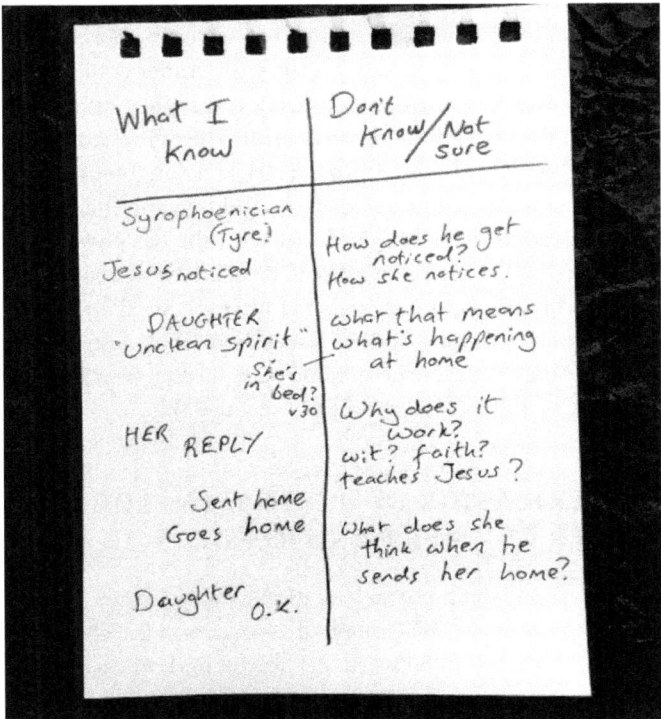

Causality in Characterization

The character "Something Else," in Kathryn Cave's classic picture book of the same name, is ostracized from the other, diverse creatures in his story and is introduced with the words:

On a windy hill

alone

with nothing to be friends with

lived Something Else.[19]

It raises the question: why?

The story that follows provides a beautiful interplay between the degree to which Something Else is excluded by others and his own experience of excluding.

19. Cave and Riddell, *Something Else*.

This difference between what a character causes and what they just experience as caused is one the reader can consider in approaching a character in a story. For each character in a story the reader could try gathering together one or two facets of characterization that they cause, and one or two over which they have little or no control. The Syrophoenician woman (Mark 7:24–30) doesn't choose to have a stricken daughter or to be on the other side of the figurative line between the children and the dogs. She does choose to beg healing from Jesus and, crucially, she has power over her response. She also has the daring to make it. Similarly, Bartimaeus (10:46–52) doesn't choose blindness or a crowd that attempts to silence him, but he does use his voice, raising it louder—and then when Jesus calls him, he chooses his response. Interesting to note, being healed, he also hears Jesus's command to "Go," but instead chooses to stay and follow.

CHARACTERIZATION BY OTHERS: ANALOGY, CHARACTER COMMENT AND READERS

Three more ways in which characterization can take place differ from the ones above. The above are self-contained as aspects of the character, whereas these involve interaction between a character and others—be they other characters or the reader.

Analogy

There is something about Buzz Lightyear that makes Cowboy Woody who Woody is, and vice versa. It's the same with King Lear's three daughters: Cordelia stands out from the other two, something she couldn't have done if they weren't there. Characterization by analogy involves the way readers compare one character with another. This characterization by analogy to other characters clearly features in biblical parables like the Good Samaritan (Luke 10:25–37) and Prodigal Son (Luke 15:11–31). In both, characters are characterized by the way they contrast with others within their story. A further example, from the Gospel of Mark, would be between the widow at the temple contrasted with the rich people making their offerings (Mark 12:41–42).

Some examples of analogical characterization are clearer than others. To some degree, every character in a story is always in comparison with every other character. However, the parallels can be starker. If David and Saul both become acclaimed by the people within chapters of each other, the contrast is waiting to be drawn, as is that between Orpah and Ruth, as they share a family tragedy (Ruth 1). Even Jezebel and Ahab stand in interesting analogy to each other in their reaction to Naboth's refusal to sell a vineyard (1 Kgs 21). To give an example from the Gospel of Mark, the response of the Syrophoenician woman describes the sufficiency of food for all. This may stand in contrast with the way in which, two stories later, the disciples repeat the panic they had at the first feeding miracle about the lack of enough to feed everyone (Mark 8:4).[20] Daniel Kirk points out that "not only is she the only person who wins an argument with Jesus in the whole gospels, she also, unlike the disciples, somehow has eyes to see, that there's enough bread, not only for the children at the table, but also for . . . whoever else."[21] Two stories after her's Jesus will again provide more than enough for all, feeding another multitude—this time a gentile one (Mark 8:1–10).

Analogy can also take the form of characters demonstrating similarity. Here again, the women of the Gospel of Mark complement one another, serving Jesus (Mark 1:30), challenging him (Mark 7:27), anointing him for burial (Mark 14:8). In the whole Gospel, as Kirk observes, "the nameless women in the gospel come off as ideal disciples in the way that the twelve never end up living up to."[22] Of course, this is also a contrast: these women stand in contrast to the male disciples. And these women *are* disciples[23] so they do create an analogy to one another within Jesus band of followers. The women are consistently faithful. At the end of the Gospel, they will be at the cross after the men have run away, and the story reveals,

> There were also women looking on from a distance; among them were Mary Magdalene, and Mary the mother of James the younger and of Joseph, and Salome. These used to follow him and provided for him when he was in Galilee; and there were many other women who had come up with him to Jerusalem." (Mark 15:40, 41)

Interesting to note that in this moment they stand with the centurion, the one character who stood declaring Jesus, on the cross, as Son of God. There are ways in which they both contrast and resemble the centurion, but both the women and the Roman, outsiders in their own ways, are present at that moment.[24]

For the women, the verses above also constitute a moment of analepsis that flashes back to Galilee, and while it may contrast with the disciples

20. The same Greek word to denote being satisfied is used in 6:42; 7:27; and 8:4, 8.
21. Kirk, "Bible for Normal People," 38:32.
22. Kirk, "Bible for Normal People," 35:55.
23. Munro in Malbon, *In the Company*, 58.
24. Malbon, *In the Company*, 60.

who ran away (Mark 14:50) these women can also remind the reader of the nameless women throughout the Gospel and indicate something of their followership, which will continue two days later at the empty tomb (Mark 16:1).

Character Comment

In the Gospel of Luke a centurion seeking healing of a servant sends some Jewish elders to Jesus, and they characterize him, saying: "'He is worthy of having you do this for him, for he loves our people, and it is he who built our synagogue for us'" (Luke 7:4, 5).

In the same way that, in direct characterization, the narrative offers up a direct description of a character, there are ways in which one character can characterize another, by commenting on them or reporting an action. At such moments, the reader is encountering two moments of characterization: the one speaking is characterizing another character but also, in doing so, shedding light upon their own character. One amusing example of this would be in 1 Kings, when the wicked King Ahab has received affirmation of the news he wanted, that God is with him in an impending battle, from all his prophets who, we will later find, have misled him. Asked by an ally, Jehoshaphat, if there are any other prophets of whom to enquire, "The king of Israel said to Jehoshaphat, 'There is still one other by whom we may inquire of the LORD, Micaiah son of Imlah; but I hate him, for he never prophesies anything favorable about me, but only disaster'" (1 Kgs 22:8a).

This negative judgment pushes the reader into a double take, as we consider the reliability of the villainous Ahab as he offers an evaluation of a critic. The reader then gets to see how these evaluations pan out once battle is enjoined.

Reader Connections

Deep down, as a reader, I ask myself what I would have done in Peter's shoes, at that fireside outside the trial of Jesus. I suspect I'd have done the same thing. To be honest, I might not even have followed that far. I'd have run away like the rest of them, in the garden. And also, at the last supper, I'd also have been crystal clear I'd never do that, and knowing how I nearly doze at certain meetings, I suspect I'd have dozed off in Gethsemane, even though Jesus told me not to.

How we relate to the buildup of characters is, in itself, part of the dynamic of characterization. It may seem strange to pick out a reader's response as a means of characterization—surely the reader is responding to everything in the story. True—there is a whole chapter on just this feature of reading, up ahead. However, there is a personal dynamic to characterization that will affect the way in which a reader builds up their construction of a character. Over the course of a story, the reader can sense a closeness to, and identification with, a character. There are also times of distance and alienation.[25] Taking Peter as an example, he is the one that stands out from the collective of the disciples, who, as "Simon and his companions," seek Jesus out on the morning of that second day of the story (Mark 1:36). Peter tops the list of the disciples (Mark 3:16) and is the one who declares Jesus to be Messiah (Mark 8:29). He is there at the transfiguration and specifically named, at the Gospel's end, when the man at the tomb instructs the women to "Go, tell his disciples *and Peter* that he is going ahead of you to Galilee; there you will see him, just as he told you." (Mark 16:7 emphasis mine). These references make Peter stand out, embodying an image of discipleship. Yet Peter also offers "a human response that is totally believable"[26] throughout the Gospel. A compelling feature here may be the way in which the character of Peter is himself in tension with the idea of an ideal disciple. Within just three verses he can faithfully affirm Jesus as Messiah, and then be Satanic (Mark 8:29–32). He professes high intentions (Mark 14:29) but also denies Jesus (Mark 14:68–70). As readers, particularly if we read as "disciples" or "followers," we are invited to find our place within the tensions opened up by characters like this.

In his study of just what it is fairy stories offer children, Bruno Bettleheim observes how child readers experience the appeal or otherwise of a character: "The question for the child is not, 'Do I want to be good?' but "Who do I want to be like?" The child decides this on the basis of projecting . . . wholeheartedly into one character."

Bettleheim observes that if that character is a very good person, then the child will want to be like them.[27] Part of the place of the Bible in the life of faith is to prompt just such a question. To Bettleheim's question we could add the reader of Bible stories also asking not just "Who do I want to be like?" but also, "and who am I like?" This tension between ideal and reality is both the experience of many biblical characters, and their readers.

25. Boomershine, *Story Journey*, 206.

26. Boomershine in Merenlahti, *Poetics*, 83.

27. Bettleheim, *Uses of Enchantment*, 10.

THE CHARACTERIZATION OF JESUS
IN THE GOSPEL OF MARK

Focusing on the Gospels, the reader may want to flick through one, not reading, but skimming and noting the one character present in nearly every scene is Jesus. Here too, there is characterization.

The Gospel of Mark could be described as a Gospel of characterization, with the first half answering the question of who Jesus is and revealing him as Messiah, and the second half outworking just what that means for this Messiah. It is also bookended by declarations that he is the Son of God. The story opens with stark and direct characterization: "The beginning of the good news of Jesus Christ, the Son of God" (Mark 1:1). Similar identifications are made by the voice of God at baptism and transfiguration (Mark 1:11; 9:7) but then, also, remarkably, by one of Jesus's executioners, the centurion at the cross (Mark 15:39). Demons also recognize his power over them (Mark 1:23–27), such that Jesus "would not permit the demons to speak, because they knew him."(Mark 1:34b). This knowing perspective is shared by the readers. We have that first verse with us, and, whether or not bystanders did, as readers we heard the declaration at the baptism.

The unfolding of that process of characterization then takes an entire Gospel, and there are three facets of it worth noting.

Firstly, the reader should bear in mind both what Jesus does and doesn't do, and what he can and can't do. Burridge describes him as bounding around the events of the story,[28] but there is also a vulnerability to this character that emerges from the first chapter. Throughout the first day Jesus emerges, calls followers, and commences a mission (1:38, 39). But then he heals a leper and his plans are scuppered. Here, the Son of God's mission is curtailed because of this healing (1:45). Despite Jesus telling the leper to say nothing to anyone about Jesus touching and healing him, the leper "went out and began to proclaim it freely, and to spread the word, so that Jesus could no longer go into a town openly, but stayed out in the country; and people came to him from every quarter" (Mark 1:45).

This ending adds a whole emotional hue to what he says and how he responds to the leper, when he is moved with pity, declares this act is his choice and reaches out and touches the man (1:41).

Throughout Mark's Gospel, the choices Jesus makes and the things he both does and does not do will shape his plans for Jerusalem. Examples include his rejection of Peter's suggested steer away from suffering and death as

---

28. Burridge, *Four Gospels*, 108.

"Satan" (Mark 8:32, 33) and his contrary declaration about taking up a cross (Mark 8:34). His choices will lead to the actions in Jerusalem and to both the things he will say in the city, and his silence at the time of trial. Again, it is for the reader to build up both what is said and done, and what isn't.

Secondly, Jesus operates against a backdrop he calls and creates. There is nothing in the Gospels that denotes anything about Jesus appearance, but there are rich indications of environment, whether these be his retreats to lakes and wildernesses or his relaxation in company that causes disapproval (2:13–17; 14:3–9). The story is always on the move with a group that includes an itinerant band of disciples including the twelve (3:13–19) along with the women (Mark 15:41), joined along the way by multitudes (Mark 3:7). Right up to his entry to Jerusalem characters like Bartimaeus swell the crowd of followers (Mark 10:52). The writer Marcus Borg observed, from a historical angle, that such crowds were not unheard of at that time, but that the Gospels give a picture of an exceptional grouping that would have included men and women, the outcasts and those of status:

> As an itinerant movement, it sometimes was offered local hospitality by sympathizers, but also no doubt slept in the open air. As a group on the move, travelling through Galilee and finally to Jerusalem, it must have been a remarkable sight.[29]

Thirdly, the characterization of Jesus involves a series of analogies that both characterize Jesus, and those with whom he is analogized. Here again, the reader is invited into this space. The Gospel opens with a beautiful analogy, in which before Jesus appears, John has begun comparing baptism by water with that of the Holy Spirit (Mark 1:8). The space between Jesus and others also opens from the moment the demons are confronted (Mark 1:27). The analogies continue: his disciples follow (1:35, 36), opponents appear (Mark 2:6, 7) and outcasts are befriended (2:17). Throughout there are opportunities for us, as readers, to situate ourselves within the spaces opened between characters, and this can be experienced in the way questions and challenges can be heard. The parables form an obvious example of this, but so do some of the questions Jesus asks. When he asks those in the house "Which is easier, to say to the paralytic, 'Your sins are forgiven,' or to say, 'Stand up and take your mat and walk'?" (Mark 2:9) or confronts the disciples, asking, "Do you not yet understand?" (Mark 8:21) or asks them, "But who do you say that I am?" (Mark 8:29) readers can hear those questions asked also to us.

---

29. Borg, *Jesus*, 128.

Ways of Reading: Characterization by Others

Compare and Contrast

David and Goliath stand in clear contrast to each other, but in this example the reader is just a stone's throw away from the exit of one character. David and Saul make a much more challenging comparison, over the course of both their narratives. Both experience the rare biblical instance of a physical description (1 Sam 10:23; 16:12), both mess up big time and are confronted by prophets (1 Sam 15; 2 Sam 12), and both lend themselves to comparison and contrast.

The reader can try comparing characters. One simple activity is to draw up a two-columned paper in which the qualities of each character are lined up either side. However, for this to work well in biblical analogies the reader should look to one side and allow it to raise questions of the other—because that is how these analogies are often working in the stories. In comparing the stories of the paralytic and Bartimaeus (Mark 2:1–12; 10:46–52) the task involves noticing something in one story and then asking it of another; the paralytic is brought by four others, but does anybody bring Bartimaeus? Such asks lead to a recognition of what both stories share in common. Both healings face obstructions: in Bartimaeus's story that stand-out characteristic of him persisting and shouting louder raises a question about the paralytic who, in this story, never says a word.

Why might that be?

And what is it about the bystanders that differs?

Why does Jesus behave so differently?

What do they each do at the close of their stories?

In analogies, one character asks such comparisons of another.

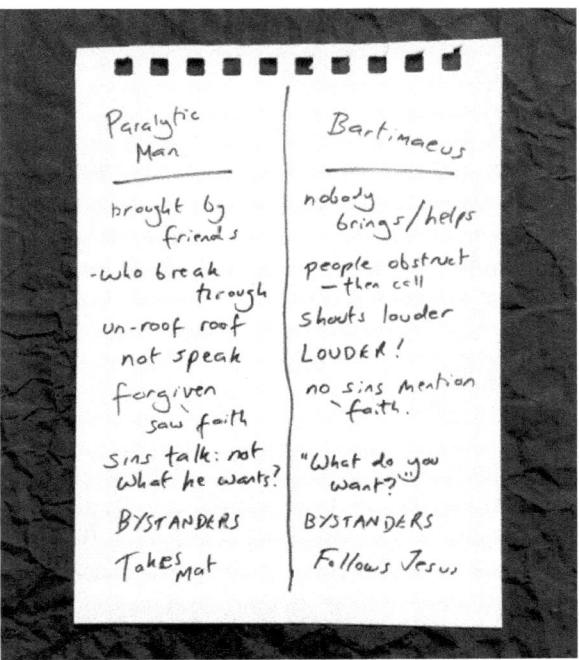

Thirds

In *Mimesis*, his classic study of ancient narrative, Erich Auerbach observed the way in which Greek heroes can remain unchanged: "Odysseus in his return is exactly the same as he was when he left."[30] Auerbach contrasted this with Old Testament characters, like Abraham and Jacob, who grow and develop over the course of their stories. The reader can look at differences that emerge in characterization, over the course of a story. One way of doing this is to consider our response to a character one third of the way into a story, and then to also consider two thirds in, and at the end. Exploring characterization in this way will involve asking, not just how we respond, but also what is influencing that response at different stages. Our response to Saul changes dramatically from the point of his reluctant calling (1 Sam 9, 10) through his downfall. In Mark's Gospel, Peter changes during the halfway mark, and his characterization is further thrown around in the last third of the story.

30. Auerbach, *Mimesis*, 17.

Distance

Defining this idea of distance, Boomershine asks those of us taking a journey through a Bible story: "On the basis of shifts of perspective and norms
of judgment, sense how close to or far from the characters you feel throughout the story."[31] He presents the alternatives of close identification and far
alienation. This isn't a simple binary and there are degrees of closeness and
distance. One way the reader can relate to a character is to imagine trying
to talk to them and, through this, imagine how we relate to them. What
would we say to Herod or Pilate when their stories conclude? How does
this differ from the women who leave the empty tomb? A further, interesting question is the degree of closeness a reader may feel to Jesus or God as
they feature in stories, and a distance that can occur between the reader and
these characters.

It is in imagined conversations of this sort with characters in Bible
stories that readers explore, not just their characterization, but also how it
matches up to the ideal of what they might have done. The space also opens
for us readers to find our way between what they do and what we think they,
and we, should have done in their circumstances.

31. Boomershine, *Story Journey*, 206.

Chapter 6

Role

This sentence has a grammar that can be laid bare, exposing the underlying sentence structure. In a similar way, structuralist theory found something akin to grammar in stories. The Russian theorist, Vladimir Propp, analyzed a large number of his country's folk tales and drew up a schedule of thirty-one "functions," as he described them. These are common features such as a hero leaving home or a villain being exposed. Different characters can perform these actions, in quite different ways[1] but in the same way that grammatical analysis will identify common features such as verbs and nouns in a sentence, Propp found certain character types in these tales performed certain functions. Propp perceived a set of spheres of action that happen in a story, and that these actions were undertaken by a set of character roles, such as a hero, a villain and a helper. Though Bible stories function differently to Propp's raw material, there is much to be gained from looking at the role characters play, functioning in a way that propels the events of a story.

ACTANTS

Building on Propp's work, the school of Structuralist theory offers some key resources for approaching character roles in stories. Structuralist theorists locate structures in language and other such structured units of meaning. Within these they highlight the vital nature of oppositions, which they see as exhibiting the structures of language. As users of language we know a

1. Propp, *Morphology*, 68.

word by distinguishing what it is from what it isn't. The word "up" isn't "down" and "red" isn't another color. By opposing and separating we build up the structures that frame language, texts and stories.

Following on from this, in an analysis that also has the benefit of widening from Russian folk tales to being more universal, the theorist, A.J. Greimas, perceived within Propp's roles a series of oppositions that make up the structure of narrative,.[2] The three binary oppositions in the Greimas structure are:[3]

- a sender and a receiver
- a subject and an object
- a helper and an opponent.

The *sender* sends something needed by the *receiver*—something that fulfills a lack or a need. In the classic secret agent drama the agency is obtaining something, or sending something to someone. In *Raiders of the Lost Ark* the government are sending something to a place of safety. That something happens to be the Ark of the Covenant. In the book of Esther, Mordecai sends salvation to the Jews. Such communication of something to someone is the spur to the action in the narrative.

The something that is sent is the *object* of the narrative and the *subject* of the story is the one who does the job of getting the object to the recipient. The volition in the story comes when the subject takes up the object, but this subject is often charged by a sender: M sends Bond to get whatever the object of the film is to the recipient. The authorities send Indiana Jones to get the Ark to safety. In the Old Testament narrative, Mordecai calls on Esther to obtain safety for the Jewish people.

The subject has the role of getting the object to the receiver but there is a power dynamic in which the subject is helped or opposed by a *helper* or helpers; they are also hindered by an *opponent*, or opponents. Indiana is helped by Marion, Bond has Q and Esther has Mordecai. These subjects are also opposed: Esther faces Haman, Bond has villains with cats on their laps, and Indiana Jones faces Nazis and a scary swordsman.

Greimas calls these six functioning points within his structure "actants" and he maps these actantial roles onto a diagram which has become quite well-known:

---

2. Selden, *Reader's Guide*, 59.

3. Greimas, *Structural Semantics*, 198.

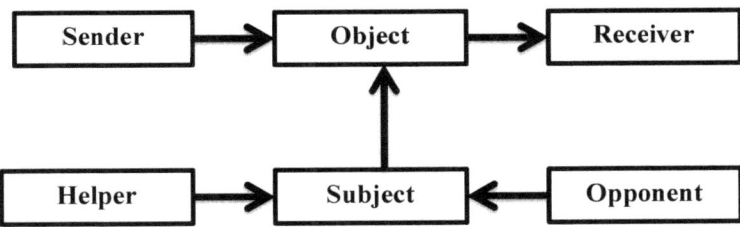

The top line is that of communication, where Sender gets the object to the Receiver. The vertical line is one of volition, along which the subject deals with the object of the story. The bottom line involves the power at play with Helper and Opponent either furthering or hindering the Subject's quest.

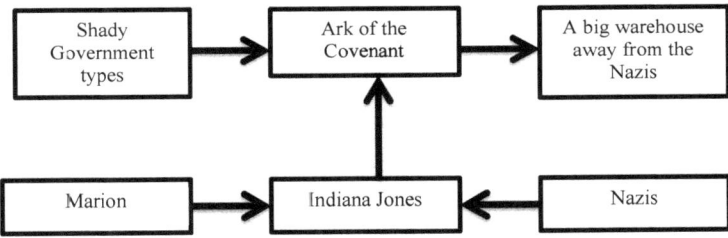

The example from Esther illustrates the fact that these spaces can be occupied by physical or abstract actants, such as salvation for the Jewish people.

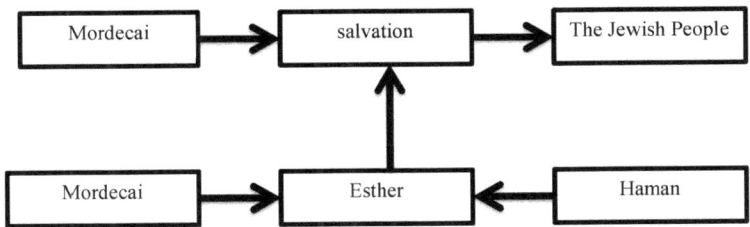

While it has its limitations this diagram can prove a useful tool for a reader to unpick the role characters play within a story. Folks will often see it and immediately start to populate it with ideas from stories they know. It can be a tool for unpicking stories, and can also open some insights into them. In the story of Jairus's daughter, Jairus sends health to his daughter, just as the story of the Syrophoenician woman sees a woman wanting health for hers. Both seek for Jesus to act as the subject, but for the story to happen there has to be a move by which communication causes volition: there needs to be a will and a way.

In both these stories, there is helper's help and the hindrance of the opponent, and both stories illustrate the interesting way in which the nodes on the diagram prompt the reader to ask: who goes in that space? For Jairus the opposition comes from mourners and those who declare the girl dead asking, "'Why trouble the teacher any further?'" (Mark 5:35b).

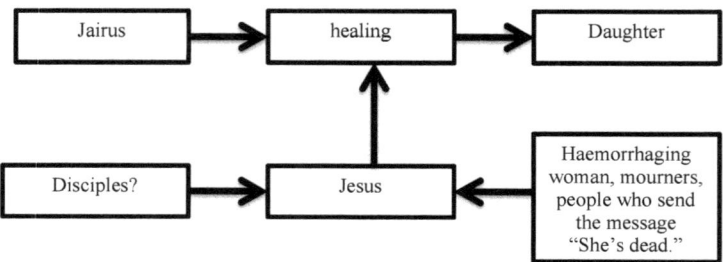

Somewhat troublingly for Jairus's diagram, there is also a woman who has suffered from hemorrhaging for twelve years. Beloved a character though she may be, she hinders Jesus progress, until the daughter dies (Mark 5:25). There is also a question in this story as to who helps? Not every actantial diagram will have a name to fill every space. So the reader may ask what role Peter, James, and John along with the parents fulfill when they progress further into the quest with Jesus (Mark 5:37, 40). Are they helpers? Do the parents come close to being opponents?

In her story, the Syrophoenician woman seeks health for her daughter: she is the sender and health is the object for her receiver. Jesus is the subject who will make this happen, but he is also the one who throws the suggestion back at her (Mark 7:27) whereas she is possibly the helper. One character can fill more than one actantial role.[4] Does her challenge (Mark 7:28, 29) help him do what he is meant to do? Is Jesus the opponent?

In a similar way, Stibbe applied this model to the narrative of John's Gospel, observing that the helper role in that Gospel remains unfilled.[5] It should be noted that, in dismissing all potential actants for that node, he does turn down some prime candidates, such as John the Baptist and others who bear witness to Jesus within that Gospel. Interestingly, Stibbe does find a potential helper: Jesus's antagonists In that Gospel, the religious

4. Patte, *Structural Exegesis*, 43.
5. Stibbe, "'Return to Sender,'" 196.

authorities who oppose him and seek to arrest him are, ironically, helping Jesus towards the goal of his mission. The story of their deliberations in John 11:45–53 makes for interesting reading in this light.

Returning to the Gospel of Mark for some final examples, it's worth mentioning that this structure works best if readers have their own crack at populating it. Part of the fun of this structure is that once taken on board, the reader may start seeing it everywhere. Whether it's the story of the loss of the garden of Eden in Genesis 2–3 or *Thelma and Louise*, it gets readers exploring how the roles and action interact in a narrative. When seen through the lens of this structure, the two feeding miracles (Mark 6:33–44; 8:1–8) have clear similarities, but also some interesting differences. Both bear the similarity of food as the object and the people as receivers. The reader asking who initiates this sending of food will find an interesting space to be occupied, as is the space opened by asking who the subject or subjects are. Who gets that bread to those hungry folks, and who helps? Which spaces do Jesus and the disciples occupy in these diagrams? And who might fill the Opponent space?

Ways of Reading: Actants

Actant roles

The structure Greimas uses presents an interesting starting point for the reader to explore a story. Clearly, stories don't always fit neatly onto such a structure, but it presents the opportunity for the sort of analysis explored earlier in this chapter.

In particular it raises questions about:

- who wants the action of the story to happen?
- who will do the action?
- what is being done?
- who will receive the result of the action?
- who may help this activity?
- who is obstructing or opposing this activity?

Underlying this, the structure Greimas presents raises questions about the communication, volition, and power in a story, and leads the reader to reflect on what is communicated by who, and what forces act upon that communication. The structure has a breadth of applications in narratives. It also has the advantage of being memorable.

Comparing Actants

Having established the actants in a few stories, the reader can compare them. This may take the form of a grid. This should not be a sterile activity of slotting characters into roles but should rather function as a way of comparing different stories for the responses they may evoke when viewed through this structure. The open spaces or question marks on the grid raise questions to a story. When the paralytic is healed, what do his friends actually want? Their friend is presented as a potential recipient of healing, but Jesus forgives his sins. Is Jesus an opponent to their object? And is their object therefore not the right one to send? The healing takes place as a proof to the scribes—so are they opponents or helpers?

	Sender	Object	Receiver	Subject	Helper	Opponent
The Leper	Leper	Healing	Leper	Jesus	??	Leper
Paralytic	Four friends	Healing	Paralytic	Jesus	Scribes?	Jesus? Scribes?
Gerasene demoniac		Deliverance	Demoniac	Jesus	Pigs??	Demons

The reader should bear in mind it is possible to use this grid as a way of unpicking the same story in different ways. The story of the leper (Mark 1:40–45) can be mapped twice onto a grid, with the second option including the earlier mission of Jesus (Mark 1:35–45) and raising the way in which the encounter scuppers this object.

	Sender	Object	Receiver	Subject	Helper	Opponent
The Leper (Mark 1:40–45)	Leper	Healing	Leper	Jesus	??	Rules about leprosy
The Leper (Mark 1:35–45)	Jesus	Message (1:38)	Neighboring Towns (1:38)	Jesus	Disciples ("Us" 1:38)	Leper

Opponent or Not

One of the facets of narrative raised by this sort of analysis is the hero and villain makeup of stories: there are those who can progress the story to a good outcome, and those who thwart it. Characters can shift between these brackets and some great drama is had when the reader or viewer is left wondering where particular characters belong in this schema. Looking across a range of stories, the reader could consider who, if anyone, has worked against the desired outcome brought to the story. The question then is, how and why have they done that? It's an interesting question to hold, particularly through Old Testament narrative, wherein characters regularly shift between the simplified "hero/villain" categories—any idea these are simple stories is soon corrected by this activity. One of the beauties of biblical literature is the complexity of the heroes. Very few remain firmly rooted on that side of the divide.

A CHARACTER'S ROLE IN THE STORY

In addition to the actantial model, there are four other pointers regarding characters and the role they take that serve to facilitate the reader's exploration of stories, namely:

- the identity of main characters
- character's statements about themselves and others
- relationships between characters
- tensions within character groups

a. Who Is the Main Character?

Identifying who dominates the action can provide an interesting insight into the workings of a story. Amit raises this question in relation to the story of Naboth's vineyard (1 Kgs 21), which although part of the Elijah cycle of tales, is one in which the prophet appears late and briefly in the narrative. One of the simplest ways of answering a question like this is just to read a story and ask "Who owned that one?" in the sense of considering, who the story is about. On that basis, the Syrophoenician woman becomes a main character in the story she shares with Jesus (Mark 7:24–30). There is also the simple maths of asking "who features most?" Both these approaches can be complemented by a grasp of the overarching plot of the story, looking at who is the focus of interest.[6] In the story of Naboth's vineyard, the scene changes from one setting to another, but Ahab is the character present throughout. Even in the times when he is not personally present, letters are being sent in his name or someone is being stoned to death for allegedly insulting him. He's also front and center in some of the main parts, such as the opening and conclusion. The net result is that Amit reads this as a story in which Ahab, rather than Elijah the prophet, or Jezebel the plotter, is the leading character. Poor old Naboth doesn't even get to own his own story (or his own vineyard!). A consequence of this is that "Ahab . . . bears responsibility for the crime, not Jezebel, nor the townspeople, nor the scoundrels, who are all only accomplices in the king's crime."[7] Read again, with this finger pointed at Ahab, the story and the role he actually plays is complex and his evil (1 Kgs 21:20) takes an interesting form. Watch what he actually does.

Similarly, in the story of the Syrophoenician woman, Jesus is a bit like Elijah in the above example, for this story is dominated by this woman from the moment she enters the house. We may expect Jesus to dominate in a Gospel in which he features so prominently but, in this regard, Jesus is similar to the character of God in much of the narrative of the Bible. Asked who is the main character in the Bible as a whole, the answer "God" springs to mind: yet review some of the narratives in the text and God is either absent or present through others or appearing for a small time. However, that small appearance can sway the whole narrative with the sort of leverage that Elijah brings to the end of 1 Kgs 22. Interestingly, the appearance of God is often at the beginning or end of a story, or both. Such stories then play out with God in the wings.

b. Character Statements about Themselves and Others

Look a character in the I. Throughout narratives the statements characters make about themselves and their experience provide an interesting level of comment, which will be explored more fully when looking at narrators in chapter eight. At this point it is just worth the reader noting the character's *I* statement and the way it can unfold something of their own sense of their role and how they act upon, and are acted upon, by other characters and events in the narrative.

---

6. Amit, *Reading Biblical Narratives*, 88.
7. Amit, *Reading Biblical Narratives*, 88.

- One of the earliest such assertions is made by Adam, in response to the call of God, when he says: "I heard the sound of you in the garden, and I was afraid, because I was naked, and I hid myself" (Gen 3:10).

- On hearing one of the men who visit Abraham declare that she will bear a child: "Sarah laughed to herself, saying, 'After I am worn out, and my lord is old, shall I have pleasure?'" (Gen 18:12).

- Elijah, when in fear of his life, offers the pained expression that "I, even I only, am left, and they seek my life, to take it away." (1 Kgs 19:10).

We noted earlier how characterization can emerge from speech and, in a later chapter, we will look at how such statements can indicate a character's point of view, but at this stage the focus is on the character's role, and the contribution the pronouns of a narrative make towards shaping it. It's through such comments that characters position themselves and are positioned by others. In the above statements Adam places himself in relation to God and Sarah in relation to the visitors and the promise of God. Another example of this is the rich young man (Mark 10:17–22) who bounds up to Jesus and asks "Good Teacher, what must I do to inherit eternal life?"

Jesus replies deflecting his question from himself as good and to a shared belief,

"Why do you call me good? . . . You know the commandments."

The man is confident: "I have kept all these."

In exchanges and comments like these characters effectively position themselves and give their perspective on the role they are talking in the narrative.

c. Relationships between Characters

Character roles are shaped by the way they interact with other characters. The reader's encounter with the character of Jesus is shaped by the way he reacts to those he heals, calls, and with whom he is in conflict. Throughout the Bible, such relationships are crucial: Adam and Eve are characters experienced through the way in which they interact with the serpent, God, and each other.

Conflict is one of the most critical forms of character interaction, and in biblical narrative there can sometimes be conflicts behind the conflict. In the Exodus narrative, Moses will face the conflict with Pharaoh, but at the outset of the conflict, the Lord has given a flash-forward summary of what will happen, and why. The Lord predicts that Moses will perform the wonders with which he has been equipped, but also declares, "I will harden his heart, so that he will not let the people go" (Exod 4:21–23). The Lord, as a character, will create this tension between wonders performed, and the stubbornness with which they are met such that as the following chapters unfold, they are the foreground of a bigger conflict in which the Lord must decisively defeat the gods of Egypt.

Similarly in the Gospel of Mark, the conflicts in which Jesus is engaged, such as his encounters with demons, are set against a background of a larger conflict. As Jesus appears, the demons respond to his arrival, knowing this bigger story and just who he is (Mark 1:24; 5:7). Theirs is a knowledge he silences (1:25) because it discloses that, behind this up-front conflict, there is the backdrop of the conflict between God and Satan. This is a conflict Jesus will reveal. When Jesus is himself accused of being "The ruler of demons" he parts the curtains and reveals the conflict going on within his ministry, observing that, when it comes to standing against Satan, "No one can enter a strong man's house and plunder his goods, unless he first binds the strong man. Then indeed he may plunder his house" (Mark 3:27).

The stage of conflict is a space the reader should observe as a key place in which the nature and roles of characters are developed.

d. Tensions within Character Groups

"I CAN'T SWIM!"

"Why . . . you crazy? The fall'll probably kill ya!"

Recalling the moment when the Sundance Kid debates with Butch Cassidy whether they should jump or not brings out a subtlety of character pairings and groupings that can be best observed in nearly any duo to feature in a narrative. Individual characters can be in conflict with themselves, but such a conflict can also be played out by a duo or collective. It's the same conflict that can battle away through the sorts of personal journeys characters undertake, explored in chapter 2. Citing individuals, television writer John Yorke observes in characters such as Michael Corleone in *The Godfather* or the boss figure in television's *The Office*, demonstrating a tension between the person they believe themselves to be and their true inner self. Yorke also observes this personal paradox is also at work in duos. He perceives it in buddy-based cop shows and also in a partnership like that of *Butch Cassidy and the Sundance Kid*. To Yorke's examples we could add Mulder and Scully, Thelma and Louise, and, of course, Bert and Ernie. Yorke also observes that superheroes can involve the splitting of a character into the two identities embodied at different times by the same individual, as with the Hulk or Batman, with "one personality hiding within another."[8]

In biblical narrative, it was observed earlier that characters can form a collective group and be characterized collectively—but this collective characterization can carry within it variety. These varied voices need not be in conflict. In 1 Samuel 9, the young Saul is looking for missing donkeys, in a quest that will lead to his anointing. He's looking for the seer who may offer some revelation as to the donkeys' whereabouts, and encounters a group of young women going to draw water. When he asks "Is the seer here?" the story goes (1 Sam 9:12, 13):

> They answered, "He is; behold, he is just ahead of you.
>
> Hurry. He has come just now to the city, because the people have a sacrifice today on the high place.
>
> As soon as you enter the city you will find him, before he goes up to the high place to eat.
>
> For the people will not eat till he comes, since he must bless the sacrifice;
>
> afterward those who are invited will eat.
>
> Now go up, for you will meet him immediately."

Bar-Efrat notes the addition and repetition in this answer and suggests what we have here is not one chorused answer, but many voices and many answers all voiced by different members of the crowd.[9] It's an example of the task of hearing the mix within the collective.

Unlike the commonality shared by those voices, sometimes the collective can take on a role that is in tension with itself. The sons of Jacob in the book of Genesis exhibit such a tension within a collective. Joseph, along with his younger brother Benjamin, is the exceptional, standout brother. There is also the standout role of Reuben, when he attempts to save Joseph (Gen 37:21–29), possibly attempting to redeem himself in the eyes of the father against whom he had offended (Gen 35:22). Judah will similarly stand out from the group in saving Benjamin (Gen 44:33). It is instances like these that reveal the inner tension within the collective grouping, and between who they could be and who they are being. In the Gospel of Mark there is just such an inner tension within the collectives of the authorities and the disciples. In the case of the former, scribes and Pharisees can appear as a single entity (Mark 2:6–7; 2:24) but this can serve to heighten the tension

8. Yorke, *Into the Woods*, 133.

9. Bar-Efrat, *Narrative Art*, 97.

when individuals within these groupings become the exception, as when one of the scribes asks about the greatest commandment (Mark 12:28–34) or when a member of the very council that had plotted Jesus's death asks Pilate for his body (14:55; 15:43). Similarly, the disciples, throughout the Gospel move and speak as a grouping (Mark 3:7; 6:35) even having common, hardened hearts (6:52). There are, however, moments in which their inner tensions appear, with James and John, or Peter, stepping out of the crowd (Mark 10:35–37; 14:29), revealing an inner tension within the collective.

It's in the scope of such groupings, just as it is in the buddies of narrative, to offer insights into an inner tension between who they are and who they aspire to be.

Ways of Reading: Character Roles

Tracing a Character's Role

Using the sort of framework introduced above, the role of a particular character, running through the course of a narrative, can be explored. To do this, the reader could simply draw a line diagram, showing the progress of a story, and consider the role a particular character has played in that storyline. This could be for a large swathe of narrative, such as a Gospel, or a more focused, single story. A focus can be what they do and what is effectively "done to" them, in a way that can highlight their agency and how they react. How it is done doesn't really matter—the reader can just have a go. Particular focus can be placed on noting:

- how they enter the story
- what they do
- what is done to them
- how they leave the story.

The rich young man (Mark 10:17–22) bounds in and fills the opening moments of his story, responding enthusiastically to the high requirement of keeping all the commandments (Mark 10:20) before falling silent and leaving in a state of shock or anger. As readers we may wonder what he expected and also to what degree he expected his expectations to remain in control of the exchange.

The Billing

One question a reader can put to any story is, who tops the bill? This can be followed by asking who comes next? There are often two main characters in a biblical story. Simply listing them in that order develops thinking about who was the main focus of this story and way they top the other two. Is the rich young man (Mark 10:17–22) top of the bill or is it Jesus? A character may have fewer verses but be seen as the main focus, as when John is beheaded, or they may feature rarely but with great significance, as when Jesus appears in the opening verses of the Gospel. The process of deciding who the reader feels is "stealing the show" can open reflection on how and why they do it.

Pronouns

One way of exploring the way characters view themselves and others is to look at all the pronouns within the speech in a story. There are also the pronouns of the narrative itself that map the way roles play out in the story. If possible, circling these in a print of the text can highlight the way these pronouns interact with each other. The rich young man (Mark 10:17–22) makes claims for himself but Jesus responds with challenging list of "You shall . . ." commandments, to which he responds to with a confident "I have . . ." It is when Jesus offers a challenge to his virtue, telling him "You lack . . ." that he faces a shock.

Like any activity that finds a way of homing in on language that is sometimes not noticed, or taken for granted, the isolation and consideration of these parts of speech can bring some life to the interactions between characters.

Collective Differences

Like the young women encountered by Saul or the brothers of Joseph, any collective is made up of individuals and the reader can imagine the diversity within that group. In some cases there are clear indications of voices within the group, as with the example of Joseph's brothers, but at other times the reader can imagine them. A reading of the wider story may prompt some thought as to what makes up that collective response. On encountering the group responding collectively, a read around the response and rereading of their collective action can prompt a thought as to what differences could be hidden within that collective statement. Imagine the conversation between midwives Shiphrah and Puah during their deception of Pharaoh (Exod 1:15–21). In the Gospel of Mark, when John tells Jesus: "Teacher, we saw someone casting out demons in your name, and we tried to stop him, because he was not following us" (Mark 9:38) you have to ask how that "we" worked their way through this. How might they have reasoned their way to that point? What differences of opinions might they have had? Is it even possible some of the things Jesus challenges in this story (Mark 9:40–50) have featured in their collective thinking or was this a knee-jerk reaction shared by all? How might these same disciples collectively have established their response to parents with children (Mark 10:13), or what might those women have said when they left that empty tomb (Mark 16:8)—how much must they have said in the process of saying nothing?

Chapter 7

Setting

LONDON. Michaelmas Term lately over, and the Lord Chancellor sitting in Lincoln's Inn Hall. Implacable November weather. As much mud in the streets as if the waters had but newly retired from the face of the earth, and it would not be wonderful to meet a Megalosaurus, forty feet long or so, waddling like an elephantine lizard up Holborn Hill. Smoke lowering down from chimney-pots, making a soft black drizzle, with flakes of soot in it as big as full-grown snow-flakes—gone into mourning, one might imagine, for the death of the sun. Dogs, undistinguishable in mire. Horses, scarcely better; splashed to their very blinkers.[1]

When Charles Dickens paints the setting in the opening lines of *Bleak House* the reader encounters an appeal to every sense. Contrast that with the setting of the miraculous feeding stories. Whereas Dickens's setting of his story is not uncommon in such novels, it does stand in contrast to the limited description in Bible stories. There are a few details about Eden, locations like the temple receive some attention, but when the waters of the sea part for Moses, the reader has to imagine the shores and sea. Even at the Sermon on the Mount the mount isn't described. In this regard, Bible story

---

1. Dickens, *Bleak House*, 49.

settings resemble those in fairy stories, which are only mentioned when they form part of the action of the story. We discover the giant's castle is atop a beanstalk, and the cottage in the woods is made of cake and sweets, because the ascent up the beanstalk and the hunger of Hansel and Gretel are events in the plot of these stories. The issue with settings is that, while characters do events and events create the storyline, settings, and the details of settings can be a lot less essential.[2] Think of a minimalist theater set with just three chairs. Creative directors can create the story of the moon landing on such a set! On such a stage the chairs could be anywhere, but the focus will be on the characters who sit—or stand—on them. Setting is sometimes evoked, but can also be unspecified and unimportant.

There are descriptions in ancient literature. The description of the Temple by the historian Josephus[3] is an example worth a read. There is also extended setting of the scene set before John in the book of Revelation (Rev 4). Furthermore, in biblical narrative, settings do feature, even if not vividly depicted. The paradise of Eden and politics of Egypt shape stories of Genesis and Exodus and Nineveh matters to Jonah—as does the big fish. To delve into the Gospel of Mark for examples, in chapter 1, Jordan matters. Chapter 2 opens at the house, and the roof plays a part. Chapter 3 has synagogue, mountain, and sea, a sea that is a feature throughout these chapters and beyond.[4] The reader may care to flick through a Bible or home in on a narrative of their choosing and consider the backdrop and props of the scene.

Whereas events in Bible stories are quite tightly set out and character features can be formed from the material of characterization, there is a lot less to shape the reader's perception of the setting. As such, readers end up bringing perceptions of their own embodiment, physicality, and movement to their experience of the story world.[5] The biblical reader sets the setting of a story. To a greater or lesser degree the reader will draw on description or fill the space with imagination, but the reader's grasp of the setting of a Bible story is usually reliant on the degree to which it features in the events or is experienced by the characters. In the Gospel of Mark, when Jesus enters Jerusalem, "he entered Jerusalem and went into the temple; and . . . he had looked around at everything" (Mark 11:11a), but nothing he saw is mentioned, let alone described. The paucity of such references to setting can highlight the rare moments when it appears. As with character description,

2. Toolan, *Narrative*, 103; Chatman, *Story and Discourse*, 141.

3. Josephus, *War* 5.

4. See France, *Mark*, 260–61.

5. Utell, *Engagements with Narrative*, 69.

there is something of the exceptional in a biblical presentation of a setting that has the effect of heightening the significance of what few references there are. Elijah's flight and despair are enhanced by the wilderness setting, the solitary tree and the cave (1 Kgs 19:1–9). If a biblical story references a growing fame in a region (Mark 1:28) or a restriction on travel within it (Mark 1:45) it matters. This paucity also opens up some of the possibilities of reading that can ensue once lack of detailed description is accepted and seen for what it is—an invitation to imagine. While debates may ensue about stables and houses in the story of Jesus's birth, or whilst the reader may have some idea what a house of the time would have been like, stories such as the nativity and healing of the paralyzed man leave an openness that the reader can imaginatively fill. A good starting point for considering such story settings is to ask: what do they do?

WHAT SETTINGS DO

As with any categorization in literary theory what follows is a set of categories imposed for the purpose of unpicking a holistic experience of reading.

a. Settings Situate a Story

Settings situate stories in specific contexts as well as against larger backdrops. Spatially, the setting places a story in a location, which can be on the scale of a land or just against a particular backdrop. When the Exodus departs from Egypt, it pays to know where that is, just as it helps to know where Abraham comes from, where Joseph ends up, where Joshua crosses and where Ruth comes from and Esther finds herself. Likewise, when Jesus crosses the Sea to the country of the Gerasenes and encounters Legion, some sense of where that is in relation to his home and background situate the story in context. Biblical narrative is rich with meaningful geography. Abraham journeys across a map as does the Exodus, and Joshua. The country unites and splits, and there is exile to Babylon. Later the book of Acts will send arrows across its own map.

With regards to setting, the Gospel of Mark opens with John and Jesus at an unspecified point along the Jordan River (Mark 1:9) and then shifts to Galilee (Mark 1:14). This is the first scene along a shoreline that will prove so important in the first half of the Gospel. Mapping the story takes the reader through various locations starting in Galilee, going north to Caesarea Philippi before moving to Jerusalem and to the empty tomb, where the disciples will be directed back to Galilee (Mark 16:7).

As well as locations on a map, setting can situate a story against a particular backdrop. Without being specific the setting can indicate a particular
type of location. If a story opens in a monastery it is immediately different from one that opens in a snowbound country house. Such settings can
be social, such as the banquet in which Herod agrees to behead John the
Baptist (Mark 6:21). It is unclear which of Herod's palaces are the location
for this event and it is even possible John was at a different palace than the
one at which the banquet took place. However, on reading the setting of a
banquet, the reader will envisage a palace and revelry, then shift the scene
to a prison. The light changes, as does the temperature and the dampness.
Where setting is concerned, particularly in biblical narrative, something
sensory is required of the reader. Whether a banquet or a prison, a sea shore
(Mark 6:33) or a boat on the sea (Mark 6:47), the reader brings an imaginative lilt to setting.

b. Settings Temporally Situate a Story

As well as placing a story in a location, the setting can also situate it in
time. Here again, setting can take different forms. In the same way there is a
geographical reference point in some Bible stories, there can also be indications of when a story took place. Examples of this would be the prophet
Isaiah fixing the story of his calling to "the year that King Uzziah died" (Isa
6:1) and the Gospel of Luke pinpoints the time of a census at the start of
the story.[6] The temporal setting of a story can also involve the duration
of a passage of time. However literally the reader takes it, the wilderness
temptation is presented as being "forty days" (Mark 1:13). The events that
then follow in most of that opening chapter are located within the passage
of one day, possibly serving as a typical example of a day in the life of Jesus.
The gospel then continues and, whereas the fourth gospel situates events
over three years, with three Passovers, the Gospel of Mark can apparently be
fitted into the time span of a month.[7]

One further type of temporal setting is what Powell labels the typo-
logical setting; "the kind of time within which an action transpires."[8] In the
Gospel of Mark, there are evening times and mornings (1:32, 35) and there
are tensions that rise specifically because events take place on a Sabbath
(2:23–28; 3:1–6).

---

6. Luke 2:1, 2, though historians struggle with this reference.

7. Burridge, *Four Gospels*, 38.

8. Powell, *What Is Narrative Criticism?*, 73.

These spatial and temporal settings are also cultural. A reading of the Old Testament presents an acceptance of polygamy and violence that can disturb the reader in a different cultural context. In the Gospels, this context can include the politics of the day, outlined below, as well as meaningful times like Passovers and Sabbaths, evoking what might be expected on that day. There is also table fellowship and the challenges Jesus poses to it (Mark 14:3–9).

c. Settings Enhance the Mood or Symbolism in a Story

Settings can enhance or develop the mood of a story: a Death Star is imposing and fearful, whereas who wouldn't want to visit a chocolate factory? Biblical settings, whether Eden or the temple, influence a story set therein, and in the Old Testament the symbol of the land is similarly and dynamically more than just a space on the map.[9] Within the Gospel of Mark, the nature of the wilderness enhances the stories of the miraculous feedings, with both including a reference to the "deserted place" (Mark 6:35) and both stories using the same Greek word (*erémos*) used in the Greek Septuagint version of the Old Testament for the desert wilderness in which the people led by Moses were miraculously fed by manna from God. Described as both "a powerful and ambivalent symbol," the wild place is both a place of lack and threat while also being a place where God is met. It is also the wilderness in which a voice begins the Gospel (Mark 1:1–4). The place is endowed with a weightiness, as is the temple, the mountain, and the sea.

Such thematic and moody connections between story and setting provide good examples of the dynamic that exists between character and setting. The demoniac called Legion lives in a setting that both tallies with the mood of the story and is an aspect of his character (Mark 5:1–5). When Jesus is being hurried along to Jairus's house, the setting becomes that of a crowd of people pressing in on those hurrying (Mark 5:24). These are characters themselves but a crowd, like a banquet, is also a setting created by a gathering.

d. Settings Create Boundaries and Transitions

Places can be significant but so too can the spaces between them. Throughout biblical literature the crossing points between places can be significant, and in the Gospel of Mark places like the sea, forming the crossing point

9. Brueggemann, *Land*.

between Jesus's homeland and the regions beyond, can be read as significant. Likewise, there are boundaries formed by the curtain in the temple (Mark 15:38) or the roof of a house (Mark 2:1–12). In the latter example of the house roof, the boundary of inside and outside creates a spatial divide between the insiders and outsiders that can hold a symbolic significance for the reader. In this instance the possibility remains open that this was Jesus's own house.[10] This is debatable but if the reader playfully entertains the idea it does add something to the story—possibly even adds a dash of fun to Jesus's immediate response to the unroofing of the roof: "Son, your sins are forgiven" (Mark 2:5).

e. Settings Can Situate a Story in a Wider Context

A biblical story can take place against a larger backdrop than the specific time and place, one possibly even of cosmic proportions. The Gospel of John opens "in the beginning" and the story that follows includes various moments when the connection between heaven and earth is opened (John 3:31–36). The disciples in Acts similarly set their experience against a bigger battle (Acts 4:23–28). The Gospel of Mark, likewise, takes place in a bounded cosmos with earth below the heavens where God dwells, with Israel at the center of this earth and the temple at the center of this entire setting, in a world set against the backdrop of the conflict between God and Satan, angels and demons. Malbon identifies this conflict as an overarching background conflict, in which the kingdom of God is announced and various conflicts indicate the end of whatever rule Satan has held.[11] The story of the Gospel of Mark takes place against this larger backdrop of Jesus bringing on the struggle, challenge, and liberation of God in a way that demons recognize (Mark 1:34) but with which the authorities of the day will struggle (Mark 3:22). Rhoads, Dewey, and Michie describe this cosmic backdrop and it's connection with the stories of the Gospel in terms that relate to events in the Gospel: "In Mark's story world, this creation is awry. Humans were created to have dominion over the rest of creation, but the actualisation in the story is the reverse of this: Humans are possessed by demons, wracked by illnesses, and threatened by storms at sea."[12] This background conflict is one with which Jesus's own disciples struggle and also one that they fail to

10. As referred to in 2:15; France, *Mark*, suggests this is a possible reading of 2:15—Levi is at Jesus house (133) See also Mark 3:19 and Goodacre, "Did Jesus Have a House?"

11. Malbon, *Mark's Jesus*, 43–54.

12. Rhoads et al., *Mark as Story*, 64.

understand (Mark 8:17, 21) but, while it may be background, "for the Markan Jesus, the conflict between God and Satan is not quite so far back!"[13]

Reading Against a Background

If a story is set against a historical background, that background can illuminate that story. There are resources that can provide the background to a biblical text, and in the same way a good translation makes biblical language accessible, a good background resource can provide some insights into temples, Babylonians, exiles, and messiahs. This section just gives an example of some light that such background can shed on the particular story of Mark's Gospel. You don't need to know what follows but if you do it may add to a reading of the Gospel.

As far as background of the Gospels goes, the bare bones which readers will know is that the land that forms the background for this story was under Roman Imperial rule. After the exile, the land entered a period termed The Hellenistic Period, under the rule of Alexander the Great and his successors. These included Antiochus the III and Antiochus the IV, who were brutal and oppressive. There was a brief moment of freedom under a family called the Hasmoneans, following the revolt of Judas Maccabeus in the second century BCE. Snippets like these may not be required, but knowing this can enhance the setting of a story in which characters are engaged in considering the identity and nature of a liberating Messiah to lead the people.

In the time of the Gospels the land was under Roman rule, delegated down to Herod the Great. This is the Herod of the nativity story, who was also a brutal tyrant. On his death in 4 BCE, the land became divided under the rule of Archelaus, who ruled a southern Judean chunk of the country; Antipas, who ruled a Northern Galilean area; and Philip, who ruled further North still. This would have included the setting of Caesarea Philippi (note Philip's name), the area of the story of Peter's declaration (Mark 8:27–30). Archelaus was eventually deposed and in his place Rome installed Pilate. The day-to-day governance of Jerusalem would have fallen to the high priest and council.

One of Herod the Great's achievements would have been the development of the temple, building the second temple, so named because it replaced Solomon's temple which was destroyed way back in the Old Testament era, after the fall of Jerusalem and at the beginning of the Babylonian captivity. Again, while it is possible to read of the journey to Jerusalem

13. Malbon, *Mark's Jesus*, 54.

(Mark 10:32–34), or of the entry to that city (Mark 11:1–11) and cleansing of the temple (Mark 11:15–18), without any of the background information above, but it is also possible to find in such background information a context that can enhance appreciation of such stories.

Ways of Reading: Setting

One Detail in the Story

To enter into a story the reader brings a sense of their own embodiment and presence to a scene. Ask someone to imagine a scene and, in their minds eye, they will be stood somewhere in relation to it. The suggestion here is that this is something to grasp—stop and look around. On reading that the setting of a story is Herod's banquet, many of us would be able to pause and, in our minds eye, have some sense of where Herod is in relation to us, along with the guests and the dancer. The reader can try a few things to further open out that vista.

The reader can enter into a story and try finding two details that would expand the scene. When Jesus approaches Bethsaida and is asked to heal a blind man (Mark 8:22–26), he first takes him out of the village. That simple detail of a story set, not in the thick of the buildings, but on the edge of the dwellings (Mark 8:23), with people gathered around, is the sort of detail that can enhance the sense of a setting. Similarly, recalling the moment of Peter's declaration that Jesus is the Messiah (Mark 8:27–30), the reader may observe that this took place between villages. The added detail that it was "on the way" (Mark 8:27) sets the scene. Interestingly, here again, Peter's eye-opening revelation also happens after they have presumably left a village, and now takes place in "the way," a setting that may relate to the opening quote from Isaiah (1:3) and "a theologically charged location for the Markan Jesus."[14]

One guide in all this: don't worry too much about accuracy. I do not know what John's dungeon was like, but I've seen enough television to grab an image from other stories to fill the gaps in my knowledge. Another guide is to consider the props in the story. Considering some of the things that would be part of a particular story the reader can visualize them and possibly even lay their hands on items, such as a loaf of bread (Mark 8:14).

14. Malbon, *Mark's Jesus*, 71.

Senses

One obvious means of embodying a setting is to visualize and imagine the place through the senses, asking what it would have looked like but also considering how those there would have felt. What is the feeling of the ground beneath the feet walking along such roads? What smells may be encountered as one leaves a village into open countryside? What noises are in the background? The miraculous feedings involve crowds that would be particularly noisy.

Interaction

Working through a story, the reader can make two sets of annotations. One is straightforward noting of when there is any mention of interaction between character and setting. The reader can simply tick that or note it. When Jesus leads the blind man out of the village (Mark 8:23) or the disciples walk the way (Mark 8:27) there is a clear indication of setting. For the more imaginative activity the reader can replace the tick with the question mark and look for those moments when the text is not specific but the imagination fills in. For example, the text does not specify how far out of the village they went. It does not record how many people followed. It does not say what sort of spot Jesus and the blind man stopped at. All these items "not told" are not omissions: they are invitations to the reader to step into the story, imaginatively filling it out.

Getting to Know the Setting

Readers don't need background knowledge to enjoy a Bible story but, equally, any morsel of insight into history, geography, and background can enrich a reading.

The same goes for maps, but with a personal turn: the reader of a story like the Gospel of Mark could consider producing their own sketch map, annotating it using some of the resources that situate the stories and journeys. This can be as scrappy as a doodle on a napkin or some annotated charted production, but if the story is taking us places, finding them can enhance the reading.

Compare and Contrast

Stating the obvious, a boat on the sea is different from a mountaintop. One way of appreciating a setting involves asking how that setting differs from another, while also considering similarities. The edge of a village differs from somewhere like a spot on a mountain. In the former Jesus heals the blind man (Mark 8:22), in the latter he appoints disciples (Mark 3:13). One may feel more remote than the other and more consciously chosen by a character, rather than the nearest convenient space. There is also a different feel and emotional response to such locations and a reader can consider their personally closest equivalent places. Similarities may be stranger to consider, but in the above examples there is a sense that both involve drawing away to a more isolated spot and both are places of closer encounter between Jesus and those who are, in ways different yet similar, called.

A BACKGROUND AND ONE READING

Throughout this book the emphasis is on literary theory and strategies, with the Gospel of Mark providing exemplification and a space to try out the material covered, but this section is much more focussed on that story. This section provides a short sweep of the whole narrative of the Gospel of Mark, providing an example of the way a wider background and reading enriches particular stories. There are three reasons for placing this in a chapter about setting. The surface one is that in a number of biblical narratives the big story is one of journey and transition. The stories of Abraham, Joseph, and Moses cross the map and the book of Acts shifts outwards from Jerusalem into the wider world. Secondly, the wider narrative arc can provide the backdrop for the particular story, so it is worth getting overall views that form the backdrop to shorter stories. The stories of Peter's declaration, Jesus's response and transfiguration is illuminated (no pun intended) by their place as within the wider narrative. A final reason: it had to go somewhere. In a book with so much dipping in and out of one Gospel, this section briefly draws together one overarching read of a Gospel that is one complete story. One health warning, though. This is a reading. It's not the meaning of the gospel or what the story is all about. It's just a reading.

At the very start of the Gospel the reader is offered an overarching explanation of the story to come, by the narrator, describing it as "the good news of Jesus Christ, the Son of God" (Mark 1:1), and in doing so offering an insight the reader will carry through the rest of the narrative. The story then begins in the wilderness with the voice crying "Prepare the Way" and John baptizing at the Jordan (1:1–9). Then, after the temptations (1:12, 13) and John's arrest (1:14). the story moves to Jesus ministry in Galilee.

In this earlier half of the gospel clues and insights are given as to who this Jesus is, building up to a hinge point at the centre of the Gospel where Peter will declare him Messiah (8:27–30). Till then, in moments such as his exorcisms, Jesus doesn't permit the demons to speak because, like the reader who received that overarching explanation at the start: "they knew him" (1:34). Within the story, just what they knew, and we as readers know, remains to be uncovered.

From the opening in Galilee, the arc of the story moves around the map, taking the story northwards, reaching the northernmost setting half way through the Gospel, before returning back to the crucifixion and empty tomb in Jerusalem. There, at the story's end, the disciples will be directed back to its original location of Galilee (16:7). In the opening chapters it is in this Galilee that the action around the Sea takes place, including the call of the disciples (1:16–18) and teaching in Capernaum (1:21) and it is throughout this Galilee that Jesus fame spreads (1:28). There follows a mission throughout Galilee (1:39) that is then curtailed following the healing of the leper who, himself, goes around proclaiming his story but in doing so, curtails Jesus's mission plans (1:40–45).

Back in Capernaum, in Galilee, Jesus experiences a run of clashes with scribes and Pharisees (e.g., 2:1–12; 2:23–28), and also with his own family (3:20–21). Followers are drawn from around Galilee and down south in Judea and Jerusalem and beyond the Jordan (3:8). One beautiful touch here is that as the crowds grow Jesus resorts to teaching by boat (4:1).

The story then journeys to predominantly gentile territories. Stories such as the encounter with the demon possessed man in the country of the Gerasenes (5:1–20) take Jesus across the sea, in eventful crossings (4:35–41). Closer to home (6:1), and a hometown where a prophet will not be honoured (6:4) there is a mission to the surrounding villages, including the sending out of the disciples (6:6,7). in a growing mission that attracts the attention of, among others, King Herod, as the narrative flashes back to the story of his mishap of an execution of John the Baptist (6:14–28).

It is at the approach to the midpoint in the story that the apostles return to Jesus and he gathers them to a quiet, grassy, deserted place—but crowds follow them, prompting the first feeding miracle. There also follows further tension with visitors from Jerusalem (7:1) and Jesus himself ventures further afield to the region of Tyre and Sidon. It is on this leg of his journey that he encounters a Syrophoenician woman who challenges him (7:24–30), and it is also here, in gentile territory, that a second feeding miracle takes place, amongst gentiles like this woman. The second feeding miracle takes this Moses-like blessing across that divide of Jew and gentile.

Following this second feeding, a section of the Gospel takes place that could be read as pivotal in the overarching storyline. Following an encounter with the Pharisees who want a sign from God (8:11) Jesus has the puzzling exchange with the disciples about their understanding, or rather the lack of it, with regards to their experience of him (8:14–21). He then heals a blind man at Bethsaida, in a healing that grows from partial sight to full restoration (8:22–26), opening a section in which the disciples come to see and declare who Jesus is. In this section, the story moves to the northernmost setting on its map, furthest away from Jerusalem that it will get. It is here that Jesus asks the disciples about his identity and Peter declares him the Messiah (8:27–30), but instead of being a graduation in learning, the story takes a turn towards Jerusalem. Jesus predicts his suffering at the hands of the authorities and his rising after three days (8:31). This results in an argument with Peter (8:32–38) followed by the transfiguration, with the voice declaring "This is my beloved Son; listen to him" (9:7, ESV). The wider story pivots on these central narratives. It's here that the tussle of ideas is not about whether Jesus is the Messiah. That has already been declared and hushed up. It's about what sort of Messiah he will be.

The journey south begins, via Capernaum, with further predictions (9:30–32) and discussions about what lies ahead (10:35–40), but it is in Jericho that the story of another healing of another blind man bookends this central section (10:46–52). The two bookended healings, bringing sight (8:22–26; 10:35–40), are the only healings of blind people in this gospel and this last one is also the final healing story in the gospel, as the healed man follows Jesus "on the way" and the story approaches Jerusalem.

Jesus reaches Jerusalem with the entrance from the Mount of Olives (11:1–11) and demonstration in the temple (11:15–18). The story has shifted, and in the events that follow much will be made of the authority of Jesus, with numerous attempts to catch him or trap him (12:13–17). After Jesus has answered and responded to a conclusive challenge (12:34) he offers his words on the temple and experience of his followers (Mark 13) before being anointed for his death by an unnamed woman at Bethany (14:3–9), following which he is betrayed and crucified.

The story began with the designation of Jesus as Son of God. From Galilee the story has proceeded to a pivot in the center, where Jesus was transfigured and a voice said "This is my Son." Now, on the cross, a different voice declares Jesus to be the Son of God. This time it is not from heaven but that of the centurion at the cross. So it is that the narrative arc comes to a moment that forms one of the largest of Markan sandwiches, in which two stories bookend content between them.

Whereas at the Baptism that opened the Gospel, as Jesus comes out of the water, the heavens open, the Spirit descends and a voice declares "You are my Son" (Mark 1:10–11), at the cross Jesus gives up his spirit and the curtain of the temple is torn in two, using the same word (*schizō*) used earlier, to describe the opening of the heavens. But this time the voice that declares "Truly this man was the Son of God" (15:39, KJV) is that of the centurion at the crucifixion.

The story concludes following the Sabbath when the women who come to the tomb find Jesus's body is not there, and a young man directs them, and the reader, back to Galilee: "There you will see him" (16:7). So we are sent back to the place where the story started, and to the start of the Gospel.

Ways of Reading: A Reading

Hopefully this demonstrates the idea of reading bigger chunks of Bible story and sweeping across the journey they offer. Although not wholly setting-related, there are a few quick thoughts to any reader who plans now to launch into the matriarchs and patriarchs of Genesis (chapters 12–50) or the tale of King Saul in 1 Samuel 8–31, or who has set their sights on Luke or Acts.

a. Read like a novel. In readings like this there are times to lose the desk and notebook and gain the armchair. A big sweep of narrative is best read quicker than some devotional or studious readings;

b. Use one sheet of paper to scribble out the story, whether a list of note words, a doodle, a diagram. This should map out where it started and ended and where it went along the way;

c. Watch out for beginnings and ends, midpoints and defining moments within the story, and make sure they get a place on the piece of paper, keeping note of main points and twists and turns of the narrative.

d. Close the Bible. Every so often along a sweeping read, close the text, rather than flick back a few pages. Allow what you have read thus far to sink in. Big, sweeping reads appeal to the gut reaction of a reader.

Chapter 8

Narration

The chief priests of the Jews said to Pilate, "Do not write, 'The King of the Jews,' but, 'This man said, I am King of the Jews.'"

Pilate answered, "What I have written I have written."

(JOHN 19:21–22)

Having spent many years as a teacher, handling the disputes between children, I am sure of two things about narratives: one, all narratives are mediated by someone, and two, depending on who does the mediation, the narrative can be a very different story. I never sorted a recess bustup where there weren't at least three versions of the same event. When it comes to the Bible, the reader can sometimes, without realizing it, assume the words are unmediated communication. A grasp of the concept of narration and presence of a narrative form of communication can illuminate a story, teasing out interesting features not just in what is told, but the telling of the teller.

SHIFTING TO READING

Up till now this book has engaged in the stuff of stories. From here on in it also engages with the stuff of reading, involving a shift from some of the features of stories, to looking at reflections on the reader. As such the practical "way" sections explore what we mean when we talk about reading, asking how readers approach stories, what is meant by "the meaning" in relation to story, and calling on the individual reader to shape something of a theory of their own experience. This will include an exploration in chapter 9 of the ways the narrative shifts between points of view and, finally, in chapter 10, a focus on reader response. Throughout we need to keep an eye on the legendary woman or man on the Clapham Omnibus, that hypothetical individual who personifies the views of a regular person. This regular Londoner reminds those of us who theorize to keep an eye on people—as in actual readers, not just theoretical constructs. As such, the following chapters will also include a mix of considerations regarding personal reading and also some thoughts for those who take some responsibility for passing on readings and sharing them, whether in a small group setting or preaching community.

As an initial exploration the reader could look at this story:

> Then they sent to him some Pharisees and some Herodians to trap him in what he said. And they came and said to him, "Teacher, we know that you are sincere, and show deference to no one; for you do not regard people with partiality, but teach the way of God in accordance with truth. Is it lawful to pay taxes to the emperor, or not? Should we pay them, or should we not?" But knowing their hypocrisy, he said to them, "Why are you putting me to the test? Bring me a denarius and let me see it." And they brought one. Then he said to them, "Whose head is this, and whose title?" They answered, "The emperor's." Jesus said to them, "Give to the emperor the things that are the emperor's, and to God the things that are God's." And they were utterly amazed at him. (Mark 12:13–17)

Consider all the questions that could be asked about this story that include the word "mean," "meant," or "meaning"—possibly even listing them before reading my ones below. One interesting take on such an activity is to list a number of such questions and then try isolating the three or four most debatable or important of the lot.

Among the possibilities there are:

- What does the story mean?
- What do the Pharisees and Herodians mean to do?
- What do the Pharisees and Herodians' words to Jesus mean?
- What did Jesus think they meant to do?
- What does the word "hypocrisy" mean?

- What did that inscription, on that coin, mean to the people in that story?

- What might that inscription have meant to the Romans?

- What did the inscription mean to others in Jesus's day?

- What did Jesus mean by "the things that are the emperor's"?

- What does this mean to me?

The question that then emerges is, where do we locate the concept of meaning when we ask such questions and consider these uses of the word? When locating the meaning of "meaning" one distinction often made is between meaning residing "behind the text," "within the text," and "in front of the text,"[1] using these distinctions to separate various features of the history and reception of a text.

- Behind the text there is a historic event, an author, the time in which events took place and the initial community for whom the text was written.

- Within the text there is the words themselves and the language on the page.

- In front of the text there is the interpretation of the text through the experience and act of reading.

The question this poses for us as readers is how we experience such a distinction. When it comes to questions about meaning are we bound by what took place behind the text? What happens when the meanings of words change? Can readers extract meaning from texts that authors didn't intend to be there? There is also the question of debatable points: where there is disagreement over the meaning of a text where do we turn for arbitration? Is the decider of meaning behind the text, or to be found in what it means for us as readers today?

1. STORY AND NARRATIVE DISCOURSE

Let's break for coffee . . .

---

1. Gooder, *Searching*, xviii. See also Pett et al., *Understanding Christianity*: Handbooks 42–44.

```
┌─────────────────────────────────────┐
│                                     │
│                                     │
│            coffee                   │
│                                     │
│                                     │
└─────────────────────────────────────┘
```

The coffee above clearly will not suffice as a hot drink: it is the signifier of one, and "signs" a hot drink to the reader. The reader on reading may have an image of what is signified, but different readers will have different images. Indeed, the reader may be drinking one, have already had one, quite like the idea, or wonder if it's decaffeinated. The distinction here is between the word (signifier) and the thing (signified).

Signified and Signifier

One of the underlying foundations to modern narrative theory arises from the work of the linguist Ferdinand de Saussure. In 1916, Saussure published the *Course in General Linguistics* which kicked off the thinking that became structuralist theory, which fed into narrative theory. In his work, Saussure provided an explanation of the linguistic sign. He dispensed with the idea there is something inherent in the way a word means what it means and that the word is somehow wedded to that meaning. The relationship is far more arbitrary. According to Saussure a sign, such as a word, is made up of two elements: the *signified* and the *signifier*. The signified and signifier work hand-in-hand in the process of *signification*. So that word "coffee" means something, but it means different things. Some will picture a cafetiere, some a jar of instant, some a steaming mug. Signification happens when the word (signifier) triggers thought of the concept (signified). But you still have to make your own coffee.

Story and Discourse

An important distinction is captured in the title of Seymour Chatman's classic unpicking of narrative theory, *Story and Discourse*. Thus far this book has delved into the events, characters, and setting of stories. These are the stuff of a story, but the same events and characters can be related in very different discourses. Readers of the Bible are used to this insight because we often read one story through three or four tellings in the different Gospels. The reader of the four resurrection accounts has had to roll away a few stones, count a few angels, and check who arrives at a tomb that may or may not be empty. However, a grasp of the difference between story and discourse draws a line between the events and the telling. Such a distinction can lift any such differences from the realm of troubling contradiction into that of diverse tellings.

In exploring the difference between story and discourse, the narrative theorist Gerard Genette uses the concepts of signified and signifier to distinguish between the story and its narrative. Story is the content—the stuff of this book thus far, including events that take place, the characters that do them and settings where it all happens. Genette describes these as: "The actions and situations taken in themselves, without regard to the medium, linguistic or other, through which knowledge of that totality comes to us."[2] In Genette's scheme that stuff is the signified. Like the coffee above there is then the medium through which that signified is related: this is the discourse. A narrative discourse is the signifier of a story.

When it comes to the Bible, this is a vital distinction, particularly for readers who see the stories therein as guiding faith and life. It's not possible to disregard the medium through which stories are experienced by the reader, yet to hear some Christians talk, you'd think they'd been stood there on the first Easter Sunday, taking down notes. Distinctions like those of Genette remind us of the nature of narrative, mediated through the signifier. Genette's distinction is also the starting point for understanding narration, and the four Gospel accounts of the resurrection provide a good example of the distinction. The Gospels contain story content signified in a various ways. Whatever happened, in history or story, on that Sunday, readers encounter a mediation of the story.

The Way of the Reader: Story and Narrative Discourse

Signification

The difference between the stuff of the story and the narrative discourse that narrates it has implications for us as readers. There is something arbitrary about the link between the word "coffee" and a drink. In the same way, the story of the denarius above, when Jesus asks for the coin, we as readers have to envisage it. Elsewhere terms like "demon," "temple," and "Son of Man" open up wide fields of meaning.

2. Genette, *Narrative Discourse*, 25.

The very form of taxation debated—the "kenson"—has history with which many readers will be festively familiar. The Greek word denotes the hated poll tax and "census" that arose from the original decree at the start of the nativity story, that "all the world should be taxed" (Luke 2:1, KJV). This census sparked a revolt by Judas of Galilee which was stamped out, but left tensions that simmered for years until it[3] sparked the uprising of 66 CE and destruction of Jerusalem in 70 CE. Judas had railed against those who paid such taxes as "putting up with mortal masters in place of God."[4] That coin has history.

However, it isn't just words that may seem somewhat historically bound that make demands of the reader. The reader also needs to bring to the text their own grasp of more common words like "knowing" and "hypocrisy." Even the word "their" between these two words prompts some thoughtfulness—by the end of this Gospel chapter, one of the scribes, who sent the trappers (the "sent" of Mark 12:1) will be demonstrating a closeness to God (Mark 12:34).

How?

"*How* does the story mean?"[5]

The separation of story from discourse can focus the reader's thinking on the workings of narration and the "how" of a story. In her study of Christ in the Gospel of Mark, Malbon makes the distinction between story and discourse or between signified and signifier when she distinguishes[6] between paying attention to what is written about, and what is written. Malbon describes the latter as the "how" of the story. The former "what is written about" is the content of events and character but the "what is written" raises the question the reader could ask: how a story comes to mean what it means to me. At this stage in our study of reading that question is put, not as a big, theoretical consideration, but more as a suggestion that the reader might want to map their experience of meaning. In answering the question the sort of features that make up the "how" of meaning may include what is read on either side of a Bible story and how a story is framed. For example, a reading of the denarius story may be affected by the preceding parable, in which Jesus challenged the authorities, such that they seek to arrest him

3. France, *Mark*, 465.

4. Josephus, *War* 2.118.

5. Malbon, *Mark's Jesus*, 6.

6. Malbon, *Mark's Jesus*, 254.

(Mark 12:1–12). It may even stretch back to the story before, where his authority is debated (Mark 11:27–33).

Reflecting on the "how" of meaning will also lead to a consideration of the way in which the story homes in and out on detail that is more or less presented. In the denarius example there is a less focussed and brief moment when "They sent to him some Pharisees and some Herodians to trap him" (Mark 12:13). It moves so quickly! Details of how they agreed this, sending, and what was discussed are passed over, whereas the crunch moment of the story is more elaborated with greater focus on detail. Instead of just stating "knowing their hypocrisy, he held up a denarius," the text reads, "knowing their hypocrisy, he said to them, 'Why are you putting me to the test? Bring me a denarius and let me see it.' And they brought one" (Mark 12:15b).

This being the crunch moment, a consideration of the "how" of the story involves the reader noticing such specific details. That is the "how" of the crunch that crunches.

But Did It Happen?

As any tabloid reader well knows, consideration of the gap between events and their narration can cause some reflection on the veracity and accuracy of the reading. When it comes to the Bible this will prompt different responses depending on what the reader's view is of Scripture and inspiration. This is not the place for historical criticism or apologetics but it is nonetheless important to note that the approach to texts described in this book be open to readers who take different standpoints on the Bible.

For those who see within these words the inspiration of God at work, I would suggest that this remains wholly compatible with also seeing stories as creative ways in which that work is worked. There may be a sense of stories having a literary shape, but that need not rule out the possibility that God's inspired word is also a great story. As one teacher on biblical literature, Pete Wilcox, puts it, "Of course the Bible is always more than carefully crafted literature, but it is seldom less than that."[7]

For those who take a more critical and liberal view of the connection between the biblical text and events related, the assertion throughout this book is that the veracity of a story as history is separate to the enjoyment and inspiration it can offer. Whether or not a multitude were fed or a tomb was empty, the story offers inspiration when read as literature. Whether or not Jesus held a denarius the challenge to him and challenge back can be, in turn,

---

7. Diocese of Sheffield, "Bishop of Sheffield's Annual Lecture," 4:40–51.

a challenge to us and our resistance or selling-out to the systems in which we live. As a Native American storyteller is quoted to say of a tale: "Now I don't know if it happened this way or not, but I know this story is true."[8]

However, for any reader with a faith orientation towards the Bible the story and discourse distinction opens up the question of how the connection between event and narrative is regarded that is worth reflecting upon. On a scale of approaches, using two stories, one more miraculous and one less, the reader may find their place on a continuum, believing that:

- The denarius story and the walking on water both happened.
- The denarius story and the walking on water might have happened.
- The denarius story happened, and the walking on water might have happened.
- The denarius story might have happened, but the walking on water didn't happen.
- The denarius story could very possibly have happened or not happened, and the walking on water didn't happen.
- The denarius story didn't happen, and nor did the walking on water

There is a reason for choosing these two stories. To most folks, including the ones on the Clapham Omnibus, it is easier to imagine the denarius story could have happened than it is to believe in walking on water. Some believe both, but on the spectrum of stories that are believed as having happened as recorded, different believers set different markers.

There are those who believe the historic and literal occurrence of

- Creation in six days
- Adam and Eve in the garden
- Jonah and the whale
- Noah's ark
- Daniel in the lion's den
- Jesus turning water into wine
- The crossing of the Red Sea
- The call of Abraham
- The walking on water
- Jesus being born of a virgin

8. Borg, *Reading the Bible*, 50.

- The resurrection of Jesus's body

- The denarius story

- The crucifixion

When teaching biblical studies to trainee ministers I offer students two walls in our classroom: the "it definitely happened" wall and the "I don't believe that actually happened" and I shout out a story from that list and students run to a wall or place themselves between them in a way that represents their view of a particular story. Interesting exercise, more interesting with a group asking "How come you are there and I am here?" One interesting occurrence is when people don't stand still. Some will run to a wall, but then think again and meander around the middle or stand somewhere, then change places, sometimes on hearing the thoughts of others. Try it!

2. AUTHORS AND NARRATORS.

Franz Kafka initially wrote *The Castle* in the first person. He then rewrote it in the third. The story didn't change but the narrative became a different one.[9] That vignette homes in on the nature of narration, which involves the ways on which the story is told. Seymour Chatman makes the distinction between *Story and Discourse* and then presents the process of discourse:[10]

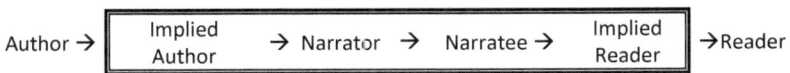

The best way to unpick this diagram is to build it up step by step.

Author & Narrator

The first distinction is between the author and narrator.

Author → Narrator

9. Onega Jaén and García Landa, *Narratology*, 8.

10. Based on Chatman, *Story and Discourse*, 151.

The narrator can be described as the "literary term for storyteller of narrative,"[11] and this is quite a familiar concept because many narratives have a first-person voice that says "I," as in the opening of Charles Dickens novel *David Copperfield*:

> Whether I shall turn out to be the hero of my own life, or whether that station will be held by anybody else, these pages must show. To begin my life with the beginning of my life, I record that I was born (as I have been informed and believe) on a Friday, at twelve o'clock at night. It was remarked that the clock began to strike, and I began to cry, simultaneously.[12]

It isn't just first-person narratives that have a narrator. In examples like *David Copperfield*, the voice is clear, even self referential. However, all narratives have a narrator, even those that never use the first person voice. That voice is always a construct and should not be confused with the author. Authors sit and write stories, but in doing so they give those stories a narrative voice, such that even an opening like Mark 1:1 should be heard as a narrative voice. That voice may feel identical with the somebody who put the words on the page—it is still a narrative voice. As will become apparent in what follows, the interplay between author and narrator can vary. The key distinction at this stage is between author and narrator, but all stories are narrated, and there is always a narrator.

Narratee & Reader

A similar distinction can be made at the other end of Chatman's diagram between a real reader (like you) and a narratee. The Gospel of Luke opens with introductory words that include Luke 1:3: "I too decided, after investigating everything carefully from the very first, to write an orderly account for you, most excellent Theophilus." This places two occupants at the other end of the continuum:

Author → Narrator → Narratee → Reader

The reader is anyone who actually reads the Gospel of Luke. The narratee is the reader written into the text. Once again, they are a feature of the story whether explicitly referred to or not. Where the Gospel of Luke is concerned,

---

11. Rhoads et al., *Mark as Story*, 39.
12. Dickens, *David Copperfield*, 11.

nothing is known about a Theophilus other than a few verses here, and in Acts. There is even a possibility that the name, meaning "Friend of God," is a literary device, constructing a sender to whom the story is written.

One place the narratee can become more explicit is in children's storytelling. In books for young children they can be quite specifically referred to, with a line like "But what do you think Alfie did then?"[13] As a classroom teacher I relished the introduction to Roald Dahl's *The Witches*, with its warning about a witch: "She might even—and this will make you jump—she might even be your lovely school-teacher who is reading these words to you at this very moment."[14] The classes I taught would puzzle a bit but also, at that moment, encounter a narratee: a reader-figure suggested and encoded into the text.

Author, narrator, narratee and reader: these four participants in the communication of a story can be illustrated by referring to the Gospel of John. The closing verses of the Gospel include the moment when Peter and Jesus encounter the disciple described a few times in the Gospel as "the disciple whom Jesus loved" (John 21:20). Peter and Jesus hold a brief exchange about this disciple and then the chapter closes thus: "This is the disciple who is testifying to these things and has written them, and we know that his testimony is true" (John 21:24). So the Gospel story is ascribed to a narrator called "the disciple." There is the speculation that leads some to conclude this disciple was John,[15] but for the purposes of our narrative diagram, we can just agree that someone has written a Gospel and there is an ascription within it that indicates that the stories are related by a community committed to this disciple. In a rare occurrence in biblical narrative, that verse also indicates a narrative "we" who is relating "these things" from "the disciple"—a small community that breaks in and offers its own voice, while also ascribing the story thus far to this disciple.

Somewhere back there we can rightly presume that someone first inscribed or told the words of this Gospel. This author could be a beloved disciple who wrote those words. Nobody actually knows. When reading those words we are experiencing the difference between the author and the narrator. That voice of the text is the voice of the narrator.

At the other end of the line the previous chapter, chapter 20, concludes, "these are written so that you may come to believe that Jesus is the Messiah, the Son of God" (John 20:31) and the "you" of that verse is an example of the narratee being addressed in the text. Over time, many people will have

---

13. Hughes, *Alfie Gets in First*.

14. Dahl, *Witches*, 8.

15. Edwards, *Discovering John*, 18–24; Carter, *Discovering*, 178–83.

read the words "written so that you may come to believe," and it makes you wonder if the original author could have contemplated the reach of those words to readers sitting where we are sitting now. The "you" of such a text is a narratee like the narratee of the children's stories above—a recipient constructed by the text who completes the diagram.

The Text

In this emerging diagram of the narrative process there are two participants inscribed in the text. As readers we identify them in different ways. When talking about the Gospel of Mark, people will often say "Mark tells us . . .," citing that narrative voice.

The narratee is less identifiable but is the audience of the text, encoded in the text. Given that these two are constructs of the text, the diagram can now gain a box, enclosing a section of this communicative process, delineating the narrative text.

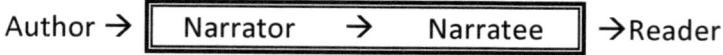

The real author and the real reader are outside the text, bringing us to a crucial distinction in the picture we form of the narrative process.

Ways of Reading: Authors and Narrators

Thinking about Authors

The focus of the theory covered in books like this will be on the story, but there is definitely a place in narrative appreciation and enjoyment for a sense of the author. The narrative reader sometimes needs to tease out just what that place is and how it works. In the Bible this can have varied impact—it's a well-known quip that if Moses wrote the books of Moses he startlingly recorded his own death, but within the historical traces of the writers of Genesis or a Luke or a John there are connections worth noting, as when we assume that Matthew used Mark as the basis for his Gospel, and in doing so inserted the reference to Matthew as a tax collector—a piece of characterization not mentioned in Mark. Such a view can illuminate Matthew and Mark. Another reference that makes this sense of author and connection particularly poignant comes during crucifixion, when Mark 15:20–21 reads: "After mocking him, they stripped him of the purple cloak and put his own clothes on him. Then they led him out to crucify him. They compelled a passer-by, who was coming in from the country, to carry his cross; it was Simon of Cyrene, the father of Alexander and Rufus." The narrator can cite the names of the sons of Simon of Cyrene with a sense of connection.

THE DEATH OF THE AUTHOR?

Some approaches to the Bible treat it as somewhat akin to a code to be cracked. In this model, the reader is like someone receiving a message in a code, such as:

> Sr, gsrh rh gsv nvhhztv. Tlg rg?

They may even work out that the three-letter word could be "the" and from that guess the second word and maybe start to figure out it's a code where a = z, b = y and c = x etc. Eventually, the reader can decode the original scrap of paper which, having served its purpose, can now be thrown away.

One of the contentious shifts in the way literary theory can guide the reading of texts emerges when considering the relationship between author and text. In the past there was a school of thought, sometimes referred to as "the intentional fallacy," that saw interpretation as being all about decoding the intention of the author. The theologian and biblical scholar Freidrich Schleimacher's views are captured by Osborne, namely, "the interpreter should align himself with the mind of the author and recreate the whole thought of the text as part of the author's life . . . to reconstruct . . . the whole process of creating the thought on the part of the author."[16] He believed that this was how the reader gathered the meaning of a text. The assertion has some apparent promise. After all, if the author of Mark's Gospel was sat here with us now we could just ask about some of the puzzles in the text, like "What did Jesus mean by 'this is my body'?" or "Why did that centurion at the cross say what he said?"

But the author isn't here so it stands to reason that however sure you are about anything in any text, you will always be interpreting. In a famous essay "On the Death of the Author," the theorist Roland Barthes raises questions like these about Balzac's story, *Sarrasine*. Barthes's response is simple and honest: "It will always be impossible to know." However many historical critics and commentaries may be written, readers will never nail down the meaning of "this is my body." That's why the narrative of the Gospel keeps us reading. Barthes makes the starkest point about the gap between an author's

16. Osborne, *Hermeneutical Spiral* 368.

intention and the text a reader holds when he declares that once the utterance of an author is in existence: "the author enters his own death."

This is not an assassination bureau against writers (I hope). Rather, Barthes challenges the way interpreters can be tyrannized by a quest to find the author's meaning, and presents the alternative, observing that a text is open to multiple interpretations. Once the author has let the work loose, having put the work out in the world where it will be read, that text is open to interpretations by readers. The notion that reading is simply a matter of decoding a message the author encoded is a misleading endeavor that fails to do justice to the fact that different readers will read texts in different ways. It is never as simple as just cracking a code and reconstructing an intended meaning. Barthes argues against such a form of interpretation, chasing the author, as limiting and closing down the meaning of a text.[17]

Reading isn't simply cracking a code. If a reader simply decoded the message above they could then discard the original coded message, but people don't do that with art and literature. They don't say "What is the *Mona Lisa* about?" then possibly agree it's all about a cryptic smile and, secure in that knowledge, discard the painting.[18]

In any text, and in a spiritually inspiring one possibly more so, the engagement of the reader requires something of their involvement in the act of reading. Barthes puts it in words by which his views on this matter have become well-known, ending his famous essay with the declaration, "The birth of the reader must be at the cost of the death of the Author."[19]

This is not to say that authors don't matter. It is rather a reflection on when and how they matter. The author of Mark is a figure of history who merits consideration and, for some of us, veneration. I'm certainly a fan. However, a focus on reaching this or any author as the means of establishing the meaning of a text simply doesn't work. Readers can't get into the mind of Mark, and are misled whenever they become falsely confident that they have achieved this impossible task.

Just to be hypothetical for a moment: what if Mark sat in on our reading? In his 1996 lecture, "The Author and His Interpreters," the writer Umberto Eco wrote as a literary theorist who had written about *The Role of the Reader*[20] but, following the success of his brilliant novel, *The Name of the Rose*, also had the experience of being a writer meeting readers who were responding to the labyrinthine complexity of that brilliant novel. He

17. Barthes, "Death," 147.

18. Barthes, "Death," 142.

19. Barthes, "Death," 148.

20. Eco, *Role of the Reader.*

acknowledged one rare situation when there was something to be said for pursuing the intention of the author as being when the author was living and accessible, but even then he suggested there could be discrepancies between the author's intention and the resultant text. Even in these cases he thought the author could appreciate the additional, potential interpretations readers could discover. He also asserted the author's right to argue against them, but acknowledged that, when an author is faced with a new interpretation, "In certain cases he can say 'No, I did not mean this, but I must agree that the text says it, and I thank the reader that made me aware of it.'"[21]

Veering away from the author as the focus for interpreting a text is not about ruling the author out, as if they never existed. We may assume a text had an author who wrote with an intention—but this approach puts a question mark over any possibility or necessity of establishing it.[22]

The model of code cracking is no friend to biblical narrative. Assertions of the author's intention, and assertions that an interpreter has captured it, can result in a narrowing and limiting approach to reading of a biblical text. There is also a risk that approaching the text with a view towards getting back to what the author intended can devalue the text itself—as when a secret code is cracked, a message decoded, and the coded scrap of paper then binned. Biblical texts have so much more to offer than just being cracked. An emphasis on extraction of a meaning can resemble the story of the man who faced a beautiful and dazzling stained glass window and complained he couldn't see through it.

There is a tendency for those who teach, preach, or interpret the Bible to promulgate "What this means," sometimes reducing stories to platitudes. The risk is such a reduction seldom matches the dynamics of the original story. The code-cracker model can also stymie the enjoyment of a reader who, instead of enjoying a story, is hounded by the notion they have to squeeze some meaning out of it. While there may be guides and challenges in literature, the first task is to read it, and, as the poet T. S. Eliot observed, to look at the text, not through it. When someone famously asked Eliot if he could explain what his poetic line, "Lady, three white leopards sat under a juniper tree" meant, he replied, "It means, 'Lady, three white leopards sat under a juniper tree.'"[23]

21. Eco, "Author and His Interpreters."
22. Barton, *Reading*, 149–50.
23. Barton, *Reading*, 148.

Ways of Reading: Authors and Reading

With all that has gone before the reader may be wondering, so why do authors matter when reading a story? How does this square with the fact that a story can draw out different responses?

With the denarius story, the fact that Pharisees and Herodians are sent to Jesus is interesting. They represent opposing camps who are joining together to destroy Jesus (Mark 3:6) and Jesus knows this (Mark 8:15), but the combination of the Roman-allied Herodians who may have supported such taxation and purer and more tax-hating Pharisees[24] leaves Jesus confronted with those who would say "Yes" and "No" to the question they put to him. The audience reading this story in the present day can also be split. There are interpreters who read this story as an example of Jesus upholding "the rights of Caesar" and "civil obedience,"[25] affirming that "obligations to Caesar which do not infringe the rights of God but are indeed ordained by God."[26] There are others who see such a reading as bourgeois exegesis.[27] In framing an approach as a reader, the question arises to what extent the views of Mark matter. If Mark was to appear and say, "I intended Jesus to be saying 'Pay your taxes'" or "No, no . . . this story is saying don't even touch those coins!" what difference would this make? Any reader encountering such differences of interpretation also faces questions about the degree to which they will be influenced, or bound, by a sense of the author's intention. What many readers also want from such an encounter is wisdom or guidance for life. It is rarely the case that the interpretation of the meaning of a story is a crude choice, like the two interpretations above. That is a crude image of such ambiguities and potential ways of reading. However, where different possible readings do arise, interpreters tend not to despair that we won't nail down a final meaning so we might as well give up on the text. There is much to be said for taking a walk down both roads. Such a tactic can sometimes discover different meanings they meet along the way.

In the denarius story, a crude fork would have two roads: along one Jesus is saying "Pay your taxes" and along another he's saying "Don't." In a way that's just the sort of dichotomy of differing views in which Jesus is being challenged to choose a side. However, one way of reading his response springs from the sort of approach explored in chapter 1, looking at what actually happens in the story. What happens is, Jesus asks for a coin. In

24. Donahue and Harrington, *Gospel of Mark*, 344; France, *Mark*, 467 questions this characterization.

25. Hunter, in Wessell, "Mark," 734.

26. Cranfield, *St Mark*, 372.

27. Myers, *Binding*, 312.

that small micro-moment we understand that he doesn't have one, and the reader could allow that detail to inform a whole reading of the story. These Roman coins used for taxation bore the Emperor's inscription "Augustus, Son of God," so the people of Jesus's day avoided using these idolatrous coins by having their own copper currency.[28] Some might have refused to even touch or look upon such an item.[29] There may even have been some shame in just possessing one.[30] Such a sense of the coin as seriously offensive changes the event of Jesus forcing someone to hand one over. In doing so, and in highlighting the inscription, Jesus puts a spotlight on the possession of such a coin and, by implication, on the dilemmas involved in buying in to the system it signified. So, when Jesus asks about the title and then wisely counsels "Give to the emperor the things that are the emperor's, and to God the things that are God's" (Mark 12:17) he uses the word *apodidomi*, translated "render" or "give," which literally means giving back, with connotations of returning something to its owner. Jesus challenges the degree to which anyone buying into a system then owes something to that power and will end up having to give it back. In Gospel stories, it's worth watching the challenges Jesus faces and watching for the ways he turns them back on the challengers. In asking for the coin he is turning the question back on those who approached him, challenging the degree to which they have given themselves over to the empire signified by such a coin.

As mentioned earlier, this chapter turns a few questions round on the reader, opening up a personal exploration of meaning and reading in narrative, so for this "Way of the Reader" section here are two provocations that keep such reflections simmering.

The Leopards

Firstly, what are we to make of T. S. Eliot's response to the leopards? Not just the words he said but the above story. There he is, with whatever was going on in his thinking when he wrote it? How satisfactory is that response? What is he saying about meaning?

If he said "Oh, that's a symbol of the trinity, and a meeting place, where the lady represents all humanity, so it's just it's a poetic way of saying 'God is with us'" could we now discard the poem, as we would a decoded message? Where does his response leave readers who ask what lines like that mean? Where does it leave anyone who thinks they know what it means?

28. France, *Mark,* 466.

29. Brandon, in Myers, *Binding,* 311.

30. Malina and Rohrbaugh, *Social-Science,* 256.

Wisdom Stories

In modern wisdom stories there is the one about an industrialist whose whole factory grinds to a halt, so he's now losing half a million dollars every day. So he sends for a machinery expert who arrives, listens to what happened, has a brief moment's thought, then walks over to this one screw on one part of the far end of the machine and takes out her screwdriver and tightens this one screw. The moment she does this, everything starts to hum and spring alive and all the machinery starts working again.

She charges the industrialist $10,000.

The industrialist takes umbrage: "$10,000, when all you did was turn one little screw? It only took you minutes!" He demands a breakdown of the bill.

The machinery expert writes it out, broken down thus: "For turning a screw: $1. For knowing which screw to turn: $9,999."

Did that really happen? There may have been some truth behind this or it may be that a bland conversation became embellished to this point, or a story that it originated in someone's imagination, but the question arises: Does any of that matter? Does it lose it's wisdom if there never was a factory? How does our attitude to the background and origin of this story compare with the denarius story . . . or the walking on water?

THE NARRATOR

The narrator is always there, but the reader hears different sorts of narrative voice. An obvious distinction would be between first- and third-person narration. Written in the third person, Mark 12:41 reads: "He sat down opposite the treasury, and watched the crowd putting money into the treasury. Many rich people put in large sums."

Imagine for a moment that it read in the first person:

"We sat down . . ."

or

"Jesus and I sat down . . ."

or even just

"I sat down opposite the treasury . . ."

This sort of first-person narrative is rare in the New Testament, and in the Old Testament tends to appear in the books of prophets like Jeremiah or

Hosea. However, looking at that verse from Mark 12, it would be a mistake to regard the third-person "He sat" as somehow more neutral and factual than the first-person "I sat," as if the former was less open to the slant the narrator places on it. All stories involve the narrative slant. In a first-person narrative that narrative voice is more obvious. In the New Testament, alongside Luke's opening ascription and some first-person moments in Acts, one of the most dazzling first-person narratives is the book of Revelation, which from the outset has John telling us "I was in the spirit on the Lord's day, and I heard behind me a loud voice like a trumpet saying, 'Write in a book what you see and send it to the seven churches'" (Rev 1:10–11a). The reader has no problem identifying the overt narrator here, on the Lord's Day hearing trumpet-like voices. Equally, the narrator becomes clearly personal when Luke, emerging as a voice within the book of Acts, relates, "we immediately tried to cross over to Macedonia, being convinced that God had called us to proclaim the good news to them" (Acts 16:10).

There is more to the personal nature of a narrative than the pronouns used by the narrator. First person narration may have a clear "I" but third person narratives can also be read with an ear for the personal voice. Narrative theorist Wayne Booth actually describes the distinction between first- and third-person narrators as "Perhaps the most overworked distinction" and adds "To say that a story is told in the first or the third person will tell us nothing of importance unless we become more precise and describe how the particular qualities of the narrators relate to specific effects."[31]

Homing in on such qualities and effects, Barthes suggested that the crucial distinction is not between the first- and third-person narrator but between the "personal and apersonal" narrators.[32] Rather than looking for the linguistic markers of third- and first-person (i.e., the use of "He" or "I" in the above examples) Barthes observes the way in which third-person narratives can be as personal as a first-person narrative. One suggested demonstration of this is to look at how easily some third-person narratives can be rewritten in the first person without radically altering the discourse. This can be interesting in biblical narratives, particularly when applied to the Gospel narration about Jesus. Looking at a story like the anointing at Bethany in Mark 14:1–10 there is an engaging exercise to be had in exploring this quality of personal presence within the narration. Imagine the narrative switched into a first-person narrative:

> It was two days before the Passover and the festival of Unleavened Bread. The chief priests and the scribes were looking for

31. Booth, *Rhetoric*, 150.
32. Barthes, "Introduction," 109.

> a way to arrest me by stealth and kill me. . . . While I was at Bethany in the house of Simon the leper, as I sat at the table, a woman came with an alabaster jar of very costly ointment of nard, and she broke open the jar and poured the ointment on my head.

Or to stay in the first person but switch the person:

> While he was at Bethany in the house of Simon the leper, as he sat at the table, I (went) with an alabaster jar of very costly ointment of nard, and I broke open the jar and poured the ointment on his head."

Or to switch again to someone else:

> But some (of us) were there who said to one another in anger, "Why was the ointment wasted in this way?" . . . And we scolded her.

The story presents a few opportunities for personal perspectives such as:

> And they scolded me. But Jesus said, "Let her alone."

or

> But I said, "Let her alone; why do you trouble her?"

Such text-play can bring out something of Barthes's insight into the personality within a narrative, imbued with Jesus. It can bring out the personality that dominates the story. In this example, even though verse 6 begins with the tag "Jesus said," the first-person words he then speaks add personal effect to the whole story:

> Let her alone; why do you trouble her? She has performed a good service for me. For you always have the poor with you, and you can show kindness to them whenever you wish; but you will not always have me. She has done what she could; she has anointed my body beforehand for its burial. Truly I tell you, wherever the good news is proclaimed in the whole world, what she has done will be told in remembrance of her. (Mark 14:6–9)

The anointing story then ends with a deed that takes place outside of the room, which those present would not have seen: "Then Judas Iscariot, who was one of the twelve, went to the chief priests in order to betray him to them" (Mark 14:9). Though, consider rewording it thus: "Then (I) went to the chief priests in order to betray him to them."

Narration at Work

Seymour Chatman talks about narrative voices being more or less overt
and covert, and in third-person narratives there are still instances where
the reader can detect the narrative voice, knowing more than any bystander
may have. In the above instance it's one that can relate not just the departure
of Judas, but also where he was headed. The distinction is not tidy and is
always more of a continuum, because in truth the narrator is a constant
presence and the degree of overtness will vary, but the narrative voice is
constantly mediating the narrative. There is never a point at which, somehow, the narrator gets out of the way leaving such a thing as pure story. It is
always more problematic than that[33] and one of the reasons for emphasizing
the constant presence of the narrator is to remind ourselves that the narrative is always mediated—there are just instances where this is more or less
overt. With this in mind, keeping a focus on examples from Mark's Gospel,
the following four features of a narrative are ones that commonly reflect a
biblical narrator at work.[34]

a. The Narrative Has Privileged Insight

When Judas stepped outside in Mark 14:9, the narrative demonstrates an
example of narrative privilege. Judas didn't say out loud "I'm just popping
off to betray Jesus," so the narrator is offering an insight any character in that
room would not have had, were they present when he left the room. Wayne
Booth describes this as the narrator's privilege: "Privileged to know what
could not be learned by strictly natural means or limited to realistic vision
and inference. Complete privilege is what we usually call omniscience."[35] The
narrators of the Bible, this one included, know what characters are thinking
even when a character does not say it. Such a narrator can relate the dilemma
in Pilate's thinking at the trial of Jesus: "For he realized that it was out of
jealousy that the chief priests had handed him over" (Mark 15:10).

    In Mark 2 after Jesus declares the paralytic's sins are forgiven, the story
relates the thoughts of some present: "Now some of the scribes were sitting
there, questioning in their hearts, 'Why does this fellow speak in this way?
It is blasphemy! Who can forgive sins but God alone?'" (Mark 2:6, 7). The
grumble is in their hearts but: "At once Jesus perceived in his spirit that they

33. Rimmon-Kenan, *Narrative Fiction*, 108.
34. See also Fowler, *Let the Reader*, 81–154.
35. Booth, *Rhetoric*, 160.

were discussing these questions among themselves; and he said to them, 'Why do you raise such questions in your hearts?'" (Mark 2:8).

What we have here is a questioning in their hearts perceived by Jesus in his spirit, with the narrative voice relating thoughts unspoken in the story. As we imagine the scene, there's a fair bit of unspoken stuff going on, but it is related in the narrative. This omniscience is the narrator's privilege.

b. The Narrative Explains

In a manner somewhat akin to the way actors may sometimes turn to the camera to explain features or events in a narrative watched on screen, the biblical narrator can also offer words of explanation to the narratee. In the Gospel of Mark, the narrator offers words of explanation, so when Jesus casts out demons, Mark 1:34 says: "He would not permit the demons to speak, because they knew him," and in doing so, the narrative offers words of explanation, that are in keeping with the overarching narrative of disclosure and hiddenness.[36]

One notable feature in Markan explanations, seen in the insight into Pilate's thinking above, is the way this explanatory activity is introduced with a "for," in which a comment is made to the narratee. These can be quite straightforward, as in "Now as he walked by the sea of Galilee, he saw Simon and Andrew his brother casting a net into the sea: for they were fishers" (Mark 1:16, KJV), and they can also offer narrative insights into inner life, as when the response of an audience is explained: "They were astounded at his teaching, for he taught them as one having authority, and not as the scribes" (Mark 1:22).

Pilate's realization, quoted above, acts both as an insight into his thinking and an explanation of the power play at work. Similarly, the parable of the vineyard in Mark 12:1–12 is rooted in the events of Jesus's final week by the narrative "for." That parable describes tenants who usurp the vineyard and kill the owner's son and, on its conclusion, the audience "were seeking to arrest him but feared the people, for they perceived that he had told the parable against them. So they left him and went away" (Mark 12:12, ESV). The "for" explains.[37]

Two points about these explanatory instances. Firstly, they often relate the past or a situation to which the reader has not been party. Each of the examples above are analeptic:[38] these people were already fishers, Pilate

---

36. See the overarching view of the story in chapter 7.
37. See Fowler, *Let the Reader*, 92–98.
38. Fowler, *Let the Reader*, 94.

realizes something that has happened before this moment, and Jesus has taught or told a parable. Secondly, they connect. They are a bit like that actor making direct contact outwards, by speaking to the camera or "breaking the fourth wall." Rhoads, Dewey, and Michie note that this can offer explanation and narrative content but also that "when the narrator turns aside from recounting the story to comment directly, the narrator establishes rapport."[39] In such instances the relationship between narrator and narratee is being developed.

c. The Narrative Shapes

Within a narrative, the connections that are made and overall shaping of the story provide other instances where narration peeps up over the overt/covert parapet. Once again, these moments of narration are not exclusively fulfilling one function or another, but when, in Mark 1:34, the narrator explains why Jesus silences the demons who "knew him," that explanation harks back to knowledge already disclosed in the first verse of the Gospel, and the declaration that this is "the good news of Jesus Christ, the Son of God" (Mark 1:1). This is knowledge the reader carries from that first verse throughout the rest of the story.

The shape of the narrative has been covered in each of the preceding chapters in this book, but here the point is that shape indicates a shaping, and that's narration at work. The Markan Sandwich is a good example of such narrative shaping. Historically, it may be the case that Jesus's visit to Jairus's daughter was actually waylaid by a hemorrhaging woman, or that the anointing at Bethany (Mark 14:3–9) took place between the plot to kill Jesus (Mark 14:1–2) and Judas going to betray him (Mark 14:10). Whether these are historical sequences or not, the sandwiching of a story can shape the reading of the portion framed and the slices framing it.

d. Focusing

In chapter 1 we explored the nature of story time, in relation to events in the narrative. A further form of narrative shaping is the degree to which biblical narrative focuses and becomes unfocused on actions, slowing down or sweeping along.[40] In Mark 12 the offerings of the crowd, including many rich people, is narrated in a sweeping: "He sat down opposite the treasury,

---

39. Rhoads et al., *Mark as Story*, 42.
40. Funk, *Poetics*, 136–46.

and watched the crowd putting money into the treasury. Many rich people put in large sums" (Mark 12:41).

When the widow appears the narrative becomes more focused: "A poor widow came and put in two small copper coins, which are worth a penny" (Mark 12:42). Recalling the consideration of story time in chapter 1, it is almost as if this narrative slows down and time is taken for her to come in and place two coins with both of them noted, as if we hear each one drop. Contrast this with Mark 14:1–2 the action of the chief priests and scribes is again covered without focus, in a summary that sums up what one presumes was a more extensive conversation: "It was two days before the Passover and the festival of Unleavened Bread. The chief priests and the scribes were looking for a way to arrest Jesus by stealth and kill him; for they said, "Not during the festival, or there may be a riot among the people" (Mark 14:1–2). The action then slows to a contrasting moment at Bethany and actions of a woman as a point of focus: "While he was at Bethany in the house of Simon the leper, as he sat at the table, a woman came with an alabaster jar of very costly ointment of nard, and she broke open the jar and poured the ointment on his head" (Mark 14:3). The narrative has slowed and the resultant focus is an example of narration at work.

Ways of Reading: The Narrator

Finding the Narrator

Reading any biblical narrative, the reader can take note of those things that make narration more overt. This can involve picking up on moments of privileged insight, explanation, narrative shaping, and focus, bearing in mind that the same words could be examples of all four. In the denarius story, from the first words, "Then they sent" (Mark 12:13a), onwards there are moments when the origin and motivation of these visitors and the insight of Jesus are narrated, in ways that show a degree of overt narration. This continues right up to the response of amazement at the end. In any Bible story such examples can be found, giving a sense of how the narrative is shaping a reading.

Privilege

The literary theorist, Wayne Booth, described the narrators insight into the inner thoughts and feelings of a character as a kind of privilege. One way the reader can engage with this is by doing a simple doodle of a scene from a story and giving thought bubbles to each character. No need for detail, but some jotted words can give some insights into the dynamic in a story at a particular point.

These can include the inner life encountered in the text, but can also expand into other bits of thinking and feeling. When, for example, Jesus asks for a denarius, a range of thoughts may be present in the one crowd. This activity can also be tried for different stages in a story

Switch Narrators

Readers may try recalling which stories they have read that were first- or third-person narratives, or where films feature narrated voices, such as *Stand by Me*. There may even be a preference for one or the other, or favorite reads may fall into one or other category. Sometimes it takes a bit of recollection to remind ourselves whether there was narrator voicing films like *Mean Girls*, *E.T.*, *The Shining*, or *Dirty Dancing*."

Looking at a Bible story, one way of experiencing narration is to think a third person narrative through as a first person, possibly switching the actual character who takes up the narration, trying on a few. The denarius story can be retold in the narrative voice of a Pharisee or Herodian, or as told by Jesus himself. If taking a disciples view, there's a need to allow tone and verbalizing aloud to give something of what is going on, feeling free to add lines to imagine a way into the story, like "It just so happens I had a denarius in my purse."

Questioning the Narrator

Readers can enter into imaginative dialogue with the narrator. However overt or covert that voice is, imaginative engagement with it can involve asking whether Jesus actually answered the denarius question, or whether the "amazed" crowd included some less amazed than others. This can also take the form of comments to the narrator, filling in gaps left, such as speculating how the person felt as they produced their denarius. Approached in this way, the narrator has become less covert and impersonal and more of a living voice. To hear a degree of overt narration is to ascribe humanity to the text, and build a rapport. In doing this the reader is focusing on both their own reading and interacting with the narratee in the story. There is a point in this sort of engagement at which the speculation becomes a form of co-creation that allows for the words "I expect" or "I Imagine" to feature in the reader's response. Such additions will always draw out something of the reader, and done in a group, something of the community that read the text.

One beautiful expression of personal responses to the Bible comes from a series of transcripts of the responses to the Bible from a group of Nicaraguan farmers and fishermen, from the island chain of Solentiname in Nicaragua. Recorded in the 1970s by their priest, Ernesto Cardenal, the Solentiname Gospels are a record of the straight-talking human responses of people oppressed by the Somoza regime of the day. They offer reflections grounded in their lives, with expressions of oppression and explorations of revolution that sit freely with the narrator of the text.[41] Faced with Matthew's account of the healing of the leper Alejandro opines that: "That was a very human act of Jesus. If someone has the power to relieve the hunger of a person who's dying of hunger, just as an example, then he ought to relieve his hunger. But the revolutionary has another mission: It's not to relieve the hunger of a few people but *all* people, right?"[42] Others comment on this reflection and their contextual experience, making for good examples of the sort of co-creation, wherein readers take the text and talk back to it, with reflections and responses that spring from whatever life experience is brought to the reading.

NARRATIVE LEVEL

The narrator is always there, but the question then arises where exactly this narrator is, in relation to the events of the story. By now a reader of this exploration of literary theory will be used to big words that cloak fairly straightforward ideas. Here's two more from Gerard Genette, that describe the concept of narrative level. The *extradiegetic* narrator narrates the base level of a story and an *intradiegetic* narrates one level up from that base.

The narrator of Mark narrates a Gospel that opens: "The beginning of the good news of Jesus Christ, the Son of God" (Mark 1:4). This is the extradiegetic level, where "extra" denotes a narrator being outside the frame of the narrative. Into this narrative steps Jesus, a character who also habitually narrates stories.

41. Cardenal, *Gospel in Solentiname*, 165.
42. Cardenal, *Gospel in Solentiname*, 165.

```
┌─────────────────────────────┐
│        Intradiegetic         │
│          narrative:          │
│       story Jesus tells      │
└─────────────────────────────┘
┌──────────────────────────────────────┐
│       Extradiegetic narrative:        │
│           Gospel of Mark              │
└──────────────────────────────────────┘
```

```
┌─────────────────────────────┐
│ "[David] entered the house of God, when │
│ Abiathar was high priest, and ate the bread │
│ of the Presence, which it is not lawful for │
│ any but the priests to eat, and he gave some │
│     to his companions." (Mark 2:26) │
└─────────────────────────────┘
┌──────────────────────────────────────┐
│ "The good news of Jesus Christ, the Son of God." │
│              (Mark 1:4).              │
└──────────────────────────────────────┘
```

In Mark chapter 2, when Jesus is challenged about the disciples plucking the heads of grain on the Sabbath, he responds to the challengers with a story of David. So this is now a narrative within the narrative, as Jesus retells the story of David being pragmatic, when he and his companions were hungry on the Sabbath: "He entered the house of God, when Abiathar was high priest, and ate the bread of the Presence, which it is not lawful for any but the priests to eat, and he gave some to his companions" (Mark 2:26). This story within the story is an *intradiegetic* narrative, built on the base story, like one level built upon another.

In Mark chapter 4 Jesus teaches with parables, again telling stories within the story, making Jesus the intradiegetic narrator, placed above the level of the first narrative. The extradiegetic narrator of the Gospel provides a base on which is told the story of the intradiegetic narrator, Jesus, telling a story. That image of levels helps understand Genette's definition of narrative level: "We will now define this difference in level by saying that any event a narrative recounts is at a diegetic level immediately higher than the level at which the narrating act producing this narrative is placed."[43]

This can be taken one step further, when an extradiegetic narrator relates a narrative in which a character tells a story (so a story is told in a story narrated within a story), but this is rare in biblical narrative. Slight examples could include the Prodigal Son's relating of his time away from home (Luke 15:21), or the contrasting story related by his brother (Luke 15:29, 30).

As with the examples of more or less overt narration, the narratives on the upper level serve the wider narrative in certain ways. Genette cites two such important functions. These internal narratives can have an explanatory function. This explanatory function is the "this is why," explaining, for example, something about the character who tells it.[44] The older brother does this in the prodigal story. A whodunit will often end with the sleuth retelling the tale of what happened on the night of the murder or films like the *Star Wars* series include moments when a character narrates a story that explains someone's past. In biblical narratives there are also moments when stories within the story explain, as when the backstory of Legion is told (Mark 5:3–5) or the experience of the hemorrhaging woman (Mark 5:26).

Secondly these narratives can have a thematic relationship with the base narratives on which they rest. The children's writer Paul Jennings tells of *The Busker*,[45] a tale in which the extradiegetic narrator needs money to suffice the whims of his demanding date, Tania. He meets a stranger who tells a chilling tale of a man who tried to buy the love of others. It has no direct bearing on his dilemma over Tania, but thematically the parallel is clear and teaches the boy a lesson. This thematic function effectively describes the way parables work within the building up of the gospel narrative. The parables of the kingdom (Mark 4:1–33) develop the theme of Jesus announcement of the kingdom of God. Later in the Gospel, the parable of the tenants in the vineyard is thematically in keeping with the events of Jesus final confrontations (Mark 12:1–12).

Thirdly the relating of the narratives can be events in themselves. To a particular generation few lines are more evocative than "Hello. My name is Inigo Montoya. You killed my father. Prepare to die." Inigo rehearses his story in *The Princess Bride* as he hunts down his father's killer, making it part of the story. Similarly, in murder whodunits the characters telling of their accounts of the night of the murder are events in themselves. A biblical example of this would be the father of the boy influenced by a spirit (Mark

43. Genette, *Narrative Discourse*, 228.

44. Genette, *Narrative Discourse*, 232.

45. Jennings, "Busker."

9:14–29) who tells the story of the disciples inability to heal him (Mark 9:18). Also, as well as being in keeping with the theme, Jesus telling the challenging tale of the vineyard (Mark 12:1–9), prompts a strong response from this hearers, such that the very telling of the story furthers the plot of Jesus final days (Mark 12:12). One of the best examples of such a narrative can be found in the Old Testament—Nathan's storytelling within the narrative of David and Bathsheba, with the denouement "You are the man" (2 Sam 12:7)—a crucial event in the story.

Ways of Reading: Narrative Level

What Type of Narrator?

In general reading there is a lot of mileage to be had using Genette's classification. Even in literature aimed at younger readers there is a preponderance of stories within stories and narrative levels. When princes stop being frogs they have to tell the story of how they came to be trapped in the body that was kissed. In biblical literature the clearest examples of levels come when characters in narratives tell narratives of their own, whether Nathan confronting David, or Jesus telling a tale. Readers can watch out for any point at which a narrative voice switches to speaking of another time or another place, and takes a shift of context. In the parable of the tenants (Mark 12:1–12), the narrative opens with Jesus who begins to speak in parables and, in doing so, shifts the scene to a man planting a vineyard, taking the narrative up one level. The reader attuned to the levels may then catch a subtle level above this when, having seen his collection agents sent away, beaten, and killed, the vineyard owner tells a narrative: "He had still one other, a beloved son. Finally he sent him to them, saying, 'They will respect my son'" (Mark 12:6). It may be few words but it pops up a level, and the story he tells is absurdly at odds with the narrative level below it. The idea is that, having insulted, beaten, and killed those who come before the tenants will now say, "Ah, we may have butchered that lot but this is his son, so everyone be extra nice!"

Absurd it may be, but one level below that, we have Jesus telling the tale. If Jesus is depicting something of God in the vineyard owner then this is a God with a love that goes to absurd lengths, "a God who is longing for a response."[46]

The vineyard owner's tale is only slight, but it's a shift to time yet to come, and so can be read as a level change, as can the rival story the tenants

---

46. Donahue and Harrington, *Gospel of Mark*, 342.

then tell of how "the inheritance will be ours" (Mark 12:7b), also clashing one narrative against another with competing narratives. What the reader watches out for is that narrative shift that tells another story, building a level above the current narrative. The other thing to then watch out for is how that narrative relates to the levels below and any narratives with which it may clash or agree.

IMPLIED AUTHOR AND IMPLIED READER

There are two further nodes in the diagram of narrative communication that can be hard to grasp, but also the enriching for biblical reading. These are the implied author and the implied reader:

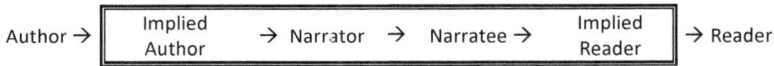

The final diagram has six occupants, with four of them enclosed by a rectangle because they are the ones the reader considers, looking within a text. The other two remain outside it. There is a symmetry to the process which can help in getting a grip on the different participants, keeping this diagram in mind as it becomes unpicked below. There is a symmetry to authors and readers—both important people, but outside the text. Then within the text there is a narrative voice of the story, and a narratee who receives, whether they are more or less overt. Between these, at either symmetrical end, there are the implied author and implied reader.

When an author writes they will have in mind an idea of a reader. As I write this I am working on the assumption, or implication, that my reader is interested in Bible stories and wants to read them. As readers read, they will imply an author. If a reader is reading a letter from a friend, their implication may be fairly accurate, but that act of implying is still part of the act of reading. The author will imply their reader and the reader will imply their author. The term "implied author" denotes that sense the reader gathers of an author, from reading the story. When exploring the Gospel of Mark, it's a fair implication that someone back there wrote this narrative, making Markan sandwiches along the way. Earlier we noted one large sandwiching of similarity between the baptism story and the moment of Jesus's death: to read in the text that sense of similarity and mirroring is to imply activity in the sandwich making. However, it is the reader who is implying. It is possible the existence of these stories sandwiched by other stories are total coincidence—unlikely, but possible. Umberto Eco testifies to readers who discerned clever features in his writings that he confesses he had not consciously written into them.[47] The point is, when reading a story, any views about any of the nodes on this diagram remain in the hands of the reader.

With the implied pair, the six places along the symmetrical diagram of narration are now in place. To locate these in an actual text, the reader may at this point want to take a quick look at Mark 12:1–12, the parable of the vineyard, in which the tenants refuse to pay their share to their landlord, killing the collectors, including the landlord's only son and resulting in their own destruction at the hands of the owner.

The text was written by a real author who is referred to as Mark. The reader is whoever just read that story. The implied author is whatever we, as readers, make of the origins of this story and the warnings being given. As readers we may imply a sense of the forthcoming doom facing Jerusalem at the time at which the vineyard story originated and, in doing so, we are also implying readers who lived at that time and may, as a result of reading, understand the turbulence of their days. The other implication could be an authorship steeped in the wisdom of Jesus, and so speaking of a hold on life that cannot be maintained, and of a need to know what you own and when you are a tenant. In this way the parable may have something to inspire in contemporary readers and may speak to false conceptions of security. Talk of tenants behaving like owners may remind some of us of the climate crisis, where the tenants of a creation have behaved too much as if they own the place, but any such implication of an author capturing the wisdom that distinguishes ownership from tenancy is just that—implied. It is implied on the part of the reader. Similarly, any sense of the message a reader could or should gather from a text is implied by the reader. The very idea we, as readers, will be on Jesus's side is, once again, implied. Hence the implied reader.

When it comes to narrator and narratee there are various levels on which this idea can operate. Firstly, at the base level there is the narrative voice of the text, narrating "Then he began to speak to them in parables" to narratees who will know what that word "parables" means. There is then another level of the intradiegetic Jesus narrating a story and those who are hearing it, and who are stung by it such that, at its ending they want to arrest him (Mark 12:12).

---

47. Eco, "Author."

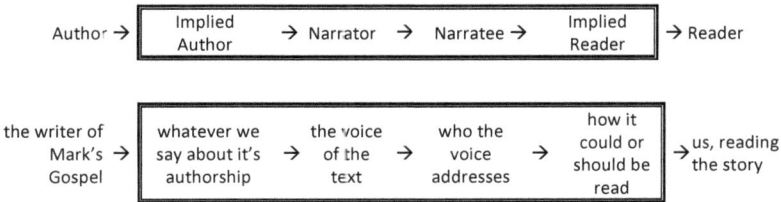

Narrator and narratee can easily be confused with implied author and reader, but the narrator is the voice the text adopts and we may imply a very different author to that text, authoring that voice. We do not know who wrote the Song of Song but various analyses of the text imply that the author has created voices in dialogue throughout the story speaking love to each other. Those are the narrative voices of the text: the woman who tells the story of her lover, "He brought me to his banqueting hall," or the man who says, "I have entered my garden" (Song of Songs 2:4; 5:1). We may imply an author who singlehandedly created the exchanges between them, but that implied author is distinct from the narrative voices they offer.[48]

In another example, the Gospel of Luke and Book of Acts open with a narrative voice, unnamed but traditionally referred to as Luke. This narrator addresses a person called Theophilus, and so there is a narrator and a narrate. The real author may have done what writers did at the time and created the recipient of Theophilus, a name which means "Loved by God." Either way, what we have here is a clear example of narrator and narratee. When, within that narrative, Jesus then tells a parable prompted, and responded to, by a Teacher of the law, the narrative moves up one level and we have another example of a narrator and narratee within a narrative.[49]

Let the Reader Understand the Reader

The model of narrative described in this chapter applies to all Bible stories, but there is one verse in the Gospel of Mark worth looking at for the unique insight it provides into reading. When, in Mark 13, Jesus speaks to his disciples in apocalyptic language, the wording he uses is full of mystery and reference to things coming. In the story the audience is four disciples, leaving the temple, having just seen the widow make her offering and following the run of parables and conflict in Mark chapter 12. Following this: "As he came out of the temple, one of his disciples said to him, 'Look, Teacher, what

48. Gros Louis, "Song of Songs," suggests there are two men and one woman narrating the poem.

49. Powell, *What Is Narrative Criticism?*, 27.

large stones and what large buildings!' Then Jesus asked him, 'Do you see these great buildings? Not one stone will be left here upon another; all will be thrown down'"(Mark 13:1–2).

There follows an exchange with his inner group of disciples, Peter, James, John, and Andrew. Within the story, Jesus privately addresses them about "When you hear of wars and rumours of wars, do not be alarmed; this must take place, but the end is still to come" (Mark 13:7) but the reader may also imply the words of the implied author to the people who both read this then and read this now. Then in the narrative, Jesus speech continues:

> But when you see the desolating sacrilege set up where it ought not to be [let the reader understand], then those in Judea must flee to the mountains. (Mark 13:14)

The words "Let the reader understand" are often enclosed in brackets in translations. They are a message outwards to implied readers. "The desolating sacrilege" is a phrase that denoted the pagan desecration of the temple by Antiochus Epiphanes in 167 BCE,[50] so while in this context it refers to something in the future, it uses the past event to describe something to come. It's a bit like if a contemporary writer were to say, "This administration will have a Watergate of its own." In the original context, Antiochus had left the stage, but the Romans were still around and those four words can be read as addressing the implied reader of that time, which would lead to the Jewish war and destruction of the temple. In this context the narrative has Jesus also tell of the coming of the Son of Man before warning: "And what I say to you I say to all: Keep awake" (Mark 13:37).

These words, addressed "to all," and the wakeup call "Let the reader understand," are overt examples of a narrator addressing narratees and, when reading such texts, the reader can imply the readers of such a text. That implication may take into account the historical context of the Roman occupation and its eventual catastrophe. However, such words can and should also resonate with contemporary readers of the Gospel, allowing the imagery of the story to resonate with the desolations and warnings of our time.

The notion of implied reader describes a pair of shoes a reader can try on, as part of their understanding and enjoyment of a story.[51] There is something to be gained from knowing that one readership of the Gospel read such words as "the desolating sacrilege" in the context of Roman occupation and in the light of the history of Antiochus. However, that is not

---

50. France, *Mark*, 371; Black, *Mark*, 268.

51. Fowler, *Let the Reader*, 33, writes of "the reader we must be willing to become."

the only pair of shoes on the shelf. Other powers and other desolations are brought to such a story by the reader, and in chapter 10 we will look at the way we, as readers, bring whatever we bring to reading. For now a reader may choose to reflect on what readings could be implied from such a narrative for those who read this text, alongside today's politics, evening news, and social media.

Ways of Reading: the Implied Reader

Historical Context

The reader can pick up a Bible story and read and respond in an enriching way for themselves, no background needed. That is the message of this book, However, the diagram above implies an author, and occupying that space can involve all the sort of historical background. It is also the case that understanding that context can enrich a reading of a text, though it's worth remembering that it is the reader who implies any link between background knowledge and a story. Knowing about a particular 'abomination of desolation' or difference between Herodians and Pharisees is one thing, applying it to the narrative involves implying something about authorship. The reader is making an implication, but these implications are worth making. On reading Mark 13 with its temple setting, believing this Gospel originated around the time of the destruction of the temple, a reader may connect the two. It's also worth noting that such connections can be countered by a different view.[52] Background can be debatable, but is also illuminating.

Telling a Story of Reading

In practical terms, the diagram of the narrative process is all about relationships between you, a real reader, and the other spaces along that continuum. Getting to grips with the reading of a Bible story involves unpicking what happens along the process, and one way of doing that is to work backwards from a starting point as a reader.

As readers, we form some idea of the implied reader. This task will vary depending on the reader's knowledge about the text, such that reading a parable like that of the tenants is different if the reader has also read Mark 1:1, declaring this to be the Gospel of the Son of God (Mark 1:1) or

---

52. Horsley, *Hearing*, 130–36.

just opened randomly at that parable. It's also different depending on how a reader understands a term like "Son of God." The construction of an implied reader involves telling a story of reading. It can include a reader considering the twists and turns in a first encounter with a story and also reflect on how, in reading a narrative the reader has read before, the reader can still be caught by a detail such as realizing Jesus has to ask for a denarius. To tell a story of reading, the real reader keeps asking what the story is doing, as story time elapses.

To tell the story of reading and construct the implied reader, the reader also enters into the process between narrator and narratee. This can be enhanced by the awareness that the narrative voice is present and narrating and the narratee is the one to whom that narrative is being related. Such a narrative presence is indicated to a greater or lesser degree and although "Let the reader understand" moments are rare in the Bible, the narratee is always a feature of the story.

There are also narrative levels, such that within the story of Jesus telling the parable of the vineyard there is a moment of clear, intradiegetic narrative, with Jesus as narrator and the chief priests, scribes, and elders as narratees.

In biblical stories the narrator and narratee rarely stand out and to keep the distinction in mind the reader would do well to note other examples from literature, such as the distinction between what we imply about the author's work when we read a novel by Charles Dickens in which there is a narrative voice like that of David Copperfield. Each of these stages along this process are constructs we figure out as readers.

Responsibility

Edward Greenstein, the biblical scholar and interpreter, tells of how he responds to objections from students who argue personal interests and agency should be set aside when reading the Bible and that readers should simply "listen to the text." In response, Greenstein says, "I open my Hebrew Bible, place it on the table, and bid my class listen to what the text says. It soon becomes clear amid the silence that whatever meaning we make of the text follows from our reading of it."[53] Greenstein observes that figures of speech about "listening" serve to objectify interpretation and negates the reader's role in making meaning.

One question this chapter raises for those of us who share readings of texts is how we present this narrative process. In preaching or teaching,

---

53. Greenstein, *Essays on Biblical Method*, xi.

or when just giving views on a Bible passage, the word "says" is a risky one. There is no "The Bible says . . ." There is only what I understand it to be saying. This is important for two reasons.

Firstly, there is a need for humility in relation to the Bible. Any one of us may have got the story wrong. There is louder debate and ambiguity over certain stories, such as whether Jesus made a racially charged comment to the Syrophoenician woman or not. Nobody knows for sure. However, the temptation is to see the loudly debatable stories as one type of text and so to assume all the others have a clear and accepted interpretation. The caution here is against any plainly accepted interpretation. A reader can read the parable of the talents (Matt 25:14–30) in line with the common reading that sees the servant who hid his talent serving as a warning against passivity and inaction, in the light of awaiting the master's return.[54] But it can also be read as a challenge to the system in which the rich get richer, in which the slave who hid their talent is the one who acted honorably by refusing to participate in the rapacious schemes of the king.[55] This is a less common take on the story, but one worth considering.

Secondly, there is a need for humility in relationships between readers. Beware the cocksure voice declaiming "the Bible says." Such an approach usually creates an unhealthy dynamic with "Bible says" spokesperson on one side passive recipients on the other. The healthier model is that of the interpretative community in which preacher and teacher take their place among others sharing a look at the text, reflecting their own reading but also being open to others.

An Ironic Note

The narrative process opens readers and viewers of stories to the wonder of biblical irony. *Irony* involves an ironist, her or his confederates and a victim.[56] It is readers or viewers of a story who become recruited as confederates in its irony, by knowing certain things that shape the experience of the characters within it, who don't know those same things. That knowledge can be a source of humour, terror or anguish. Even as Scar is telling Simba he has done a terrible thing in killing the king, we know Scar actually did the deed, and we know this, even as Simba runs. We also know Juliet isn't dead, though Romeo thinks she is. We also know that God has chosen David to be king over Israel even as Saul is struggling with the rivalry of this young

54. Carson, "Matthew," 518.

55. Malina and Rohrbaugh, *Social-Science,* 150.

56. Liesbeth Korthals Altes,, "Irony," 262.

pretender. And as Nathan tells David the parable that will trap him (2 Sam 12), we know.

Irony occurs when the implied author has tipped off the implied reader with some understanding that is unknown to characters, or sometimes even at odds with the narration of the narrator. In the latter case the dynamic creates an unreliable narrator who may be ill-informed, misleading, or delusional. Without spoiling plots, *Atonement*, *Shutter Island*, and *The Usual Suspects* are good examples, as is *Grease*'s opening song, "Summer Nights," with Danny and Sandy's different narratives of their summer, and the added irony they are telling clashing narratives in the same schoolyard.

When reading from the first verse of the Gospel of Mark that this is "The beginning of the good news of Jesus Christ, the Son of God" (Mark 1:1), the reader now knows something that is hidden from the characters in the story—something the characters hearing the parable of the tenants don't know. When the owner sends his son and believes "They will respect my son" (Mark 12:6), the reader is a confederate in irony.

In the Gospel, this confederacy can take the form of the implied reader carrying that awareness into a reading of Peter's declaration that Jesus is the Messiah ("Christ," Mark 8:29) followed by his argument with Jesus over what should happen to such a Messiah. In a way that reflects the partial sight of the blind man, in the healing story preceding this moment, Malbon observes: "Peter is half-sighted . . . he can see a Christ powerful in healing and teaching; he cannot see a serving and suffering Christ."[57] Nor will he get it, the closer the narrative moves to the suffering. Once again, rather than Peter or one of the twelve, it will be one of the women of the Gospel who, in a moment of irony, sees what is coming and anoints Jesus for his burial (Mark 14:8). Malbon describes such occurrences as "deflected Christology."[58] Throughout the Gospel the identity of Jesus clatters off those around him[59] but through this clattering it is built up in the implied reader.

The Bible is brimming with irony.[60] The reader knows about Jonah, even as the storm sets in or knows about Esther before her king does. In exploring this further, the reader may care to take an excursion into the Gospel of John, where the person of Jesus and the confederacy of the implied reader is established from the outset and makes for some genuine humor. A prime example is that of Nathanael, sitting under a fig tree and

57. Malbon, *Mark's Jesus*, 142.

58. Malbon, *Mark's Jesus*, 130–31.

59. "The teaching of Jesus in Mark's Gospel has little effect on hearers at the story level." Fowler, *Let the Reader*, 76.

60. Good, *Irony*.

hearing about Jesus from Nazareth, asking "Can anything good come out of Nazareth?" (John 1:46), only to later discover Jesus could see him under the fig tree (John 1:48).

A more moving example can be found in the Johannine narratives of the trial and crucifixion of Jesus, in which questions about Jesus's identity, the agency of those who act and the interplay between what the characters think is happening and what the implied readers believe to be taking place is as ironic as the moment when the supposed ruler of the moment, Pilate, writes a text: "The chief priests of the Jews said to Pilate, 'Do not write, "The King of the Jews,"' but, "This man said, I am King of the Jews."'"

Pilate answered, "What I have written I have written" (John 19:21–22). It's a moment brimming with narration and irony.

Narration and Reader

Throughout this chapter the reader has remained the one who constructs the meaning of the text. In literature, people often refer to "the work" when they are referring to the book or text. Lategan draws out the role of the reader, which will be covered in chapter 10, observing that: "The marks on a printed page are signifiers which do not even form a series, just a display. The joining of these signifiers to signifieds according to specific codes takes place in the reader's mind, not in the text."[61] This chapter has explored the stages of the narrative process and identified a series of names along it. However, the reader does the work. The reader relates to the stages of the narrative process and gathers the significance of the printed page. If you check the first line of this book, I did warn you—you're doing all the work.

61. Lategan, "Coming to Grips," 11.

Chapter 9

Point of View

It has been said that you should never criticize someone until you have first walked a mile in their shoes. It has also been pointed out that, this way, you have a mile head start if they get angry at the criticism. Also, you have their shoes.

Narratives offer the reader different pairs of shoes in a story. To start with an example, when you read this opening to a story, what do you see?

> People were bringing little children to him in order that he might touch them; and the disciples spoke sternly to them.
> (Mark 10:13)

What picture forms in your thinking (because I bet you see something)? How does this situation feel? Who's side do you find yourself on?

Throughout a story the events are being narrated from a particular point of view.[1] In narrative theory, point of view is the position the narrative adopts in relation to the story. It's a bit like the lens the narrative deploys, through which readers perceive. In one of the best explorations of this aspect of biblical narrative, Adele Berlin asks us to consider the difference between the experience of seeing a play at the theater and watching a filmed version. Watching a theatrical production as spectators, we have a set place from which we can see some things, and not others, but we can also choose to look at one part of the stage rather than another. If the verse above was an

---

1. Point of view has elsewhere been called focalization. I find the former term plainer and connotative of the range of uses of the term both in literary and day-to-day parlance.

event on a theater stage, the lighting may highlight the people and disciples but an audience member can still choose to look across at Jesus, while such action is taking place in the spotlight. Contrast this with the cinema. Here the same story could be told, but a director will be in charge of what we see. The direction of the film will sometimes result in a long shot and at other times be a close-up. The camera may focus on one face or corner of the action, and the viewer can't then look in another part of the scene. In the verse above, a camera could operate in a way somewhat akin to the mind's eye of a reader, visualizing an anguished look on a parent's face or imagining a particular disciple's stern rebuke. Biblical narratives, like most prose stories, operate in a similar way.[2] The narrating of a story is done in a way that mediates the events through a point of view that can alter during the narrative. Chatman applies three uses of the term "point of view" in day-to-day speech to the way it is used in relation to narrative, based on the perceptual, conceptual, and the interest at play.

Perceptual

The *perceptual* involves the scene literally as viewed from a point, as in "From Ted's point of view the cows looked far away," or simply "Ted saw the cows." In the story started above, verse 14 continues the narrative: "But when Jesus saw this, he was indignant and said to them, "Let the little children come to me; do not stop them; for it is to such as these that the kingdom of God belongs" (Mark 10:14).

As that verse begins, like the shift of a camera, the reader may now be seeing events as Jesus saw them. Between those two verses the language of the narrative shifts the reader's perceptual point of view.

Conceptual

The *conceptual* point of view is not about physical vision, but instead expresses how something relates to a person's attitudes, opinions, or ideas, as in the most usual use of the phrase in statements that begin: "From my point of view." The statement "From my point of view the future is looking good" expresses a viewpoint and "He's just corrupt—that's my point of view on the matter" an opinion. Equally "I have a bad feeling about this" is a conceptual point of view.

2. Berlin, *Poetics*, 44.

Mark 10:14, quoted above, gives an insight into what Jesus is thinking and feeling about the situation. There are some verbal tags that can make this more explicit. Elsewhere, when a scribe accepts Jesus's evaluation of the commandments (Mark 12:28–34), at the close of the story the narrative offers a conceptual evaluation: "When Jesus saw that he answered wisely, he said to him, 'You are not far from the kingdom of God" (Mark 12:34). This interesting use of the same word "saw" denotes a conceptualization; Jesus wouldn't see an answer, but this is about how he evaluated it, capturing his point of view on the Scribe's opinions.

Interest

Point of view can also be a matter of *interest*, asking "who's interests are served by what happened?" This usage captures from who's point-of-view a particular occurrence is advantageous or profitable. If the votes change in an election, this could be beneficial to a particular candidate and, as a result, to those who would benefit from their victory: from their point of view, that change is a good thing. Chatman points out the possibly confusing nature of this category of point of view, in that unlike the other two, which involve active perception or conceptualisation, the interest point of view is passive.[3] Indeed, the beneficiary may not even be aware of it. In the example of the story of Jesus and the children, the moment when Jesus sees what is going on and is open to their approach, rebuking the disciples, serves the interests of those children and parents. From their point of view it's a good thing.

Mark 10:14 offers all three types of point of view identified by Chatman. The disciples obstruct the families: "But when Jesus saw this (perceptual), he was indignant (conceptual) and said to them, "Let the little children come to me; do not stop them (interest)" (Mark 10:14a).

Point of View at Work

The concepts of point of view and narration work together, but also need to be distinguished. They can be separated by observing the way in which a story, such as Jesus's welcoming the children, is told, deploying different points of view, while maintaining a consistent narrative voice. This makes for the important difference in how a reader approaches these narrative features, as point of view is a bit more like plot and characterization, in that

---

3. Chatman, *Story and Discourse*, 152.

it can be unpicked a bit more in analyzing a story. In the example quoted above, the reader experiences a shift, as the barrier to the approaching children becomes seen from Jesus's point of view and the interests of the disciples and families shift at this point. There is a significant change in point of view, but the narrative voice remains consistent.

Narratives can also vary in the degree to which a point of view is lodged with one character, making it either character-bound, or external to any one, particular character.[4] As the parents bring their children the point of view is less bound than when it switches to Jesus sight and response. At that point the reader reads through Jesus's eyes. The story then moves back out to a wider, external impression of the whole scene: "And he took them up in his arms, laid his hands on them, and blessed them" (Mark 10:16). Clearly, in this story there is a tension between the disciples' point of view and that of Jesus. Such a tension emerges throughout the second half of the Gospel.[5] Having declared Jesus as Messiah (Mark 8:27–30) the tension concerning what it means, and will mean, to be Messiah, results in a tension between the conceptual point of view of Jesus, which is shared with the viewpoint of the narrator, and that expressed in instances like his disagreement with Peter (Mark 8:31–33), representing one of the examples of the disciples' "flawed conceptual point of view."[6]

Ways of Reading: Point of View

How We Read

Point of view is about how we experience what we read. When reviewing the material of this chapter, the reader should pick up a story and have a read, watching for this narrative feature. One suggestion is to look at a less familiar story—if the reader hasn't taken a focused look at Manoah and his wife (Jud 13) or the sorry tale of Ananias and Sapphira (Acts 5:1–11), then these are the sorts of stories to read while being conscious of the way, as readers, we step from shoes to shoes as perception and misunderstanding shift the reader from one point of view to another. The reader can keep an eye on how the story is visualized, and which character's thoughts and

---

4. Chatman, *Story and Discourse*, 153 see also Mielke Bal on character bound and external uses the term "focalization."

5. Fowler, *Let the Reader*, 73.

6. Fowler, *Let the Reader*, 73.

feelings are affecting the reading. There is also the question of where sympathies lie and how the reader perceives the interests of different characters are progressing.

Focalizing and Defocalizing

The reader could look across a series of stories in a macrosequence, such as a gospel or a longer narrative like the book of Esther, finding within these longer stretches the way in which one story opens as another closes down. How do we, as readers, know that the scene has changed and we have defocalized from one story, and are focalizing on another? One way of doing this is to imagine the filming of the story, but to do so with a particular focus on what angle the camera would take upon a scene, and how wide the vista would be. The reader can even turn full Spielberg and think about where the close ups would happen and where the narrative requires a wider scene. At what point would the camera home in on a point in the story and what would it be? This could result in a sketched storyboard capturing, for example, something of the moment when Peter and Ananias meet and the deception unravels (Acts 5:3).

Meetings

Watch out for characters meeting. In biblical narrative a common way of focalizing into a story is to bring on the characters and begin their encounter with each other. The reader can ask: who is meeting who? What do they each bring? Then, following a meeting, the reader can explore how they departed the scene. From the point of view of interest the reader can also explore what they brought into this scene and took from it. This can be an interesting way to unpick some of the longer stretches of narrative, such as the tale of Balak and Balaam (Num 22–24). So much of biblical narrative thrives on encounters between individuals that can make for a good focus.

INDICATING POINT OF VIEW

When exploring point of view, narrative theorists will sometimes use the alternative term "focalization." This describes the way in which, as a reader experiences a story, they create something of the image and sound of events that happen and the characters and settings of their happening.[7] For this to

---

7. Funk, *Poetics*, 102.

happen, the reader will at times home in on certain features of the story, focalizing on them, before changing to another scene and other events.[8] There are a few telltale ways in which the reader can experience this focalizing of narrative.

a. The Narrative Focalizes and Defocalizes

Looking through the larger sweeps of narrative, such as the book of Exodus, or an entire Gospel, with the chapter numbers and subheadings removed, the story can read like a single, continuous narrative. However, there are demarcating moments that home in:

> Moses was keeping the flock of his father-in-law Jethro. (Exod 3:1a)

> Then they came to Jerusalem. And he entered the temple. (Mark 11:15a)

In instances like these the story is homing in on a moment, focalizing in on it.

There are also ways in which the narrative defocalizes. Sometimes these can be conclusive ends to a story. In other instances, the story merges with the narrative that follows on. Funk observes certain common defocalizers such as the change of the locale or the time, the ending of a conversation or, in gospel stories, a response by an individual or crowd, such as "And they were utterly amazed at him" (Mark 12:17b).

Between such focalizing and defocalizing markers the narrative almost slows down. Jesus's approach to Jerusalem, above, condenses an extended event into a few words, but, harking back to the analysis of story time in chapter 1, events then move from a summary to something more akin to a scene, with more detail and a focalizing upon Jesus cleansing the temple.

In biblical writing one key moment of focalizing and defocalizing is the arrival and departure of characters, whether literally, as when the widow enters the temple (Mark 12:41–44) or when characters who were presumably present beforehand are picked out and become the focus of the story, as when one of the scribes present in the temple begins a discussion that becomes the focal point (Mark 12:28).

---

8. Funk, *Poetics*, 74, focalizing and defocalizing.

b. Behold

If you have a King James Authorized version of the Bible, just flick through the Gospel of Matthew and look for the word "Behold," used sixty times within its twenty-eight chapters:

> Now when Jesus was born in Bethlehem of Judaea in the days of Herod the king, behold, there came wise men from the east to Jerusalem. (Matt 2:1, KJV)

> While he spake these things unto them, behold, there came a certain ruler, and worshipped him, saying, My daughter is even now dead: but come and lay thy hand upon her, and she shall live. (Matt 9:18, KJV)

"Behold" summons the reader to look and see the subject matter beheld. In the first example it is a wide angle on the entire story, focalizing in on a particular macrosequence of events. In the second, the point of view is shifted within the story. For the reader of Matthew 9, this may involve inhabiting something of the experience of a bystander, noticing this ruler approach. It could also take us into the point of view of Jesus, seeing this person approach. A similar example of the "behold" aligning our vision with a character's point of view would be the moment when Joseph, having heard Mary's news, plans to break their engagement, but "While he thought on these things, behold, the angel of the Lord appeared unto him in a dream (Matt 1:20a). This offers the reader a deeply personal viewpoint, stepping into and beholding Joseph's point of view.

In Old Testament narrative, this function is served by a Hebrew word "hinneh," often translated "Behold." Adele Berlin offers an example of this from the story of Isaac, when: "He [Isaac] lifted up his eyes and saw, and hinneh there were camels coming" (Gen 24:63).[9] Up to now, the narrative has been following the camel train but "suddenly the camera gives us a shot from a different angle—that of Isaac viewing the caravan from afar." The text could have read "He saw *that* there were camels coming" but, Berlin suggests: "This would have given a view external to Isaac. The present form is more dramatic . . . it provides a kind of 'interior vision.'"[10]

In the Gospels, this sort of beholding is found in Matthew and Luke, such that a story that also appears in Mark can gain a "behold" in these gospels. The same people may crowd around the same house but "Behold, some men were carrying a paralysed man on a bed" (Luke 5:18, author translation).

---

9. Berlin's translation from *Poetics*, 62.

10. Berlin, *Poetics*, 62.

c. Verbs

Starting from Eden, when "the woman saw that the tree was good for food" (Gen 3:6) there are verbal indicators that can locate the perceptions or thoughts in a Bible story. An example from the Gospel of Mark occurs when Jesus walks towards the disciples, on the water, and the focalization shifts from his point of view to theirs. Initially, the boat is on the sea and he is on the land and "When he saw that they were straining at the oars against an adverse wind, he came towards them early in the morning, walking on the sea. He intended to pass them by" (Mark 6:48).

The reader sees this through Jesus's eyes and becomes party to his inner thinking and intention, then the point of view shifts to the disciples, in both perception and conceptualization: "But when they saw him walking on the sea, they thought it was a ghost and cried out" (Mark 6:49). Words like "see," "saw," "heard," and "thought" often open ways into a character's point of view. After James and John have asked for places of honor from Jesus the narrative switches to the point of view of the other disciples: "When the ten heard this, they began to be angry with James and John" (Mark 10:41).

With verbs like this, stories such as the story of Bartimaeus provide a sensual treat of the blind man's point of view (Mark 10:46–52), enlivening the story.

d. Naming

In the story of Babe, a pig finds himself on a sheep farm and learns to be *The Sheep Pig*, of the original book's title.[11] The changes over the course of the story are subtly reinforced by the way the pig is named. It's Babe who asks "Why can't I learn to be a Sheep-Pig?"[12] When first bringing Babe home, Farmer Hogget simply announces him:

> Farmer Hogget . . . never wasted his energies or his words.
> "Pig," he said.

The name sticks. Later, when first taking the pig out to the sheep—and questioning his own sanity in believing this pig may herd them—the farmer's summons is a simple

> "Come, Pig," said Farmer Hogget.[13]

11. King-Smith, *Sheep-Pig.*
12. King-Smith, *Sheep-Pig*, 29.
13. King-Smith, *Sheep-Pig*, 49.

It is later in this story, once Babe has triumphed, that the farmer's changed point of view is indicated with a simple "his" and a new name that changes how Babe is referenced:

"'That'll do," said Farmer Hogget to his Sheep-Pig. "That'll do."[14]

The way a character is named can focalize the reader into a particular point of view. In the Old Testament, the very names of a character can denote something of what will become of them and how the reader may view them. Changes in names and the way characters are denoted shape point of view. When Judas appears in Gethsemane, he's described as "Judas, one of the twelve" (Mark 14:43). He approaches with a hostile crowd and the naming changes: "Now the betrayer had given them a sign" (Mark 14:44).

Similarly, when Jesus tells the parable of the tenants this subtle shift in naming can be seen at the parable's climax. The owner sends many who are beaten and killed, but at the climax, "He had still one other, a beloved son. Finally he sent him to them, saying, 'They will respect my son'" (Mark 12:6). When the son is sent the naming shifts. The tenants do not see him as "the son": "Those tenants said to one another, 'This is the heir; come, let us kill him, and the inheritance will be ours'" (Mark 12:7).

From their point of view "The son" is "the heir." One interpretation is that, seeing the son coming, the tenants assume the father is no longer alive, but has died.[15] They see the arrival of the son as being that of the rightful inheritor and believe, if he is disposed of, they will be heirs. Jesus then caps this story off with a further play on naming, as a stone receives a new name from different points of view: "Have you not read this scripture: 'The stone that the builders rejected has become the cornerstone'" (Mark 12:10).

When it comes to the naming of Jesus, the titles by which he is called throughout the Gospels merit studies of their own and this is not the place to explore terms such as "Son of Man," or "Son of Humanity." However, the reader does not need to understand all the complexities of a title to note the use of that name and way the name changes. In the Gospel of John, the naming of Jesus is a running feature of the narrative. From the first chapter, with "the word" being God, and becoming flesh (John 1:14), through to John the Baptist naming Jesus, later in that chapter as "Lamb of God" (1:35), the opening chapter bandies various names around. This then continues through the Gospel, such that one particular healing story of a man born blind actually becomes a story about naming, with the Pharisees asking who has done this illicit act on a Sabbath, naming such a one "a sinner" while the

14. King-Smith, *Sheep-Pig*, 118.
15. Lane, *Mark*, 418–19; France disputes this *Mark*, 461.

healed man variously names Jesus as "The man called Jesus" (John 9:11) and "a prophet" (John 9:17). The gradual process of everyone seeing who Jesus is reaches a climax in this story when Jesus affirms the man's point of view and, when challenged, condemns that of his opponents: "Now that you say, 'We see,' your sin remains" (John 9:41).

This is an example of a story in which it isn't just the naming of characters in the narrative, but also the names they use for other characters, that gives voice to varying and changing points of view.

The Gospel of John moves on, to include highlights of naming, as when Jesus and Pilate engage over the naming of a king (John 18:33–38)—an argument Pilate takes to the limit when labeling the cross of Jesus to the chagrin of the chief priests (John 19:19–22)—and the culmination of the Gospel in the labeling by Thomas of the risen Jesus: "My Lord and my God" (John 20:28b). It's a Gospel that shifts points of view, with naming being one of the significant ways of shifting.

e. Inner Life

When Babe, the Sheep-Pig, is suspected of attacking sheep, Farmer Hogget is about to shoot him—but the event is narrated from Babe's point of view: "He saw the boss . . . carrying something in the crook of one arm, a long thing, a kind of black shiny tube."

The reader gets what that long tube is, even as: "The boss was pointing the black shiny tube at him, and he sat down again and waited, supposing that perhaps it was some machine for giving out food."[16] The thinking presented, including the differential awareness of guns and food machinery, access Babe's point of view.

In biblical narrative, the inner life of a character can shift narration to their point of view, as when during the Exodus story the response of Pharaoh is continually referred to in words like "When Pharaoh saw that the rain and the hail and the thunder had ceased, he sinned once more and hardened his heart" (Exod 9:34a).

A character's "inner life" involves their conceptualization of their situation. It's a moment that a fellow character in the narrative may not have been aware of, as it's internal to the character. This can include Eve experiencing the fruit of the tree as a delight to the eyes, and desiring it (Gen 3:6), or, in the Gospel of Mark, Herod's perplexity on listening to John (Mark 6:20). In such instances of inner life, the reader is taken into someone else's shoes and stands where they stand in relation to events.

16. King-Smith, *Sheep-Pig*, 82.

In biblical terms an oft-repeated example would be all those instances where a character's beliefs are presented. When Jesus walks on water, the disciples think they have seen a ghost (Mark 6:49); Jesus, in turn, is intending to pass them by (Mark 6:48b). Both are examples of the inner life, here switching the reader's viewpoint from that of Jesus to the frightened disciples.

Inner experience is one of the ways in which the reader accesses the interest point of view indicating how one character perceives their outcome in the story or that of another. Following Jesus's confrontation with the demons the crowd are amazed at what Jesus accomplished (Mark 1:27) and the exchange over the healing of the paralytic ends with the crowd, who "glorify God" (Mark 2:12). Such summative statements can serve to draw a line under the way the story has served the interests of characters, leaving them conspiratorial (Mark 3:6), amazed (Mark 5:20), grieving (Mark 10:22), or cautiously warned away from challenging Jesus (Mark 12:34).

The Inner Life of Jesus

In the Gospels the reader is given insights into the inner life of Jesus, encountering his compassion for a crowd (6:34) or his distress (14:34). There is an interesting example of this, returning to the leper of chapter 1. A puzzling moment is rendered differently by varied texts of the New Testament. In Mark 1:41, the leper has approached and Jesus is described as "moved with pity" (NRSV), or "compassion" (NLT), though the reader may note a footnote indicating the text could also read "moved with anger." This is one of those moments when there are variants between the ancient manuscripts. Often, in such cases, translators will regard the more difficult reading as the original. This is based on the understanding that a scribe of old may have baulked at Jesus getting angry and so changed the response to pity, but that it is hard to imagine a scribe taking the opposite journey and making a compassionate Jesus angry. However, what this does exemplify is that the cause of a character's emotion sometimes has to be figured out or inferred. Why would Jesus be angry? It would be out of character for him just to be peeved at a leper, but he could have been angry at the way such folks were treated, or that such a one feels a need to come and kneel. For the reader, part of the fascination of such instances is that they offer a point of view and we step into another's shoes—or sandals—but still need to figure out what we're doing there. So could it be that, if touching a leper makes him unclean, he foresees what is coming in verse 45—the interruption of the mission begun in vv. 38 and 39?[17] One reading would be that he sees himself about to do something that scuppers his mission, and is angry that this is how it has to be—but he still reaches out.

Ways of Reading: Indication Point of View

Verbs

Home in on verbs. These will guide the reader to grasp the ways in which point of view is established and shifted over the course of a reading. These can include verbs of perception and conception, but note should be made of other verbs and their subject. Verbs of speech are also worth noting. What characters say involves a disclosure of their point of view.

When a young man runs up in Mark 10:17, the verbs and point of view remain with Jesus. The runner approaches him, followed by the kneeling, but the perception remains with Jesus who "Looking at him, loved him" (Mark 10:21a). It is only after the call to sell all and follow that the story shifts to the young man's inner response, which reflects back over the whole story: "When he heard this, he was shocked and went away grieving, for he had many possessions" (Mark 10:22).

The very next verse, Jesus "looks around" at the disciples, who have been there all along, and reflects on what they have all seen (Mark 10:23). Watch the way verbs like these guide point of view in a story.

Retelling the Point of View

Imagine it was you, and you now get to recount the story. The reader can take a narrative and imagine a character retelling it from that character's point of view. One way of doing this is to imagine the story being related one year on. By now Jesus has been and gone, but what would that rich young man say, or what would one of the disciples recall? There are some excellent examples of such retellings that can take a reader back into a story but creating one's own is also recommended. One tip: inject a bit of honesty—don't assume a devoted perspective towards God or Jesus but be as human as the characters. This is the point at which your Syrophoenician woman can let rip and express her shock and even disgust at what she experienced as arrogance, or your rich young man can get angry at the straw that broke the camels back (or at least prevented it passing through the eye of a needle).

17. Lane, *Mark*, 87.

Connections

One way of exploring the point of view in a story is to map out the way various characters respond to, and perceive the others in the narrative. Taking a sheet of note paper, the names of characters can be recorded in its corners—bearing in mind there are collective characters that can take up one corner as a group.

Parents   Disciples

Children   Jesus

The story may contain four or more characters, or may not have that many. In the story of the rich young man the reader has Jesus, the young man, and, looking beyond the encounter to Jesus's conversation that follows, the disciples, who were there all along. Given the discussion that follows, there may be a case for giving Peter a corner of his own. As ever, readers can give such things a go and see what works for them.

Having given corners to characters the task then involves starting with one corner and drawing a line to another, and then labeling it with the views, feelings, and responses that the reader imagines that first character would have perceived and thought about the other. The same can then be done for another corner to corner, and another, till the page is a web of points of view.

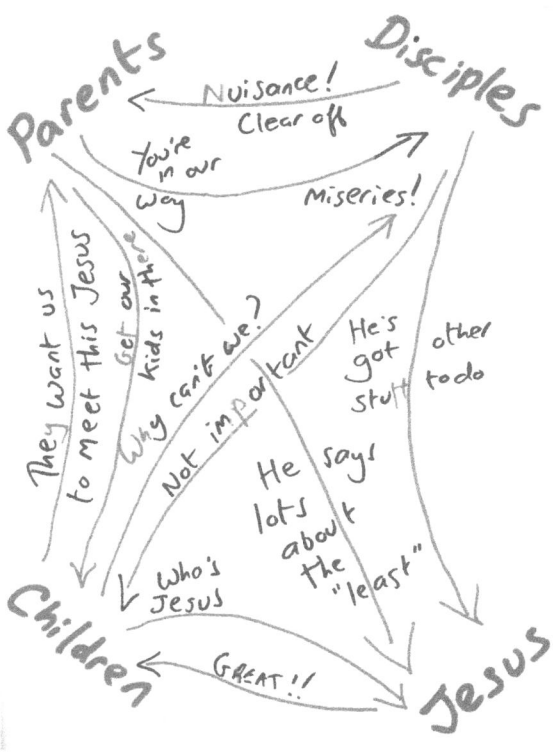

In group settings this can also be done by individuals or groups taking up roles and actually going to corners of the room and looking across and being called upon to express their character's point of view.

Questions

One final note that is more geared to groups and sharing. The reader who is tasked with passing on and sharing Bible stories, whether through teaching or preaching, can find in the concept of point of view a rich resource for homing in and focalizing on the views, thoughts, and interests of the characters in a story. It presents a rich seam for narrative exploration, and one productive outcome of using this concept is when we find ourselves sat in a group, reading a story, and completely disagreeing about what is going on for a character within that narrative. When a room is alight, fired up by varying points of view within stories such as the rich young man or the Syrophoenician woman, and arguing across the room, the points of view have made their points.

DANCING

When Babe sees Farmer Hogget's feeding tube, I see a gun. There are varying degrees to which the reader may or may not align with points of view in a narrative. Sometimes the narrative ensures the alignment, as when it states that Manoah's visitor in Judges 13 is "the angel of the Lord" (Jud 13:3). In the Gospel of Mark, the first verse gives the reader a perspective on the story, from the outset. Such insights recruit the reader, aligning us with the narrator. Also, irony in a story arises from the reader confederating in a perspective at odds with that of characters. Such a dynamic process of alignment can be perceived taking place through the Gospel of Mark. Rhoads, Dewey, and Michie delineate two competing claims to represent God, within the Gospel: that of Jesus and that of the authorities. They observe the way in which, over the course of the story, "The narrator has guided the reader to accept Jesus claim and reject the authorities' claim—by aligning the narrator's point of view with the point of view of Jesus about the rule of God."[18]

Malbon detects a further tension at play here. She presents a creative tension in the Gospel of Mark, between the narrator and the narrator's Jesus, such that the story becomes seen from the point of view of this particular character.[19] This is actually similar to what happens when Babe sees Farmer Hogget's "black, shiny tube"—the reader gets to see the story through the eyes of, what might be termed, a "reflector character."[20] Malbon stresses these two points of view are not in conflict with each other, but there is a tension, and crucially, tensions like these are creative in any narrative in which they occur. In the example of this Gospel, the narrator is pointing to Jesus but Jesus is always deflecting the attention and honor away from himself to God. Such points of view are in step with each other, but more like dancers, creatively in step with each other's steps, than feet marching in unison. The reader who has read chapter 1 verse 1 knows who this Jesus is, but the character will never use those words about himself—it is steps like this that that make reading the Bible like dancing.

18. Rhoads et al., *Mark as Story*, 122.

19. Malbon, *Mark's Jesus*.

20. Stanzel quoted in Malbon, *Mark's Jesus*, 241.

Chapter 10

Reader's Response

Are you still here?

I only ask because after two tough chapters on narration and point of view, this last one is all about you.

1. READER RESPONSE INTRODUCED

So, reader, what are you dong?

> If at this moment someone were to ask "What are you doing?" you might reply "I am reading," and thereby acknowledge the fact that reading is an activity, something *you do*. No one would argue that the act of reading can take place in the absence of someone who reads—how can you tell the dance from the dancer?[1]

These words come from Stanley Fish, a literary theorist who has argued for the importance of the reader in constructing the meaning of texts. Reader response theory is the school of thought in literary theory that ascribes a key place, in the construction of interpretations of texts, to the reader. It starts from the belief that you can't separate an interpreting subject from whatever it is they are interpreting.[2]

Any reader reading the resurrection story in Mark 16:1–8 brings assumptions and knowledge that will shape their reading. While that may be

1. Fish, *Is There a Text*, 22.
2. Mailloux, "Reader-response Criticism?," 414.

relatively uncontroversial, it gives rise to a number of debates between different reader-orientated approaches, though they share this familial resemblance.[3] However, there are significant differences within this family that tend to divide around the question of just how much the meaning of a story is shaped by the response of the reader, and the degree to which there is a shaping power held by the text. Theorists divide over the extent to which responses to a text are shaped by the text or are the act of the reader.

One of the best ways to explore this debate is to look at the divide between two such theorists: Wolfgang Iser and Stanley Fish.

Wolfgang Iser and Stanley Fish

The theorist Wolfgang Iser writes beautifully about reading, describing a fixed text that is interpreted and "puts limits on response"[4] as akin to:

> Two people gazing at the night sky may both be looking at the same collection of stars, but one will see the image of a plough, and the other will make out a big dipper. The "stars" in a literary text are fixed; the lines that join them are variable.[5]

For Iser there are two poles to a literary work.

> The artistic pole is the author's text and the aesthetic is the realization accomplished by the reader.[6]

The artistic stars, in the interpretation of stargazers, become aesthetic ploughs and dippers so the resultant image is one of a relationship between a fixed text and a reader. This relationship emerges within the gaps of the text—a bit like joining the dots in constellations to create saucepans or bears.

Gaps are the breaks in the narrative[7] which the reader has to fill. Looking at a text, it helps to imagine them as vertical and horizontal or, to use the terminology, syntactic, and paradigmatic.

The *syntactic* gaps[8] seem to run horizontally along the line of the text. When reading that, at the start of his trial: "They took Jesus to the high priest" (Mark 14:53) the reader quite naturally connects the "they" with the

---

3. Freund, *Return of the Reader*, 8.

4. Mailloux, "Reader-response Criticism?," 424.

5. Iser in Freund, *Return of the Reader*, 146.

6. Iser in Freund, *Act of Reading*, 21.

7. Vorster, "Reader in the Text," 26.

8. Iser uses the term "syntagmatic" in *Act of Reading*, 225. I am following Vorster in using "syntactic."

crowd who arrested him a few verses beforehand (14:46) and not with the disciples who ran away (14:50). In doing so, the reader fills a gap. Such syntactic gaps can vary in their degree of openness.[9] It's not clear if Judas is still one of the "they" at this point, though he was there at the arrest.

Paradigmatic gaps draw out the reader's image of the objects and wording in the text[10] and the way in which these can change as we read.[11] The reader will imagine the "they" of the "crowd" in a way that is personal to each reader. Likewise, when "They took Jesus to the high priest" (Mark 14:53), words like "high priest" and the act summed up as "took" open gap the reader fills with their own response to such words. There is a personal dictionary of impressions and experiences a reader will deploy as they make sense of these words.

Gaps are basic to reading. They are as basic as the very act of connecting the words "gaps" and "are" in that last sentence. It is the debate as to just how great the gaps are in texts that create the opening for the more radical stance of Stanley Fish. Whereas for Iser there is something fixed and agreed about a phrase like "Gaps are . . .," Fish would assert the role of the reader in formulating a meaning of that two-word scrap of text.

In his work since 1970, Fish has warned against the supposed objectivity of any text, describing it as an illusion, and a dangerous one at that "because it is so physically convincing."[12] For Fish, interpretation is a subjective experience. It's all about what a text does.[13] At it's most extreme this stance says a text doesn't exist unless there is a reading. Reading is "something that happens to, and with the participation of the reader,"[14] so for Fish, reading is all about "the developing responses of the reader."[15]

Between these two writers we have an engaging bust-up with Fish accusing Iser of steering a safe middle way,[16] avoiding the difficult logical conclusion of a reader orientated approach. He even titled an article on this matter, "Why No-one's Afraid of Wolfgang Iser,"[17] taking Iser to task for suggesting there is something determinate about a text,[18] when in reality all

9. Rimmon-Kenan, *Narrative Fiction*, 128.

10. Iser, *Act of Reading*, 228.

11. Vorster, "Reader in the Text," 26.

12. Fish, *Is There a Text*, 43.

13. Freund, *Return of the Reader*, 93.

14. Fish, *Is There a Text*, 25.

15. Fish, *Is There a Text*, 27, 46.

16. Fish, "Why No One's Afraid," 3.

17. Fish, "Why No One's Afraid," 13.

18. Freund, *Return of the Reader*, 145.

such things are still filtered through the reader's perception. Iser, in turn, replied to Fish, in a piece called "Talk Like Whales."[19] He accused Fish of collapsing the distinction that exists between perception and the perceived, asserting "what can be seen will be there," raising the specter that the alternative is the replacement of what is given, there and seen, with interpretation itself.[20] I'd suggest this critique is actually an accurate assessment of Fish and one which I suspect he may happily own, and with which I agree.

That's the debate, in a brief tussle and, while I veer more to Fish's side of this debate, in the approach to biblical texts that follows, this book will take both these exponents of the role of the reader along with us for the read.

Reader Response Implications

For the reader of Bible stories there are a few implications of reader-oriented approaches that can shape the approach to texts, and stories in particular. One critical question raised by this turn to reader response is, why isn't reading a free-for-all? How is it we can and do end up agreeing on what a text means? What is to stop the reader from interpreting "They took Jesus to the High Priest" (Mark 14:53) as meaning the disciples took Jesus to a cafe? The first step is to explore agreement.

a. The Text Is Always Mediated

Both Iser and Fish highlight the role of the reader. They both shift away from a text being just a text towards the presence of reader mediation. At times, that mediation may result in greater or lesser agreement between readers: there will possibly be general agreement that the arrested Jesus is being taken for trial and not to a café called "The High Priest"—but that agreement lies this side of the text, with the readers. That affirmation of the role of the reader is important in some of the more open questions, such as what attitude to taxation Jesus adopts in the denarius story or whether he was needlessly offensive to the Syrophoenician woman. It's also there in smaller questions, such as that of the make-up of the crowd taking Jesus for trial. The answers to such questions always lie on the reader's side of the text, with the possibilities that open up in the sections below.

---

19. Iser, "Talk Like Whales."
20. Iser, "Talk Like Whales," 84.

b. This Is Just How Things Are

There is the famous story in Boswell's *Life of Samuel Johnson* where the two men are chatting after church about the views of Bishop Berkeley, who posited the idea that matter did not exist and all experience was a matter of the senses at work, hearing and feeling what was, in effect, not there. Boswell commented that even though they did not believe this to be true, it was hard to refute it, at which point "I never shall forget the alacrity with which Johnson answered, striking his foot with mighty force against a large stone, till he rebounded from it, 'I refute it thus.'"[21] Of course, the refutation was just as much a matter of sensory experience, even if it did stub a toe. Boswell was just observing how things actually are. Similarly, the approach to reading being presented here isn't a stance or crusade so much as an observation of how things just are. It could be where the Bible is concerned, given the authoritarian way in which it is handled in some circles, a healthy observation. Iser challenges us to accept what is there and what is given, but in doing so exposes the dilemma that, where the meaning of a text is concerned, we have no way of saying anything about it other than interpretation. So what if someone does come up with an interpretation that is wrong? Can we still refute it? Absolutely! However, this approach suggests the only way we do this is through community.

c. Community

Paraphrasing the philosopher Richard Rorty, "objectivity is an agreement of everyone in the room."[22] When we read a text, anarchy does not ensue and you and I remain fairly confident neither is reading the arrest of Jesus as a café outing. Fish suggests the reason for this is the agreement that ensues within the interpretative community. One of the blessings of such an image is that it opens the possibility for the community to change. A community can agree and disagree, be creative or conservative, bring in the marginalized, seek to persuade and sometimes accept there is a difference of views in the room.[23] It also raises the challenging question of who is let into the room. Hopefully a recognition that this is how interpretation works can open those doors a bit wider.

---

21. Boswell, *Johnson*, 281.

22. Brueggemann's paraphrase in *Postmodern Imagination*, 8.

23. For a really well written, engaging alternative to the reader orientated approach see Vanhoozer, *Is There. . .?*

Ways of Reading: Reader Response

Delving into debates this approach can provoke, this section encourages reflection on the role of the reader.

Ask Yourself

The debate raises the question of the given and what the text is, along with whether or not it is interpreted. In doing so it raises the question of what there would be on this page if you were not reading it. There are also other questions, not about specific stories but more about the reading experience, and the reader may want to consider a few:

- What happens when you read?
- How would you describe the experience you have when reading a text?
- What are the constraints that stop the anarchic free-for-all of interpretations?[24]
- Consider your reading community—whether the one where you learned to read or the one to whom you would give an account of reading in which you currently engage. How does this shape your reading?
- To what extent is the text independent of the reader or constructed by the reader's reading?

Imagine Being Punched!

This debate even comes to fisticuffs! However, they are ones that raise an image to ponder. At one point Iser challenges Fish's approach observing we may blink when we are punched but the blink is not the punch.[25] However, it could be said Fish's approach isn't reducing the punch to the blink. The whole interpretation, including sight of the fist, pain, ascription of motive to the puncher combine and is, after the initial shock, interpreted as a punch. After all, if the punch is an accidental consequence of a swung arm that catches me, was I punched?

24. Freund, *Return of the Reader*, 104.
25. Iser, "Talk Like Whales," 85.

2. READERS RESPONDING: TEXTS

Having explored the debate about the role of text and reader, in this chapter both will be considered, starting with the text, and features that can be assigned to the text. Just to note that as with so many of the literary features explored in this book, for the purpose of working with the process of reading, the following sections create artificial subdivisions within something experienced as a holistic act of reading a text.

a. The Text: Parts and Whole

In "Rumpelstiltskin," when the goblin initially appears and helps the princess out, readers may welcome a helpful soul, even if he makes us somewhat uneasy. When he then requires her baby, the unease becomes acute, such that when the princess acquires means to defeat him we are now rooting for his downfall. Throughout the story the reader's overall impression of the goblin is revised by parts that build into a whole view that changes, and reflects back upon, the parts. Small changes change the whole story.

There is a cycle to the reading process in which the reader reads, bit by bit, and builds up a sense of the whole text, whether that be words in a story that shape the whole or events building an overall plot. Culler uses the term "models of unity" to describe the way readers integrate the parts of a reading to an overall interpretation.[26] This is a circular process. Reading the story of Jesus's trial before the high priest (Mark 14:55–65) the reader who reads that the council were looking for a basis to execute Jesus (Mark 14:55) then reads "For many gave false testimony against him, and their testimony did not agree" (Mark 14:56) within a context in which to place these spurious testimonies. This is not random; these parts are part of the whole story of a stitch-up. That same reader takes in the straightforward and clear answer Jesus gives, when questioned (Mark 14:62) and integrates this into an overall understanding of the trial. The holistic story presents a stitch-up. Within it, testimonies don't agree—so the whole story is now one of a botched-up stitch up! And within this the testimony of Jesus remains clear and true.

Reading with a view towards the model of unity provides a way of charting how overall response and particular moment interact within the reading of a story. The reader encounters parts, such as the declaration that Jesus remained silent (14:61), in a story in which he then speaks (14:62), and it is parts like these that grow the whole story. It is also wholes, like the extent to which Jesus is or is not responding, that call upon the reader to

26. Culler, *Pursuit*, 68–70.

ask why the silence gets broken. Observing that cycle of part and whole can open up fresh encounters with a well-known tale.

One final example of part and whole interrelating, particular to Mark's Gospel, is the interaction of part and whole in a Markan sandwich.[27] The inquisition at which we're looking features as the filling for one of the Markan sandwiches in the Gospel, in which the reader can look to Peter's story, outside in the courtyard, bookending the trial by the high priest. Here again, the reader can reflect on the dynamic relationship between the whole sandwich and the particular filling, and vice versa.

b. The Text: Open and Closed

When questioned as to whether or not he is the Messiah, Jesus replies, "I am; and 'you will see the Son of Man seated at the right hand of the Power,' and 'coming with the clouds of heaven'" (Mark 14:62) and nobody knows what he meant.

There are opinions: some believe he was referring to a second coming, others to the cross as a demonstration of power. There is less ambiguity about what Peter meant in response to his questioners in the courtyard (Mark 14:66–72). To use a distinction from Umberto Eco, some texts and stories are more open, and some are more closed. At the *closed* end of the scale, Eco places comic strips that "Apparently aim at pulling their reader along a predetermined path, carefully displaying their effects so as to arouse pity or fear, excitement or depression, at the due place and at the right moment."[28] While this may not do justice to the complexities of modern graphic stories, the word to hold to there is "path." In a closed text, the path is clearer and laid out. The contrast is with the *open* text which is more akin to wandering in woods: "a garden of forking paths. Even when there is no well-trodden paths in a wood, everyone can trace his or her own path."[29] Eco describes reading as being like the forked pathways, the taking of directions, and even the experience of being lost, affirming the choice of the wandering reader. Once again in literary theory an apparent distinction is more of a continuum than an either/or, and there are degrees of open wandering or closed path, but to enjoy a story a reader really needs to wander in the woods.

One indicator of the closed or open nature of a text is the degree to which the reader experiences a more or less active role in reading. The reader can look at a Bible story and consider: is this like a pathway or does it feel

27. See chapter 2.
28. Eco, *Role of the Reader*, 8.
29. Eco, *Fictional Woods*, 6.

like a wander? To some extent, it falls to the reader to strike off the beaten track. Reading the story of Peter's denial of Jesus can involve choosing to wander down pathways, such as:

- considering what the servant girl meant by "with" when accusing "You also were with the Nazarene" (Mark 14:67b ESV);

- considering how the murmuring against Peter spirals from servant girl to bystanders;

- observing that Peter does not just deny being with Jesus but also professes complete ignorance as to what they are talking about.

Some of the paths may be dead ends, but these can also be a place to wonder.

c. The Text: Happenings

Comedian Rowan Atkinson created a Father of the Bride[30] speech in which the grizzled dad at a wedding takes the opportunity to "say a word or two about Martin," and proceeds to extol Martin's virtues:

> As far as I'm concerned, my daughter could not have chosen a more delightful, charming, witty, responsible, wealthy (let's not deny it), well-placed, good-looking and fertile young man than Martin as her husband.

Then he continues:

> And I therefore ask the question, "Why the hell did she marry Gerald instead?"

Something happens, as this single line brilliantly capsizes all that went before.

Fish describes reading as "something that happens to, and with the participation of the reader"[31] and consequently he sees the interpretation of a text as involving "the structure of the reader's experience rather than any structures available on the page."[32] This sense of interpretation as happening over time is shared by Iser who also describes the reading process as dynamic,[33] akin to a journey through the text: "We look forward, we look back, we decide, we change our decisions."[34]

30. Atkinson, "Wedding."
31. Fish, *Is There a Text*, 25.
32. Fish, "Interpreting the 'Variorum,'" 468.
33. Iser, *Act of Reading*, 108–9.
34. Iser, *Implied Reader*, 288.

This may be easier to envisage in a text that reveals something new as the story unfolds, but how does this happen in a text which the reader has encountered many times before, knowing all the surprises and the ultimate ending? In actual fact, this approach to a text happening is one of the ways a reader may be able to experience encountering, yet again, a story read many times before. One approach involves the implied reader and an exploration of the story from the standpoint of a first encounter. The reader may know what the neighborly Samaritan in the parable does (Luke 10:29–37), but how might a virgin reader, treading this path for the first time, respond at the approach of a perceived enemy towards the poor victim? A reader can wander through a narrative observing how each new step along the way develops the experience of reading, such that, to give an example, when the high priest reacts to Jesus's answer to the question "Are you the Messiah?" (Mark 14:61), the reader can allow the shock of the response to be felt again, as if for the first time. While such readings are somewhat artificial[35] the "virgin reader" approach is not a pretense of faux ignorance, but rather a consideration of how the story builds up.

Mapping the way response happens involves experiencing the construction of meaning as a dynamic rather than static experience,[36] one that Fowler suggests bears some resemblance to the view of language in the time when Mark was written, when language was regarded as being active and happening and "an utterance or a text represented an active unit of force, not a passive object for analysis."[37]

d. The Text: Language

servant girl

warming

with

denied

out

These are all words gathered from the first few verses of the story of Peter's denial (Mark 14:66–68). Among them there are some standout words like "denied" but also some inclusions that are very common words, such as "with." How the reader reacts to these words will vary according to a reader's prior experience of them and how they figure in reading.

35. Moore, *Literary Criticism*, 83.
36. Fowler, *Let the Reader*, 47.
37. Fowler, *Let the Reader*, 50 drawing on Tompkins's work on Longinus.

The theorist Norman Holland looked at the varied responses readers gave to the use of the word "Fathered" in one line of a William Faulkner story. Different readers gave a range of responses but Holland summed up that range with the observation that

> Since the text presents just the one word "fathered," one cannot explain by means of the text alone why one reader would find that word heroic, another neutral and abstract, and a third sexual. . . . We can explain such differences in interpretation by examining differences in the personalities of the interpreters. More precisely, interpretation is *a function of identity*.[38]

The very words of the text will be a matter of personal interpretation. Even if my perception of "denied" substantially matches yours, a responsive reading should acknowledge, and can enjoy, personal connection with the language of the text.

One interesting approach to the language of biblical narratives can be found in Anna Carter Florence's *Rehearsing Scripture*,[39] in particular her focus on verbs. She advises, "If you're looking for a way to make scripture relevant, start reading the verbs."[40] Carter Florence observes the way in which verbs remove the distance between reader and text, observing that "most of us enter scripture nouns-first" with the result that our reading can be distracted by things that are not so familiar. In the trial story this would include a courtyard, a high priest, chief priests, a temple, and a Messiah, whereas the verbs are shared with the reader's experience. In the trial story the verbs of following, warming, staring, cursing . . . and denying—these are actions we will have encountered, albeit in different experiences of our own. They comprise familiar features of the identity that reads the story.

e. The Text: Gaps

The review of reader response approaches included the two types of gap: syntactic and paradigmatic. The former runs horizontal across a line of text and the latter engages with the vertical gaps, filled by the reader's concept of the words in the text. In the preceding sentences there is an example of syntactic gap-filling whereby a reader connects the word "syntactic" with the word "horizontal," and there is also a paradigmatic exercise in which the reader brings to the reading their understanding of a word like

---

38. Holland, "Unity Identity Text Self," 123, italics mine.
39. Florence, *Rehearsing Scripture*.
40. Florence, *Rehearsing Scripture*, 21.

"paradigmatic." The very act of reading involves filling such gaps, applying interpretation that fills in indeterminacies.[41]

The difference Iser and Fish demonstrate is between the degree to which the text already sets something in place and the degree to which it emerges out of the act of reading, but whatever view is taken on this debate, the fact remains there are gaps for the filling. In the example of the trial of Jesus before the high priest, it is the reader who connects the "they" in "They took Jesus" (Mark 14:53) with the people in the preceding verses, just as it is the reader's imagination that will supply the distance at which Peter followed (Mark 14:54). What that distant following implies and why he does this is also up to the reader, as is the servant girl's prior experience, why she chose to raise it, how she ascertained who Peter was and why she said what she said (Mark 14:67-69). And there are more: the whole text draws the reader into the gaps between words, the gaps within the poetics, and the underlying gap in understanding as to why this whole event is taking place.

Ways of Reading

Unlike earlier chapters, in this one the reader activity is collected together, gathering five sets of activity in one place, to reflect the fact that a reader's actual response involves bringing and keeping these various strands of response to the text together.

Ways of Reading: Parts and Whole

In exploring event, character, and setting, previous chapters have all given ways of reading the lines and chunks of stories. The activities in this section focus on doing things with the experience of reading. The focus here is on the way the act of reading integrates parts into whole encounters with a story, and also the way that whole shapes response to the parts. As with other activities, the recommendation to the reader is to look wider and try these ways of reading out on other stories. The reader could look back through the Gospel or, as always, there's a whole Bible of stories out there.

Part to Whole

The reader can pick a word, a phrase, or a sentence, jotting it down. That's the part. When it comes to the whole, the reader then defines a frame—whether

---

41. Iser, *Act of Reading*, 111.

it's one Bible story or a few in a row. The part can be treated like a lens through which the whole is read, and vice versa. If selecting the word "denied," the story often termed "the denial" is now read with that word in mind. This would be the same if the chosen part were a phrase, such as the clause "But again he denied it." Read through this lens, the reader may observe the repeated nature of the denial and, in turn, may contemplate the fact that Peter remains there, even after the first exchange. It could even spill into the next bit of text, with a reading of how Jesus responds to charges, the ambiguous answer to Pilate, and his eventual silence. Read through this lens, the reader may ask, is this a different sort of denial?

Likewise, that frame of bigger story can become the lens through which the chosen part is returned to and reread, with the trial before Pilate shaping the reader's understanding of the word "denied." The circular interaction from the part to the whole and back again is, in part, the experience of reading.

Close the Book

Sometimes the way to read the Bible is to close it. A model of unity in a Bible story is a holistic integration of a reading experience and, to fully grasp that, the reader can just close a Bible and consider the overall impression of the story and then think through some of the parts that are integrated into this whole. It can also be interesting to note just what does stay in the mind, once the book is closed.

Often, faithful readers want to press on and come up with some reflection or application of the text, but the stage described here is one of just holding the story and gathering its parts into a whole.

Ways of Reading: Open and Closed

The focus of play here is on the degree to which the act of reading is more like a singular pathway or a ramble in the woods.

Question Marks

One of the simplest things a reader can do in exploring openness of a text is to annotate it with question marks in the margin, possibly printing a copy of the text to allow maximum scribble down the margin. Each question could be regarded as the text opening to the reader, and one question the reader should be asking is, why am I marking this with a question? What is it that places a question here? There are very few things learned from the text that don't lend themselves to a question, and few knowns that don't opens the unknown. We read that Jesus ceased replying to Pilate (Mark 15:4). The question can arise: why? We read that Pilate used to release a prisoner, but why would he do that? (Mark 15:6).

In this activity, the reader can regard questions as being a bit like wedges. The task is almost to find the opening and drive them into the story—even if they seem petty. In Mark's story of the trial before Pilate when Jesus is bound and led to his trial (Mark 15:1) there is a question of what that would have looked like? Did they go en masse? In the trial itself the bigger issue of what is to be understood by the title "the King of the Jews" opens a very different type of question. Exploring response in this way is not about furnishing the answers so much as noticing the questions.

Different Kinds of Reading

Eco's image of the singular path or the rambled wandering provides a useful metaphor for consideration of the difference between more closed and open texts. In the same way a ramble requires a different type of walking, so open texts require a different kind of reading.

The suggestion here is simple: the reader can use an open text to reflect on the nature of the opening. In engaging with the Bible it is sometimes interesting not to find a way through an openness or an undecided question and come down on one side or give one answer, but just to allow a ramble in the space that is opened. The reflection can, in turn, inform the way we understand a particular open text. Looking back through the Gospel, those narratives that leave open some unresolved questions present space to wander, and the time taken to read them before moving on will differ. The final verses on the cross take time to read, as does the resurrection narrative in Mark 16:1–8, and what the women actually do at the end.

Opening

When the text is open, the question is "How open?" The reader can contemplate the degree to which the path has wandered off any beaten track. When Pilate begins his questioning with "Are you the King of the Jews?" the meaning of such a phrase is also open, and Jesus's cryptic "You say" (Mark 15:2), variously translated as "You say so" (NRSV) and "It is as you say" (NKJV), is gaping wide. What does Jesus mean?

The reader may be aware that answers or explanations of the term could be found in a commentary, but this should not deter anyone from allowing the text to open to them and engage their own response to those words. Open texts invite our thoughts; in reality, when an opening opens, such as the one that widens when the reader asks what the soldiers were doing when they mocked Jesus as "King of the Jews" (Mark 15:18), nobody has a final answer that imposes closure. This story will lead to the cross which, although explained and explored by theologians of salvation, also remains as open as an opening can be.

Ways of Reading: Happenings

The focus of this section is to explore ways the story unfolds as the reader reads, finding ways of mapping the developing responses of the reader, specifically looking at those twists and turns that shape the happening of the reader's experience.

Mapping Response

I can't be the only viewer of popular dramas who shouts outrage at the screen when a favorite character is being killed off or exclaims with pure joy when a delicious denouement unfolds.

Tracking the happening of a narrative is about following the reader's experience—telling a story of reading. Response is a whole experience, but in looking across a story, one way of charting it as it happens is to look for a few of the following:

- What were the emotions experienced at different points in the story? How have emotions grown and shifted over the course of the read?

- What words would you, as the reader, say back into the story? Can we verbalize the way we respond to certain moments? When the crowd are motivated to call for Barabbas, what does a reader say to that crowd, or those who stir them up, or the dynamics of what this will mean?

- How do the reader's hopes relate to the story? As readers we bring to a reading a developing sense of how we would want the story to progress. This may involve a will that the crowd would call for the release of Jesus rather than Barabbas, or that the whole scene would become a revolution. Spotlighting such hopes is not about prediction but emotion. What would we want to happen at a particular moment in the narrative?

The words "A few of the following" at the top of this list are important. This is not an exhaustive listing, but the suggestion that gathering a sense of the experience across a page is one way of telling a story of reading.

Roller Coaster

Linked to the previous activity, the reader can track the course of emotion and response over the course of a story. Are there points at which things dip down sadder or climb up in hope? Looking across the stories of the Gospel as a whole, are there moments of surprise or even humor? The reader could draw a graphic of the emotional roller coaster the story takes them through, showing the ups and downs. In the case of Jesus's trial there is the story of the prisoner release with its small glimmer of possibility when Pilate continues to question and challenge the crowds (Mark 15:14).

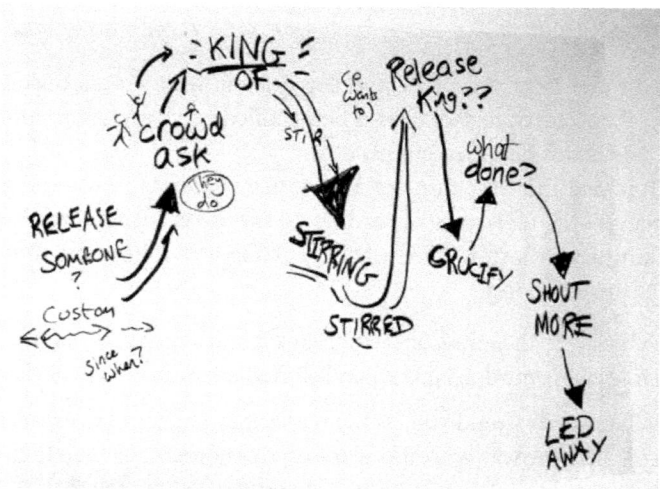

Virginal Reading

One implied reading a reader may want to try out is that of the virgin reader engaging in a first read, not knowing the twists, turns, and outcome of a story. Of course, the Bible reader often does know the outcome, but why let that stop us? A virginal reading traces the course of the reading experience afresh. At the outset of the trial before Pilate there is a moment when his sympathies towards Jesus seem apparent, when he asks: "Do you see how many things they testify against you?" (Mark 15:4, author translation) That's not a comment about the specific things being said. It is a comment about the stacking up of a case and is more a comment on Jesus's silence than any accusation—but for the virgin reader there is a glimmer of hope here. This judge can see what's going on. Similarly, when Pilate then responds to the prisoner release by asking the crowd about Jesus and when the narrative presents his inner awareness of the jealousy of Jesus's accusers, that initial hope may grow. Then what happens?

Rediscovering that first read is one way of reflecting on that sense of the text as something happening to the reader, who is never just a passive object.

Ways of Reading: Language

You may or may not have been spat at. You may or may not have particular views on spit. The focus of this section is on the language of the text and the personal nature of a reader's response to it.

One starter suggestion, away from the Gospel of Mark: just read a Bible story, a section of a Gospel, or a piece of Old Testament narrative, then close the Bible and give it thirty seconds, then jot down the words that stood out in that story, considering why, and what they mean to you.

Word Pools

The reader can consider what they regard as the three key words in a story they have read. If jotting notes that are restricted to three to five words, which would be selected? These need not be from the text—it is a good idea to avoid just having ones lifted from it. So the story of release of Barabbas by Pilate may net a word like "King," but may also net a word like "coercion"—which may not be in the text but may be encountered within the story. There is also the little used word in the text that still stands out for the reader. In this case, an example may be the word "realized."

One graphic way of gathering these is to draw a simple pond-shaped blob and gather the words inside it.

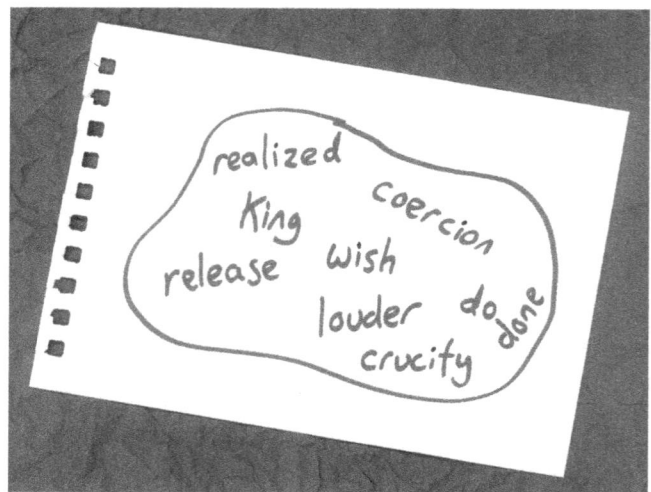

Having chosen three to five words the reader could then rank them in order of significance. Here again, this is not about whether they dominate the text so much as their impact on the reader.

Two questions that address the relationship between the reader and the language are: why have I chosen these? And what do they mean to me?

Find a Phrase

There are numerous activities that can be undertaken, that work with the particular strings of words used in a story. One first step is for the reader to just pay attention to one or two standout phrases—ideally one—from a particular story. The words can change on different readings, but in any one encounter a particular string of two or three words can provide a focus for reflection on a Bible story.

The search for such a small phrase can challenge the reader's sense of what is taking place. The phrase when Pilate "realized that" Jesus was being set up carries within it a concentrated moment that is crucial to the story and his character. Similarly, when it comes to the crucifixion, there is a reference in Mark 15:29 to "those who passed by." When picturing the cross readers often imagine it set apart with characters stood around, at its foot. In reality it was possibly on the road, in public view, to those passing by about their daily life. The idea of someone just passing by a roadside spectacle stands in juxtaposition with the significance of the cross, to readers of this story.

Verbs

Drawing on the excellent work of Anna Carter Florence the reader should take specific note of the verbs in a story and the way they offer a closeness to experience and narrow the distance that nouns can sometimes present. When relating to a story, words like "compelled" and "offered" may resonate with the reader's actual experience more than nouns like "cross" and "myrrh."

Two suggestions she makes amongst a host of other great ideas is to watch out for the order of the verbs, pointing out that Noah needed to build the ark before he brought the animals in, and the meaning-making that results from such an order.[42] Following such an order, the trial before Pilate begins with "Pilate asked," followed by an accusation from the chief priests; the crowd then asks for a prisoner to be released, and there is an answer from Pilate suggesting Jesus, and a stirring by the chief priests for Barabbas. Florence also suggests watching out for who gets which verbs, keeping an eye on which verbs get attached to a particular character. Again, the trial narrative presents some interesting insights into Pilate through his verbs and the way his asking and realizing unfold across the story.

Distance and Connection

Having read a story the reader can revisit the language by looking out for certain types of word in a biblical narrative. These can vary from person to person, and it can be interesting to explore these with a group. Some word types stand out as capturing something of our relationship with the text, illustrated below by examples from the story of Peter's denial:

- Words that stand out as ones in common use . . . but not very common (e.g., "denied," "courtyard")
- Words that stem from the particular context (e.g., "high priest," "Galilean")
- Words common to me but with a special emphasis here (e.g., "with," "out")

The particular context of words may merit some background research. Readers can also explore small, common words that make a big difference: a word like "the" in Mark 14:67, where the servant girl accuses Peter: "and you were with the Nazarene" (author translation)—that definite article is vital.

---

42. Florence, *Rehearsing Scripture*, 36.

My Words

The approach here, and throughout this book, sees interpretation as connected to the identity of the reader. Having undertaken activities such as the ones above, the reader can also consider a text and look for the words that have particular, personal resonance. Stand out words like "spat" (Mark 15:19) or "compelled" or "carry"(Mark 15:21) can connect to personal responses or formative experiences.

It could be words from a particular experience or just ones that evoke a strong feeling but the purpose is to locate that personal connection.

Ways of Reading: Gaps

This section explores the gaps in a text that the reader "fills in" including the horizontal bridging along its lines and the vertical ways those words mean what they mean within such lines. This relates directly to the previous section on "language" and also brings to light the reader's role in establishing the cohesion of a text.

Inference

Any act of reading involves inference. When the soldiers lead Jesus away and call together their "whole cohort" (Mark 15:16),[43] the reader brings their idea of how many that may have been. When he is clothed in a purple cloak the reader infers the reason why (Mark 15:17). The reader can take any story and look across it for the degree to which we, as readers, bring inferences to gaps, such as their idea of what a whole cohort gathering would have been like. This does not require research into ancient cohorts. It is more to do with the manner and behavior of the crowd, envisaged at that moment in the narrative, reflecting on an imagination that fills the gaps.

Holding Moments

So what does the reader imagine when "After mocking him, they stripped him of the purple cloak and put his own clothes on him. Then they led him out to crucify him" (Mark 15:20). The text is sparse and the event is huge.

---

43. France, *Mark*, 637, points out the term need not be taken to literally denote hundreds of soldiers.

When reading any narrative the reader can pause at one verse or one sentence and work through their response: how am I imagining this? What would this have been like? Taking one line or verse, the reader can look at the connections being made across the text, with the sense of who is doing what to whom, why they are doing it, and what effect it will have. Here again, the reader is finding and reflecting on the gaps we fill when we read.

Watch Pronouns

In the verse above from Mark 15:20, the reader connects "they" and "him" with the soldiers and Jesus, as they are the only group or individual currently within the narrative. It isn't always this straightforward. When the Leper is healed in Mark 1:45, Jesus instructs him to tell no one. The NRSV translation reads, "But he went out and began to proclaim it freely, and to spread the word, so that Jesus could no longer go into a town openly" (Mark 1:45a) but the actual Greek reads "he was no longer able." The assumption is being made that the "he" was Jesus—an assumption I would support. However, it could have been the Leper—give that reading a go.

The point of this reflection is to encourage the reader to watch the pronouns in a narrative, remembering the way each clause in a text has gaps the reader fills.

Ways of Reading and Responding

These activities are gathered together to reflect the holistic experience of reading. Any reflection on response should ideally range across all five areas of consideration. It should also be noted that this section subdivides what, in reality, the reader experiences as a whole.

To take the story of Jesus final hours as an example, a part like the darkness over the land (Mark 15:33) is one of those moments that casts a shadow over the whole story. As a happening in the story it changes it and, while it is hard to imagine a virginal reader of this story, the reader can still reflect on how it changes the course of the unfolding narrative. Language like 'darkness' will relate to particular readers in particular ways and it is the reader who will fill the gap as to why this is taking place and what it is like. With Jesus's final cry of "My God, my God, why have you forsaken me?" the story opens out with a cry that can be wandered through. The language of "forsaken," and the gaps the reader fills in response, come together at this point, and the particular story happens upon a turn that engages our language and gap-filling, as the centurion declares a part of the story that may take the reader a whole way back to the first chapter of the gospel: "Truly this man was the Son of God" (Mark 15:39 KJV).

3. READERS RESPONDING: READERS

Reader response approaches raise the question: "Who is the reader?"[44] A biblical text, like the Gospel of Mark, has a rhetorical orientation, pragmatically molding and shaping the reader such that Fowler posits the idea that the Gospel "is designed to construct its own reader."[45] So this final strand of literary theory, applied to stories of the Bible, focuses on the reader, including who they are and how they are shaped and constructed by the experience of reading. Such an exploration involves both the nature of readers in their diversity, coming to a text, but also the nature of reading, and what readers do. In the sections below this will be explored through looking at the identity of the reader, their experience of the wider world of texts, and the community in which they may be situated. Again, the activity here is well-described in Jonathan Culler's phrase: to grasp the meaning of a story we need to tell the story of the reading.[46]

The Reader's Engages

> Two people gazing at the night sky may both be looking at the same collection of stars, but one will see the image of a plough, and the other will make out a big dipper. The "stars" in a literary text are fixed; the lines that join them are variable.[47]

Returning to Wolfgang Iser's depiction of reading as akin to the lines that lead to constellations, however fixed the stars and individual the interpretation, it is possible for someone to say "I see a plough" while another sees a bear, but it is also possible for one to outline to the other how their dots configure. This may be a bit more akin to lying on grass describing pictures in the clouds, explaining which protrusion is a trunk and which is an ear. Similarly, our readings will imply responses that the text could evoke. These can be singular and feel clear; they can also offer scope for diverse responses that can be explained and considered. In the story of the empty tomb, in

44. Fowler, "Who Is 'The Reader.'"

45. Fowler, *Let the Reader*, 57.

46. "To speak of the meaning of a work is to tell a story of reading," Culler in Freund, *Return of the Reader*, 87.

47. Iser in Freund, *Return of the Reader*, 146.

Mark 16:1–8, it remains beautifully unclear why the women continued on their way to the tomb when they themselves recognized a dilemma: "They had been saying to one another 'Who will roll away the stone for us from the entrance to the tomb?'" (Mark 16:3).

Engagement involves the real reader bringing their identity and experience to the text, leading to their reading. That involves wondering why these women continue, and also entertaining possible reasons why. This approach should liberate readers. However, the way Bible reading is treated in some quarters can make it seem as if there is only one pure and correct reading—sometimes fobbed off as the one the author intended—and the job of reading is to acquire that and that without it the reading is wrong. Sadly, this just closes reading down. It restricts readers, as there is no way the reader can ever acquire the thoughts of the writer, so they are cowed by those who fake the assertion they have done just that. Alternatively, faced with the concept of the implied reader, another possibility presents itself: the reader can allow a story not to narrow down into one meaning, but instead entertain as many as they wish to explore. This involves the reader being open to various implied readings, trying them on and seeing what each offers. What if these women were faithfully remembering something of Jesus's promise to rise (Mark 9:31), or experiencing a despair that means they just keep walking? If no reading gets shut down, every reading is open, and you can try them on, one by one.

Similarly, at the close of the Gospel, the women have been told by the young man in the tomb:

> "But go, tell his disciples and Peter that he is going ahead of you to Galilee; there you will see him, just as he told you." So they went out and fled from the tomb, for terror and amazement had seized them; and they said nothing to anyone, for they were afraid. (Matt 16:7, 8)

The reader must decide whether these women failed in their task, or whether their silence didn't last, and the reader does not have to come down on one final answer. In reality, such a tension is what every reader is engaged in when encountering the biblical text. Engaging with one particular reading can be like trying on a reading and experiencing what that means for us, as readers—telling that story of reading.

The Reader's Changes

One of the joys of Maurice Sendak's *Where the Wild Things Are*[48] is the way in which, at the start, as Max charges around his home, there is a constrained and small image bordered by a large white border which dominates the page. As he enters the place where the Wild Things are this border slims and diminishes, as the pictures grow and almost draw the reader in, till by the time we join Max on the Wild Rumpus there is no border and no words, just the double-paged experience.

Stories don't just resonate with the reader. They draw the reader in. There is a sense in which, in any act of reading, we give ourselves over to what the text will do to us This can be even more the case when facing a biblical narrative, often read with a faithful connection to the text. In describing the Gospel of Mark, Fowler captures a feature the Gospel shares with much of the biblical text: "The narrative does not strive to convey meaning as referential content as much as it strives to achieve communion with its audience by means of a forceful event that takes place through time."[49]

Narrative taking force through time is a good description of John Dominic Crossan's approach to parables. Crossan demonstrates the way in which parables start with a framework of expectation that could present itself to a story. An example would be the assumption that a pharisee will be acceptable and a tax collector unacceptable[50] or a priest and Levite will help a man in need at a roadside, and a Samaritan will not.[51] Crossan demonstrates how, in a parable, such expectations are challenged and the story forges a different direction. This extends to the stories of the Gospel, with different and radical revolutions ringing their changes, such that the people who remove a roof or massively outnumber the food available experience such a parabolic crossover in what happens. It can also be seen in the way of the cross where the despair of Mark 15 brings the reader to Mark 16. Elsewhere in the Bible it is why the least remarkable of Jesse's sons will be anointed as king (1 Sam 16:1–13) or why the diminishing of Gideon's armies will end in victory (Judg 7:1–8). In approaching Bible stories, the reader is drawn into an upending of expectation.

Stories engage readers and change them. This power to effect such change is at work at the very close of the Gospel of Mark, and the women being sent with a charge that they don't carry out. One approach to this is

48. Sendak, *Where the Wild Things Are.*

49. Fowler, *Let the Reader*, 57.

50. Crossan, *Dark Interval*, 102.

51. Crossan, *Dark Interval*, 107.

to set it within the schema that has appeared elsewhere in the Gospel of the plan for the ministry of Jesus being put to followers who do not get it, such as when the disciples fail to grasp his teaching or plans. Van Oyen observes that this pattern always results in new teaching and a new way forward such that "failure is not the last word of the scheme."[52] In the instance at the empty tomb he suggests the instruction to the women and their response opens a "participatory function on the part of the readers" which Van Oyen describes: "The story demands to be continued, but since there is no continuation by and for the characters in the Gospel, only one person can continue it: the reader."[53]

The Reader Reflects

The process of reading also involves continual reflection on what we are reading. This is how the reader builds up that unity of the story they read and their story of a reading.

The urge to reread is natural in the Bible's shorter stories, particularly when the reader reflects on some of the twists and turns to be encountered within the space of a few verses. On a wider scale, the ending of Mark's Gospel sees the man at the empty tomb instructing the followers that Jesus "Is going ahead of you to Galilee; there you will see him, just as he told you" (Mark 16:7b). This can be seen as directing the readers, sending us back to Galilee, where the story began in chapter 1. Jesus comes from and returns to Galilee, and Van Oyen interprets in this instruction a call to the reader to reread the Gospel as an answer to the question: "Where can we meet Jesus? On the one hand, the readers are thus invited to reread the past (the early Jesus) and, on the other hand, to hope and find their bearings to the future."[54]

In biblical stories the process of reflection and revisiting can be a vital part of living with short stories. If a reader is inclined to read Bible stories regularly, this will inevitably lead to a revisiting of some. However, the reader changes as a person, and so has the opportunity to encounter each read with that renewed sense of personal response.

There is a story about Cardinal Timothy Dolan, the Archbishop of New York, who, while on a Jesuit retreat, was invited to pray imaginatively—a practice common within Ignatian spirituality. Cardinal Dolan undertook just such an imaginative piece of reflection with the story of Christ's birth. He imagined himself into the stable, but then he had a surprise. In

52. Van Oyen, *Mark as a Novel*, 134.
53. Van Oyen, *Mark as a Novel*, 134.
54. Van Oyen, *Mark as a Novel*, 133.

his imaginative prayer, and to his surprise, Mary handed him the baby. He found himself cradling Jesus, an experience that changed his reading of a narrative he had read many times before.[55]

The Reader's Community

As readers, we always have a community around us that shapes our responses. Where the Bible is concerned this can be a sense of our fellow readers, or it can be an actual grouping, such as a church or class. Whatever form it may take, that sense of community shapes the reader's response.

The community is essential in shaping reader response. One of the challenges that can be and often is presented to Stanley Fish's approach is the way it remains too open to diverse and peculiar readings. Fish himself raises the question, if reading is a matter of personal response, "Why should two or more readers ever agree?"[56] The answer is to be found in the reading community. This can be an actual, real group or more of a sense of how others read. In this context, the community is also those who taught us to read. Such communities, whether physically present or not, are with readers as they read, and such communities create the context that leads to shared reading practices.

What is to stop a reader reading the words "He is going ahead of you" (Mark 16: 7) as meaning that Jesus is taking up ballroom dancing? Using a similarly absurd reading of a poem, Crosman posits this same question: what is to stop such eccentric interpretations? Suppose someone reads it that way? Is there anything in the text to prevent this? His answer is that there isn't, but faced with such readings, Crosman suggests the task would be to ask the reader to offer up the context and thinking that led to their interpretation.[57] He's presenting a community and a conversation. In this way, a more reader-orientated approach could be seen as healthier and more open, because ultimately it lands in community and in the authority that arises from sharing readings. As Fish reassures, "An infinite plurality would be a fear only if sentences existed in a state in which they were not already embedded."[58] For Fish, the bed is the interpretative community.

55. Martin, "Gift of Imagination."
56. Fish, *Is There a Text*, 171.
57. Crosman, "Do Readers Make Meaning?," 153.
58. Fish, *Is There a Text*, 307.

What Community?

So, who is in this community? The reader may want to give some thought to their reading community and make an assessment as to who influences their reading and experience of the Bible. Note again, the community referred to isn't necessarily a specific bunch of people but rather a feature of reading. It's the sense of those around us influencing the way we read and the sense we make of the text. As such, the reader could ask, is it a community that constrains the reader or one that leads to flourishing? When Fish uses the term, he does not refer to a gathering of like-minded interpreters, but rather a sharing of interpretative strategies.[59] When reading of the empty tomb there are those who will have certain boundaries on interpretations that may be down to their belief in the accuracy of Bible stories and the historical resurrection of Christ, and there are others who will be quite at ease with the idea the story is not literal and there was no physical body gone to Galilee.[60] Both types of reader can and should read the story as it is. Each will be differently shaped in the potential they have to interpret the text, and such shaping comes from community. It should always be possible to challenge those communities, and any community that unduly constrains a reading or understanding of the text is not so much an interpretative community as a constraint which a reader may or may not respect and welcome, but which they may want to consider.

Ways of Reading: Readers

This is another section with a slight variation, again gathering all the suggestions in one place for the same reason—the experience of reading and being a reader is a holistic one that relates to all these aspects. Here again, the activities in the book thus far are all about the reader taking note of their own reading. This section focuses on that reader.

Ways of Reading: The Reader Engages

The focus here is on the reader who engages with texts, asking the question "Who is the reader?"

59. Fish, *Is There a Text*, 171.
60. See the discussion in Wright and Borg, *Meaning of Jesus*.

Your Story of a Reader

One way in which a reader can reflect on the experience of reading involves mapping it over time. Such a map can be a general one, recalling the experience of learning to read and being introduced to the texts this skill has opened. It then also has a specific edge of narrating the experience of reading and engaging with the Bible. For some readers this will have changed over time—many people on a journey within Christian faith shift in their approach and attitude towards the Bible.

The activity can be done in note form or as a written activity or just doodling and scribbling, but one way to do this is to take a strip of paper and fold it in half and then quarters and, at one end, write the year in which you first recall reading or being read to and at the other, the current year.

The next step is to calculate the stages at half way and at the quarter marks, and jot on any notes that spring to mind as you do this.

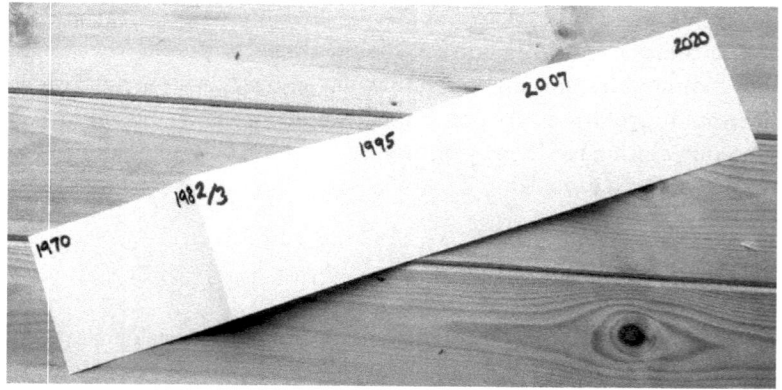

This is now a timeline and the reader can populate it in two ways. Firstly, recalling moments of significant experience with the Bible. For me this would include a teenage experience of encountering the Gospels, and reading Matthew 5 and the Sermon on the Mount for the first time and being bowled over by those words.

The second approach is to then note gaps and ask what my experience or opinion of the Bible was at those times. What, if any, was my experience of the Bible in my mid-twenties? Through reflections like these the timeline becomes populated.

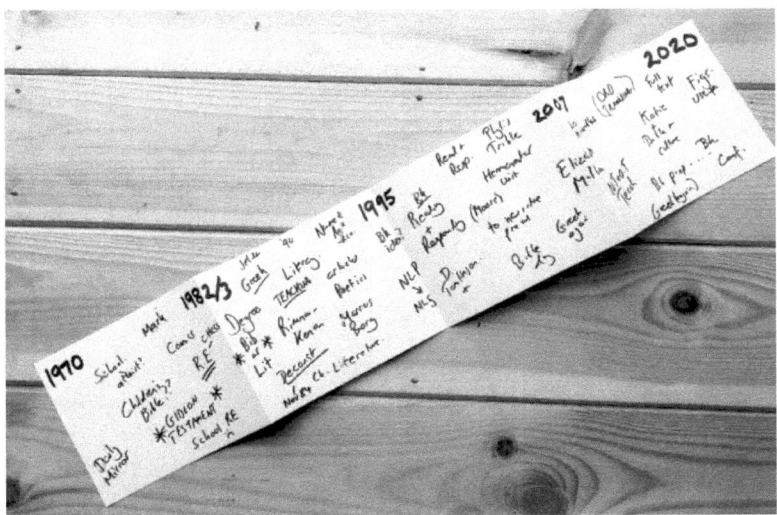

As with all such activity, there is no need to be bound by rules. An alternative is to take the start as the first time the reader seriously read the Bible and map onwards from there. Depending on the age of that encounter the two lines may differ radically. The purpose of the exercise is to reflect on yourself as a reader.

Another Reader

Many years ago there was a British television series for children called *Mr. Benn* featuring a character who would visit a costume shop, and choose a costume such as a cowboy outfit or a magician's outfit. Having donned the garb he would then open another door in the changing room and find himself in a world suited to the costume, whether the wild west or a fantasy land. It was a great back-to-front approach, in which the world entered was suited to the costume, rather than living vice versa.

   For the reader of the Bible there is the potential to engage with a different persona as a way of engaging with one's own reading. On encountering a story the reader can imagine how it would be read through the lenses of another reader. This isn't about happening on an alternative approach. The activity here is to deliberately, and sometimes contrarily, consider an alternative reading to a common one or the readers personal interpretation thus far. The reader may even be fortunate enough to be able to actually engage with someone reading from a radically different perspective. Sam

Wells presents one striking example of how different a story that is taken for granted can be when read from a different perspective:

> When you're reading the story of the Exodus, it's a different story if you read it with an Egyptian Christian sitting next to you. Because we just loosely talk about how . . . the Red Sea closed over the Egyptians, and they were all slain and we think "Wonderful God" and well done Moses and Miriam led the dancing. But what if you've got an Egyptian Christian who hears the word "Egyptian" and sees their being crushed as being the price of God's people being free?[61]

Readers will often be reading alone or without representation from the sort of diverse insights Wells highlights to hand, but the principle is a good one offering a nudge to read with a sense of alternative insights. Throughout, the reader is reflecting on how this alternative reading informs and influences their own, in a way that can challenge and inform.

Ways of Reading: The Reader Changes

Stories aren't just looked over. There is an active engagement that changes the reader. Appreciation of the reader's response to stories involves exploring such changes.

Stories that Change

The playful reading of a Bible story should be free from any forced application. However, it would be misguided to ignore the way in which these stories inspire change. The reader should ask of a story, what change might this story make? Care should be taken to note that this is not about imitating what particular characters in stories do. It's about the reader bringing realities of life that they carry as a reader and simply asking the question: what change could this prompt, nudge, suggest, or inspire?

As readers we don't need to be stood outside a Roman trial or find a friend's tomb empty to find something of ourselves in a Bible story. As was noted above, we may share the verbs of a story without its nouns. The same goes for the emotions.

As ever, some form of scribbling can enable us to discover something of ourselves in the text. Exploring this idea, the reader can use a piece of paper folded in half, with the emotions encountered in the story jotted on one side.

61. Wells, "Improvising Faith," 48:16–52.

On the other, it is up to you. The reader can jot notes of any personal memories or experiences that resonate with the emotions on the left. One necessary caution is not to feel to drawn to holy words. While the story of Peter's denial may be a story that can challenge faith and prompt bolder witness, it can also be a story that just speaks to fear and that sense of being caught in a system and a moment where speaking out would be just too hard.

Overturning Expectations

Our problem as modern readers is that we often know the story we are reading but that need not stop readers exploring the overturning of expectations in stories such as the parables and stories such as the resurrection and tracking some of the expectations that are overturned by them, simply using Crossan's criss-cross pattern.

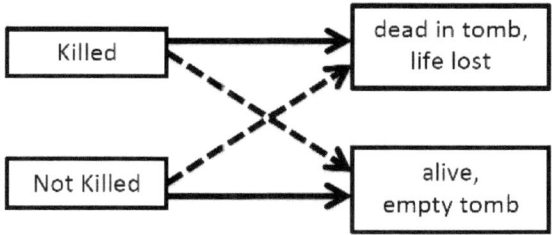

The resurrection story opens with the experience of the women and their expectation, but also reverberates back to Jesus teaching about life, earlier in the Gospel: "For those who want to save their life will lose it, and those who lose their life for my sake, and for the sake of the gospel, will save it" (Mark 8:35).

One example Crossan cites[52] is Jesus's table fellowship which, in an adapted version of his diagram, would see us depicting such stories as Jesus's meal with Levi (Mark 2:15–17) in diagram:

---

62. Crossan, *Dark Interval*, 92.

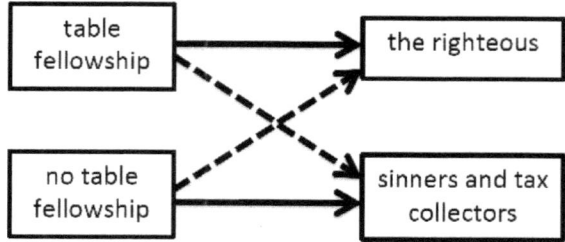

The reader may want to consider this crossing over in relation to the story of the anointing at Bethany (Mark 14:3–9). Looking across the unexpected occurrences of the Bible there is also the crossing of the Red Sea in the book of Exodus:

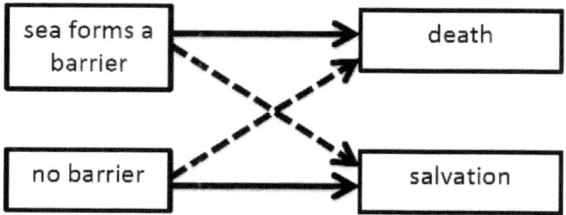

Crossan's simple criss-cross demonstrates ways in which the tracking of the norm and the expectation brings home the inversion of normality in the outcomes of the stories. As with all such strategies, the game's afoot for the reader to explore the overturning of expectation in their own reading.

Ways of Reading: The Reader Reflects

The worst thing readers can do is smother a story with overthinking. However, Bible stories do leave themselves open to revisiting and reflecting.

Imaginative Reading

The story of Cardinal Dolan, above, opens the reader to the Ignatian Exercise of imagining oneself into a story. In his *Spiritual Exercises*, Ignatius encourages this with the scene at the birth of Christ. The reader reads the text a few times and then closes their eyes and imagines the scene, including what they see and hear. There are also smells and senses to evoke, including how hot or cold the scene is, or what tension may be felt in this context.

The reader can then watch a significant character—often Jesus in a Gospel story—and follow them in their words, gestures, and actions. This is not an activity designed to factfind or gather points of interest: the emphasis is on the reader's experience of the story and immersion in it.

All of Me

How does all of me affect my reading of a story? A reader can read a story and then isolate, among everything else they know, five things about themselves that influence their response to a story. The reader's task here is to come up with the real experiences and opinions we hold that will shape our reading. One simple way of nudging us to respond is to aim for five things in and about ourselves that shape a personal response that may differ from that of others. Personally speaking, I can understand hearing that news at the empty tomb and wondering if I'd got it wrong, or this was all nonsense—but that's a Thomas for you. There is something about a set of five that restricts us to selectivity while also prompting us to think of a good few responses, so the reader can list off on the fingers of a hand five things they think, believe, or know that influence their response to this story.

Ways of Reading: The Reader's Community

As was mentioned above, the reader should take note of their community and how they shape the text. There is a whole other book to be written on how readers can work in community to share the reading of stories, but two standout suggestions are worth considering here. These activities here provide two simple ways of playing with Bible stories in a community.

Along the Line

Exploring a story, a group of readers can agree on a line that can be drawn from one extreme to another. In the denial story one extreme could be "Peter's actions were understandable and fine" and at the other "Peter did an unforgiveable thing." Alternatively, at the resurrection they could consider extremes prompted by the women and their response to their instructions. The line can then be physically created in a room with one extreme at one end and the other extreme at another. There are various ways readers can allocate places along the line. One way is to randomly stand at distances along the line and consider the position adopted. Faced with extremes of response to the resurrection story, between "The women in the story should have done as they were told" and "The response of the women was okay" the reader stood at either extreme has a clear position, but what about someone a third of the way along the line?

Another approach is for readers to simply stand where their personal view takes them. This may differ from where they would like to think they would stand. It may reflect a gut reaction or an understanding of tensions in the story. The main reason for this activity is to encourage those participating to talk to each other up and down the line about "Why I am here and not where you are?" with the resultant opportunity to share differing stances in response to a story.

Sharing and Connecting

This is an activity focused on gathering and sharing responses and then connecting them. It is adapted from the "tell me" approach of children's author and teacher Aiden Chambers.[63] Chambers describes his approach as "a way of asking particular kinds of questions." He worked with teachers in drawing out children's responses to texts, banning "Why?" questions, such as "Why did you like this book?" His questions adapted for biblical readings are as follows:

- What struck you about the story?
- What made you feel negative, or angry, or upset?
- Was there anything that puzzled you?
- Were there any patterns—any connections—that you noticed?

That last question would involve the reader identifying anything perceived as a pattern or a structure, such as the three different denials in Peter's story or the connection the person in the empty tomb makes with other locations and characters.

The idea is that a group face a long flipchart with these questions at the top and, working through them one at a time, offer a few words or phrases as responses to the question.

---

63. Chambers, *Tell Me*.

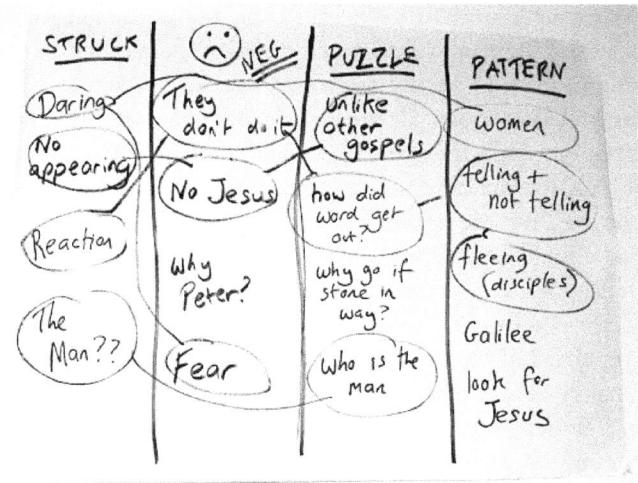

Once this is complete, the group then identifies topics or references that appear in more than one column and draw lines between these.

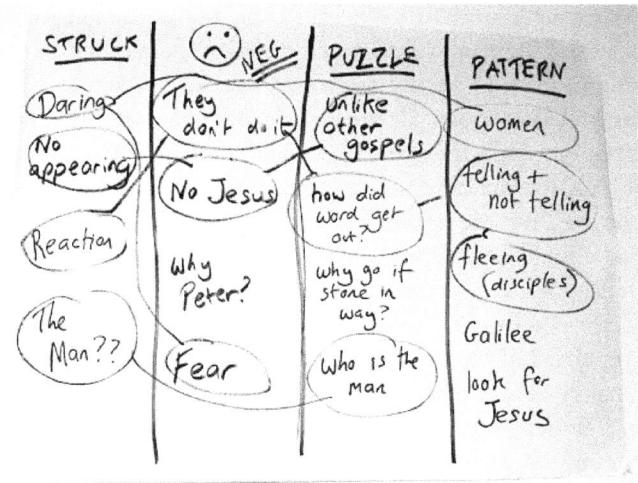

This then leads to a collective dive into the story, as Chambers suggests that the item with the most lines joining it is a topic that can be put to discussion. One starting point could be: why did this one get so many lines? What might this tell us about the story?

Intertextuality

Our culture is riddled with references across works, with one text referencing another. When E. T. goes out at Halloween he passes a child dressed up as Yoda, from the *Star Wars* films. It's a nice reference that was followed by George Lucas putting E. T.-like characters in a small snippet of *The Phantom Menace*.[64] David Fincher's *Fight Club* has a dig at consumer culture and, apparently, there is a Starbucks cup in every scene of the film.[65] An image of Mickey Mouse appears in some way in most Disney films. As readers, our approach to texts is described by Barthes: "*I read the text* . . . This 'I' which approaches the text is already itself a plurality of other texts."[66]

The term *intertextuality* was coined by Julia Kristeva to describe the way in which a text is not a static object but dynamic and related to a world of other diverse and different texts.[67] It denotes "the multiple ways in which one text echoes, rewrites, or is otherwise intertwined with other texts."[68] This can involve clear and specific links, such as the connection between the crowd thinking Jesus is calling for Elijah from the cross (Mark 15:35) and the character of Elijah in the Old Testament. There is also a view of intertextuality, captured by Barthes in the quote above—that all texts are, by their very nature, intertexts, because they use the language shared with all other texts.[69] Both approaches to the idea of sharing between texts have something to offer, as texts share both the clarity of some of the specific instances while also sharing language and ideas that are universal.

At the more specific and limited end there are various taxonomies of examples but, for biblical examples, three of the main ones readers will encounter in the Bible are citations, allusions, and echoes.[70]

A citation is where a specific text is referenced, usually an Old Testament text cited in the New, such as when the Gospel opens with the quote from Isaiah: "As it is written in the prophet Isaiah, 'See, I am sending my messenger ahead of you, who will prepare your way'" (Mark 1:2).

Allusion occurs when a few words are used that connect with another text. Brown notes the connection between Jesus's accusation that the authorities of the day have turned the temple into "a den of robbers" and

---

64. R2D2 and C3P0 also appear in hieroglyphs in Lucas and Spielberg's *Raiders of the Lost Ark*.

65. Furn, "Easter Eggs."

66. Barthes, *S/Z*, 10.

67. Martínez Alfaro, "Intertextuality."

68. Moore, *Poststructuralism*, 130.

69. Moraru, "Intertextuality," 259.

70. Hays, *Echoes*; see also Brown, *Gospels*, 116–21.

Jeremiah 7, in which the word of the Lord condemns the people for their abominations and warns against the false security they gain from having "the Temple of the Lord" (Jer. 7:4) only to then ask, "Has this house, which is called by my name, become a den of robbers in your sight?" (Jer. 7:11a).

A specific allusion is made whenever the title "Son of God" is used in the Gospel, which may be alluding to references to the king in Psalm 2:7 and Israel in Deuteronomy 14:1. When moving from citation to allusion, the task falls upon readers to identify the allusion and consider the links that may be evoked by such language. Terms like "Son of God" and "Son of Man" are subjects of entire works in themselves, all chasing a sometimes-elusive allusive.

An echo is heard whenever the reader of one text has a sense of the evocation of another text. Hays gives the example of Barack Obama's 2008 victory speech referencing imagery used in speeches of Martin Luther King.[71] Echoes, by their very nature, are subjective and require the reader to make the connection. An example of this could be the way the feeding miracles of Mark's Gospel echo the provision of manna from God to the people, when they were led by Moses. However, unlike the Gospel of John, where the feeding miracle follows directly on from Jesus claiming that Moses bore witness to him (John 6:32), there is no such reference in Mark, so it is up to the reader to detect those things that echo across the narratives. Like Moses feeding, the story takes place in a wilderness. There is also a reference to the people being like sheep without a shepherd (Mark 6:24)—a possible allusion to Moses description of the people (Num 27:17). Equally the reader may make a link between this story and other miraculous feeding stories in the Bible, involving Elijah (1 Kgs 17:15–16) and Elisha (2 Kgs 4:43–44). Such echoing is both ambiguous, but also liberating. The ball is coming back to the reader's court if the reader detects an echo, then an echo has occurred.

This more open approach to intertextuality allows the story to resonate, not just with clear and tied citation or allusion, but also with personal experience of other texts and of life itself. The story begs the question, what experiences the reader brings from other reading that are even remotely akin to that turnaround of scarcity to provision depicted in such a tale of miraculous feeding. Some readers hear in the feeding miracles echoes of the Eucharist, with the breaking and giving allusion shared across the stories of the miracle and the Last Supper (Mark 6:41; 14:22).

Unlike allusions and citations which are more specific and tied down, echoes are often open to the experience of the reader. While the reader does

71. Hays, *Echoes*, 12.

not require a course in Old Testament narrative to read the Gospel story, familiarity with its stories can provide enriching resonances when reading the Gospels. The reader may also sense the echo of stories beyond the biblical text. The miraculous feedings can echo with stories such as such as *Babette's Feast* or the old story of Stone Soup.

The Soup Stone

There is an old folk tale, of which there are many variants. In the version I know, the inhabitants of a poor village gather together because they are facing starvation as food supplies have dwindled to nothing. The wise old rabbi admits that, for years, he has been keeping secret a soup stone that will make one large cauldron of soup. If they boil a huge pot of water, he will drop the stone in and it will make a nourishing soup for all. The villagers boil a massive pot of water and their rabbi steps forward, unwraps his precious stone and drops it into the pot. One woman is so touched by this action that she rushes home and finds some cabbage leaves she has been hiding and brings them, and adds them to flavor the soup. Another villager sees her doing this, and so dashes out and returns with a slightly mangled but edible turnip. Someone does the same with some carrots they have been hoarding and then, lo and behold, some more cabbage is found by another. In time everyone adds something till the meal is ready, with more than enough.

Then, just before they all eat and are satisfied, the rabbi grabs the ladle and says "Hang on! First I must remove that old pebble I chucked in!"

In literature, there are also intertextual echoes that simply spring from the way stories work. Escape stories will echo each other, as will disaster movies and spy thrillers, as will stories of the miraculous provision of food to hungry people. The resurrection stories of the Gospel resemble Aslan in *The Lion, the Witch and the Wardrobe*, but there are also echoes in the stories of *E. T.* and Harry Potter. To what extent such echoes were devised by the real author may be of interest in literary history; for readers of the Gospel it's about being open to the potential for intertextual echoes to illuminate reading.

One example of a reading that illuminates two stories would be the echoing Malbon describes in the story of the anointing (Mark 14:3–9) and the widow's offering (Mark 12:41–44),[72] sharing, as these women do, a contrast between themselves and the men around them. They also share generosity, with the giving of all the widow had and the anointing with an

72. Malbon, *Mark's Jesus*, 226.

ointment that would cost a year's wages. There is also a shared connection to sacrifice as the widow gives her all, and Jesus is anointed as he approaches his giving up of his life. Malbon also observes the symmetry is broken as Judas hands over Jesus for money, whereas the widow handed over her money as an offering.[73] Intertextuality can also be a matter of what is not shared between stories, when so much else is.

Beyond the Bible, art galleries are full of intertextual depictions of Bible stories. There are also interesting uses of biblical themes or scenes in a different text, whether that be the way artists, comedians, or cartoonists use tropes from a story. Read well, these texts can reflect back on the stories they reference.[74]

Two final intertextual points. Firstly, faced with an example like a reference to a verse elsewhere in the Bible or an echo in one story of another, the reader may reflect on what impact that intertextual reference is having. Is it connecting old story with new and somehow validating the latter with the former? Or is it evoking the former within the latter? There may be historic reasons for this.[75] It is worth bearing in mind the distinction between intertextual connections that offer some insight into words used in a text and ones where the connection is more thematic and illuminating of the story. The cry from the cross of words from Psalm 22 needs an explanation, offered in the text itself, but it is also open to what the reader makes of a reading of that Psalm as part of their encounter with the crucifixion story.

Secondly, when it comes to a Gospel, one obvious intertextual connection will be with the other three. It's up to the reader to what extent a reading of a story such as the resurrection requires referencing of the other gospel accounts. For some readers this will be essential and driven by faith conviction. I would just nudge the reader in the direction of not always rushing off to parallel accounts. Try also reading like the early church that just heard the Gospel of Mark and experiencing that resurrection story with an ending that echoes out to us in a way that is distinct from any other.

Ways of Reading: Intertextuality

In a way this section is one of the most open in the whole book. The idea that a story, as a text, forms a web of meaning with other texts, opens every story to an array of texts and cultural reference. This is a section in which

73. Malbon, *Mark's Jesus*, 226.
74. Thomas, "The Mote in Thine Eye."
75. Brown, *Scripture as Communication*, 227–28.

readers could devise their own activity, forming their own webs of meaning, alongside the suggestions below.

Comparing and Contrasting Stories

Alongside following up citations and allusions there are echoes shared between Bible stories, and the reader can look at two stories side by side and consider, for example, the echoing of Hannah's story (1 Sam 1–2) in that of Mary (Luke 1). However, the breadth of approach to intertextuality taken here raises the question about echoes between Hannah's or Mary's story and that of Peter at the denial or the women at the empty tomb. Randomly placing two Bible stories side by side can provide an intertextual adventure. Those faced with lectionary readings in churches that allocate readings alongside each other may encounter this joy more regularly than others. Bear in mind, this is about echoes, so faint traces of the dilemma Hannah and her husband face may resonate with any New Testament story. The question this poses is, what is the echo we're hearing?

Cultural References

Any Bible reader will also, hopefully, enjoy a wide cultural experience. The enjoyment of intertextuality lies in playfully holding cultural experiences alongside the Bible's stories, and vice versa. It shouldn't spoil a trip to the theater to identify within a play's tension the intertextual echoes of a biblical story, particularly those that become a focus for ongoing reading and response. Just like Moses had to flee because he kills an Egyptian, Simba of *The Lion King* flees the Pride Lands after believing he is responsible for his father's death.[76]

You start seeing the Bible everywhere.

76. Thomas, "The Mote in Thine Eye."

Conclusion

"He is going ahead of you to Galilee; there you will see him, just as he told you" (Mark 16:7).

Those words form the conclusion to the way of one story, and offer a signpost to readers of that Gospel. Likewise, though this book is primarily about all stories, the following of the way of that particular Gospel story leads to a similar conclusion. Off you go. Bible stories are open to readings that consider events, trace a plot, encounter characters, and step into settings. There is also an experience of reading narratives and responding to them, but this book is also an encouragement to enjoy them by working with them, engaging in a personal reading that wanders over boundaries and allows questions that may remain open.

The conclusion is to go back to the start of any story, choosing which one you choose from all the Bible has to offer, reading in the way stories work, because the way is never-ending, and there is more to be done.

I did say you'd be doing all the work.

Bibliography

Alter, Robert. *The Art of Biblical Narrative*. New York: Basic Books, 1981.

Amit, Yairah. *Reading Biblical Narratives*. Minneapolis: Fortress, 2001.

Atkinson, Rowan. "The Wedding c. The Father of the Bride." Track 6 on side 1 of *Live in Belfast*. Recorded September 19–20, 1980. Arista, 1980, vinyl.

Auerbach, Erich. *Mimesis*. Princeton: Princeton University Press, 1953.

Baines, Nick. "Seeing Through the Eyes of Others." *Nick Baines's Blog* (blog), January 13, 2010. https://nickbaines.wordpress.com/2010/01/13/seeing-through-the-eyes-of-others/.

Bal, Mielke. *Introduction to the Theory of Narrative*. Toronto: University of Toronto Press, 1988.

Bar-Efrat, Shimon. *Narrative Art in the Bible*. Sheffield: Almond, 1989.

Barthes, Roland. "The Death of the Author." In *Image, Music, Text*, 142–48. London: HarperCollins, 1977.

———. "Introduction to the Structural Analysis of Narratives." In *Image, Music, Text*, 79–124. London: HarperCollins, 1977.

———. *S/Z: An Essay*. Oxford: Blackwell, 1990.

Barton, John. *Reading the Old Testament*. London: Darton, Longman & Todd, 1984.

Bell, John. *Present on Earth*. Glasgow: WGRG, 2002.

Berlin, Adele. *Poetics and Interpretation of Biblical Narrative*. Almond: Sheffield, 1983.

Bettleheim, Bruno. *The Uses of Enchantment*. Harmondsworth: Peregrine, 1978.

Black, Clifton. *Mark*. Nashville: Abingdon, 2011.

Blevins, Kent. *How to Read the Bible Without Losing Your Mind*. Eugene, OR: Wipf & Stock, 2014.

Booker, Christopher. *The Seven Basic Plots: Why We Tell Stories*. London: Bloomsbury, 2005.

Boomershine, Thomas E. *Story Journey*. Nashville: Abingdon, 1988.

Booth, Wayne C. *The Rhetoric of Fiction*. Chicago: University of Chicago, 1961.

Borg, Marcus. *Jesus, a New Vision*. London: SPCK, 1993.

———. *Reading the Bible Again for the First Time: Taking the Bible Seriously but Not Literally*. New York: Bravo, 2002.

Boswell, James. *The Life of Samuel Johnson*. London: n.p., 1817.

Bremond, Claude. "The Logic of Narrative Possibilities." In *Narratology*, edited by Susan Onega and Jose Angel Garcia Landa, 61–75. Longman Critical Readers. London: Longman, 1996.

Brown, Jeannine K. *The Gospels as Stories*. Grand Rapids, MI: Baker, 2020.

——. *Scripture as Communication: Introducing Biblical Hermeneutics*. Grand Rapids, MI: Baker, 2007.

Brueggemann, Walter. *The Bible and the Postmodern Imagination*. London: SCM, 1993.

——. *The Land*. 2nd ed. Philadelphia: Fortress, 2002.

Burridge, Richard A. *Four Gospels, One Jesus*. 2nd ed. London: SPCK, 2005.

Burridge, Richard A., and Graham Gould. *Jesus, Now and Then*. London: SPCK, 2004.

Cardenal, Ernesto. *The Gospel in Solentiname*. Eugene, OR: Wipf & Stock, 2020.

Carson, D. A. "Matthew." In *The Expositor's Bible Commentary with the New International Version of the Holy Bible: Matthew, Mark, Luke*, 8:3–599. Grand Rapids, MI: Zondervan, 1984.

Carter, Warren. *John: Storyteller, Evangelist, Interpreter*. Peabody, MA: Hendrickson, 2006.

Cave, Kathryn, and Chris Riddell. *Something Else*. London: Puffin, 1994.

Chambers, Aidan. *Tell Me: Children, Reading and Talk*. Stroud: Thimble, 1993.

Chatman, Seymour. *Story and Discourse: Narrative Structure in Fiction and Film*. Ithaca: Cornell, 1978.

Clines, David J. A. "The Ancestor in Danger: But Not the Same Danger." In *What Does Eve Do to Help? and Other Readerly Questions to the Old Testament*, by David J. A. Clines, 67–84. Sheffield: JSOT, 1990.

——. "Story and Poem: The Old Testament as Literature and as Scripture." *Interpretation* 34 (1980) 115–27.

Cohan, Steven and Linda M. Shires. *Telling Stories: A Theoretical Analysis of Narrative Fiction*. London: Routledge, 1988.

Cooke, Sam. "Touch the Hem of His Garment." Track 1 on *The Man and His Music*. RCA Records, 1986, compact disc.

Craffert, Pieter F. *The Life of a Galilean Shaman: Jesus of Nazareth in Anthropological-Historical Perspective*. Cambridge: Clarke, 2008.

Cranfield, C. E. B. *St. Mark*. Cambridge: Cambridge University Press, 1959.

Crosman, Robert. "Do Readers Make Meaning?" In *The Reader in the Text: Essays in Audience and Interpretation*, edited by Susan Suleiman and R. Inge Crosman, 149–64. Princeton: Princeton University Press.

Crossan, John Dominic. *The Dark Interval: Towards a Theology of Story*. Allen, TX: Argus, 1975.

Culler, Jonathan. *The Pursuit of Signs: Semiotics, Literature, Deconstruction*. London: Routledge, 1981.

——. *Structuralist Poetics. Structuralism3 Linguistics and the Study of Literature*. London: Routledge, 1975.

Culpepper, R. Alan. *Anatomy of the Fourth Gospel*. Philadelphia: Fortress, 1983.

Dahl, Roald. *James and the Giant Peach*. London: Puffin 2007.

——. *The Witches*. London: Puffin, 1983.

Dannenberg, Hilary P. "Plot." In *Routledge Encyclopedia of Narrative Theory*, edited by David Herman et al., 435–39. London: Routledge, 2005.

Dickens, Charles. *Bleak House*. London: Penguin, 1971.

——. *A Christmas Carol*. London: Puffin, 1984.

——. *David Copperfield*. London: Penguin, 1996.

——. *Great Expectations*. Ware: Wordsworth, 1992.

DioceseofSheffield. "The Bishop of Sheffield's Annual Lecture 2019 - Bishop Pete Wilcox." *YouTube*, March 19, 2019. https://www.youtube.com/watch?v=_6Mq5j8xZ88.

Donahue, John R., and Daniel J. Harrington. *The Gospel of Mark*. Collegeville: Liturgical, 2002.

Eco, Umberto. "The Author and His Interpreters." *Umberto Eco Readers* (blog), Novmeber 18, 2007. http://umbertoecoreaders.blogspot.com/2007/11/author-and-his-interpreters.html.

———. *The Role of the Reader: Explorations in the Semiotics of Texts*. London: Hutchinson, 1979.

———. *Six Walks in Fictional Woods*. Cambridge, MA: Harvard University Press, 1994.

Edwards, James R. "Markan Sandwiches: the Significance of Interpolations in Markan Narratives." *Novum Testamentum* 31 (1989) 193–216.

Edwards, Ruth. *Discovering John*. London: SPCK, 2003.

Enns, Peter. *How the Bible Actually Works*. London: Hodder & Stoughton, 2019.

Fish, Stanley. "Interpreting the 'Variorum.'" *Critical Inquiry* 2.3 (1976) 465–85.

———. *Is There a Text in This Class? The Authority of Interpretive Communities*. Cambridge: Harvard, 1980.

———. "Why No One's Afraid of Wolfgang Iser." *Diacritics* 11.1 (1981) 2–13.

Florence, Anna Carter. *Rehearsing Scripture*. London: Canterbury, 2018.

Forster, E. M. *Aspects of the Novel*. London: Penguin, 1927.

Fowler, Robert. *Let the Reader Understand*. Harrisburg: Trinity, 1996.

———. "Who Is 'The Reader' in Reader Response Criticism?" *Semeia* 31 (1985) 5–23.

France, R. T. *The Gospel of Mark: A Commentary on the Greek Text*. Grand Rapids: Eerdmans, 2002.

Freund, Elizabeth. *The Return of the Reader: Reader Response Criticism*. London: Methuen, 1987.

Funk, Robert W. *The Poetics of Biblical Narrative*. Sonoma, CA: Polebridge, 1988.

Furn, Daniel. "16 of the Best Movie Easter Eggs." *Radio Times*, August 4, 2020. https://www.radiotimes.com/tv/sci-fi/best-movie-easter-eggs/.

Genette, Gerard. *Narrative Discourse*. Ithaca, NY: Cornell University Press, 1980.

Goldingay, John. "Biblical Narrative and Systematic Theology." In *Between Two Horizons: Spanning New Testament Studies and Systematic Theology*, edited by Joel B. Green and Max Turner, 123–42. Grand Rapids: Eerdmans, 2000.

Good, Edwin. *Irony in the Old Testament*. Philadelphia, PA: Westminster, 1965.

Goodacre, Mark. "Did Jesus Have a House in Capernaum?" *NT Blog* (blog), March 2, 2006. https://ntweblog blogspot.com/2006/03/did-jesus-have-house-in-capernaum.html.

Gooder, Paula. *Searching for Meaning: and Introduction to Interpreting the New Testament*. London: SPCK, 2008.

Greenstein, Edward. *Essays on Biblical Method and Translation*. Providence, RI: Brown Judaic Studies, 1989.

Greimas, A. J. *Structural Semantics an Attempt at Method*. Lincoln: University of Nebraska Press, 1983.

Gros Louis, Kenneth R. R. "The Song of Songs." In *Literary Interpretations of Biblical Narratives*, edited by Kenneth R. R. Gros Louis and James Ackerman, 2:243–58. Nashville: Abingdon, 1982.

Guellich, Robert. *Mark 1—8:26*. Vol. 34A of *Word Biblical Commentary*. Nashville: Nelson, 1989.

Gunn, David M. *The Fate of King Saul*. Sheffield: Continuum, 1980.

Hays, Richard B. *Echoes of Scripture in the Gospels*. Waco: Baylor University Press, 2016.

Holland, Norman. "Unity Identity Text Self." In *Reader-Response Criticism: from Formalism to Post-Structuralism*, edited by Jane P. Tompkins, 118–33. Baltimore: John Hopkins University Press, 1980.

Horsley, R. *Hearing the Whole Story: The Politics of Plot in Mark's Gospel*. Louisville: Westminster, 2001.

Howker, Janni. "A Plot of My Own." *Times Education Supplement*, April 7, 1997. https://www.tes.com/news/plot-my-own-0#.

Hughes, Shirley. *Alfie Gets in First*. London: Bodley Head, 1981.

Iser, Wolfgang. *The Act of Reading: A Theory of Aesthetic Response*. Baltimore: John Hopkins, 1978.

———. *The Implied Reader*. Baltimore: Johns Hopkins University Press, 1978.

———. "Talk Like Whales." *Diacritics* 11 (1981) 82–87.

Jennings, Paul. "The Busker." In *Unreal*, 53–80. London: Puffin, 1995.

Johnson, Bradley T. *The Form and Function of Mark 1:1–15: A Multi-Disciplinary Approach to the Markan Prologue*. Eugene, OR: Pickwick, 2017.

Kazmierski, Carl R. "Evangelist and Leper: A Socio-Cultural Study of Mark 1.40–45." *New Testament Studies* 38.1 (1992) 37–50.

King-Smith, Dick. *The Sheep-Pig*. London: Pufffin 1983.

Kirk, Daniel, et al. "The Bible for Normal People: Episode 69: Daniel Kirk—Five Things You Need to Know About the Gospel of Mark." *The Bible for Normal People* (podcast), November 26, 2018. https://thebiblefornormalpeople.podbean.com/e/episode-69-daniel-kirk-five-things-you-need-to-know-about-the-gospel-of-mark/.

Korthals Altes, Liesbeth. "Irony." In *Routledge Encyclopedia of Narrative Theory*, edited by David Herman et al., 261–63. London: Routledge, 2005.

Lategan, Bernard. "Introduction: Coming to Grips with the Reader." *Semeia* 48 (1989) 3–17.

Lane, William. *The Gospel of Mark*. Grand Rapids: Eerdmans, 1974.

Lawson, Mark. *Idlewild*. London: Picador, 1996.

Lewis, C. S. *The Lion, the Witch and the Wardrobe*. London: HarperCollins, 1980.

Loomans, Diane, and Karen Kolberg. *The Laughing Classroom: Everyone's Guide to Teaching with Humor and Play*. Novato: H. J. Kramer, 1993.

Mailloux, Steven. "Reader-response Criticism?" *Genre* 10 (1977) 413–31.

Malbon, Elizabeth Struthers. *In the Company of Jesus: Characters in Mark's Gospel*. Louisville: Westminster John Knox, 2000.

———. *Mark's Jesus: Characterization as Narrative Christology*. Waco, TX: Baylor University Press, 2009.

Malina, Bruce. *The New Testament World*. Louisville: John Knox, 2001.

Malina, Bruce, and Richard Rohrbaugh. *Social-Science Commentary on the Synoptic Gospels*. Minneapolis: Fortress, 1992.

Marcus, Joel, *Mark 1–8: A New Translation with Introduction and Commentary*. New York: Anchor, 2007.

Martin, James. "The Gift of Imagination in Reading Scripture." *The Bible for Normal People* (podcast), February 3, 2020. https://thebiblefornormalpeople.podbean.com/e/episode-113-james-martin-the-gift-of-imagination-in-reading-scripture/.

Martin, Wallace. *Recent Theories of Narrative*. Ithaca: Cornell, 1986.

Martínez-Alfaro, María Jesús. "Intertextuality: Origins and Development of the Concept." *Atlantis* 18 (1996) 268–85.

Merenlahti, Petri. *Poetics for the Gospels? Rethinking Narrative Criticism.* London: T. & T. Clark, 2005.

Moore, Stephen D. *Literary Criticism and the Gospels: The Theoretical Challenge.* New Haven: Yale University Press, 1989.

———. *Poststructuralism and the New Testament.* Minneapolis: Fortress, 1994.

Moraru, Christian. "Intertextuality." In *Routledge Encyclopedia of Narrative Theory,* edited by David Herman et al., 256–61. London: Routledge, 2005.

Myers, Ched. *Binding the Strong Man: a Political Reading of Mark's Story of Jesus.* New York: Orbis, 2008.

Oegema, Gerbern. "The Coming of the Righteous One in 1 Enoch, Qumran and the New Testament." In *The Bible and the Dead Sea Scrolls: Scripture and the Scrolls,* edited by James H. Charlesworth, 381–96. Waco, TX: Baylor University Press, 2006.

Onega Jaén, Susan, and José Angel García Landa, eds. *Narratology: An Introduction.* London: Longman, 1996.

Osborne, Grant. *The Hermeneutical Spiral.* Downers Grove, IL: InterVarsity, 1991.

Patte, Daniel. *What Is Structural Exegesis?* Philadelphia: Fortress , 1976.

Paul, Ian. "Did the Syrophoenician Woman Teach Jesus to Be Jesus?" *Psephizo* (blog), August 28, 2018. https://www.psephizo.com/biblical-studies/did-the-syrophoenician-woman-teach-jesus-to-be-jesus/.

Pett, Stephen, et al. *Understanding Christianity: Text, Impact, Connections; Resource Pack.* Birmingham: RE Today, 2016.

Powell, Mark Allen. *What Is Narrative Criticism?* London: SPCK, 1993.

Propp, Vladmir. *The Morphology of the Folktale.* Mansfield, CT: Martino, 2015.

Proust, Marcel. *Swann's Way & Within a Budding Grove.* Vol. 1 of *Remembrance of Things Past.* London: Penguin, 1981.

Resseguie, James. *Narrative Criticism of the New Testament: An Introduction.* Grand Rapids, MI: Baker Academic, 2005.

Rhoads, David. "Jesus and the Syrophoenician Woman in Mark: A Narrative-Critical Study." *Currents in Theology and Mission* 47.4 (2020) 36–48.

Rhoads, David, et al. *Mark as Story: An Introduction to the Narrative of a Gospel.* Minneapolis: Fortress, 1999.

Rimmon-Kenan, Shlomith. *Narrative Fiction: Contemporary Poetics.* London: Routledge, 1983.

Ryken, Leland. *How to Read the Bible as Literature.* Grand Rapids: Zondervan, 1984.

Schweizer, Eduard. *The Good News According to Matthew.* Atlanta: John Knox, 1975.

Selden, Raman. *A Reader's Guide to Contemporary Literary Theory.* Brighton: Harvester, 1985.

Sendak, Maurice. *Where the Wild Things Are.* London: HarperCollins, 1963.

Shepherd, Tom. "The Narrative Role of John and Jesus in Mark 1.1–15." In *Biblical Interpretation in Early Christian Gospels: The Gospel of Mark,* edited by Thomas Hatina, 1:151–68. London: T. & T. Clark, 2006.

"Simon Smith: 40." *The Lent Project* (blog), n.d. https://lentproject.wordpress.com/resources/visuals-video-painting-and-design/simon-smith-40/.

Smith, Frank. *Reading.* Cambridge: Cambridge University Press, 1978.

Springer, Mike. "Alfred Hitchcock Explains the Plot Device He Called the 'MacGuffin.'" *Open Culture*, July 9, 2013. https://www.openculture.com/2013/07/alfred-hitchcock -explains-the-plot-device-he-called-the-macguffin.html.

Sternberg, Meir. *The Poetics of Biblical Narrative: Ideological Literature and the Drama of Reading*. Bloomington, IN: Indiana University Press, 1985.

Stibbe, Mark. "'Return to Sender': A Structuralist Approach to John's Gospel." *Biblical Interpretation* 1.2 (1993) 189–206.

Telford, William R. "Jesus Christ, Movie Star: The Depiction of Jesus in the Cinema." In *Explorations in Theology and Film: An Introduction*, 115–39. Oxford: Blackwell, 2004.

Thomas, Huw. "The Mote in Thine Eye: An Analysis of the Bible in Cartoons." *Journal for Interdisciplinary Biblical Studies* 3.2 (2021), forthcoming.

Tolmie, Francois. *Narratology and Biblical Narratives: A Practical Guide*. Eugene, OR: Wipf & Stock, 1999.

Toolan, Michael J. *Narrative: A Critical Linguistic Introduction*. London: Routledge, 1988.

Utell, Janine. *Engagements with Narrative*. London: Routledge, 2016.

Van Oyen, Geert. *Reading the Gospel of Mark as a Novel*. Eugene, OR: Cascade, 2014.

Vanhoozer, Kevin. *Is There a Meaning in This Text?* Grand Rapids: Zondervan, 1998.

Vorster, Willem. "The Reader in the Text: Narrative Material." *Semeia* 48 (1989) 21–39.

Walker, Alice. *The Color Purple*. London: Women's Press.

Watchmojo.com. "Top 10 4th Wall Breaks in Film." *YouTube*, March 13, 2014. https:// www.youtube.com/watch?v=jTaN6wyMwCY.

Wells, Sam. "Improvising Faith (N223)." *Nomad* (podcast), May 6, 2020. https://www. nomadpodcast.co.uk/sam-wells-improvising-faith-n223/.

Wessell, Walter W. "Mark." In *The Expositor's Bible Commentary with the New International Version of the Holy Bible: Matthew, Mark, Luke*, 8:601–793. Grand Rapids, MI: Zondervan, 1984.

Wilcox, Pete. "Imagining the Good News: Inhabiting and Commending the Beauty of the Christian Faith through Storytelling and Poetry." https://www.stpeterscollege. org.uk/bishops-lecture-2019.

Wright, N. T. *The New Testament and the People of God*. Philadelphia: Fortress, 1992.

Wright, N. T., and Marcus Borg. *The Meaning of Jesus*. London: SPCK, 1999.

Yorke, John. *Into the Woods: How Stories Work and Why We Tell Them*. London: Penguin, 2014.

Index

Lightning Source UK Ltd.
Milton Keynes UK
UKHW020856160122
397207UK00005B/321